Dynamic
Web Programming
A Beginner's Guide

About the Authors

Marty Matthews has worked with computers in various capacities—from a programmer to a software company executive—since the days of early mainframes. As a result he has considerable insight into how best to use computers and has applied this to authoring or coauthoring over 70 books, including ones on desktop and web publishing, Microsoft Office, and Microsoft operating systems. Recent titles include *FrontPage 2003 QuickSteps; FrontPage 2003: The Complete Reference; Microsoft Office 2007 QuickSteps;* and *Windows 7 QuickSteps.* Marty lives with his wife, Carole, on an island in Puget Sound.

John Cronan has over 30 years of computer experience and has been writing and editing computer-related books for over 17 years. His recent books include *Build an eBay Business QuickSteps, Second Edition; Microsoft Office Excel 2007 QuickSteps;* and *Microsoft Office Access 2007 QuickSteps.* John and his wife, Faye (and cat Little Buddy), reside in Everett, Washington.

Dynamic
Web Programming
A Beginner's Guide

Marty Matthews
John Cronan

New York   Chicago   San Francisco
Lisbon   London   Madrid   Mexico City
Milan   New Delhi   San Juan
Seoul   Singapore   Sydney   Toronto

The McGraw·Hill Companies

Library of Congress Cataloging-in-Publication Data

Matthews, Martin S.
    Dynamic web programming : a beginner's guide / Marty Matthews, John Cronan.
        p.   cm.
    Includes index.
    ISBN 978-0-07-163344-4 (alk. paper)
    1. Web sites—Design.   2. Web site development.   I. Cronan, John.   II. Title.
    TK5105.888.M3657   2009
    006.7—dc22   2009034488

McGraw-Hill books are available at special quantity discounts to use as premiums and sales promotions, or for use in corporate training programs. To contact a representative, please e-mail us at bulksales@mcgraw-hill.com.

Dynamic Web Programming: A Beginner's Guide

1 2 3 4 5 6 7 8 9 0   DOC DOC   0 1 9

ISBN   978-0-07-163344-4
MHID   0-07-163344-8

Sponsoring Editor   Roger Stewart

Editorial Supervisor   Janet Walden

Project Manager   Smita Rajan, Glyph International

Acquisitions Coordinator   Joya Anthony

Technical Editor   Greg Kettell

Copy Editor   Jan Jue

Proofreader   Deborah Liehs

Indexer   Valerie Haynes Perry

Production Supervisor   Jean Bodeaux

Composition   Glyph International

Illustration   Glyph International

Art Director, Cover   Jeff Weeks

Cover Designer   Jeff Weeks

To our spice in life:
Carole and Faye

Contents at a Glance

Contents

ix

Acknowledgments

A number of people helped make this book what it is, among them:

Greg Kettell, technical editor, corrected many errors and added considerably to the book. Thanks, Greg!

Joya Anthony, acquisitions coordinator, kept us on track. Thanks, Joya!

Jan Jue, copy editor, did the yeoman work of turning our poor attempts into readable text, while always being a joy to work with. Thanks, Jan!

Smita Rajan, project manager, kept all the players moving forward turning the manuscript into a book. Thanks, Smita!

Janet Walden, editorial supervisor, gave the book its final polish. Thanks, Janet!

Roger Stewart, editorial director, whose belief in us and this book made it possible. Thanks, Roger!

Introduction

People generally start building web sites with text and graphics on a page and proceed through several levels of formatting and layout. All of this, though, is *static* content and can be created with common text-editing and layout programs. Creating a *dynamic* page, where the content changes in response to user events, requires programming and the possible use of a database.

Dynamic Web Programming: A Beginner's Guide uses a hands-on approach to take you from building an advanced static web page to one with a variety of dynamic elements. To do this, five of the most commonly used web programming languages (X/HTML, CSS, JavaScript, PHP, and MySQL) are introduced, explored, and demonstrated through the creation of common dynamic web elements.

You are assumed to have some experience creating static web pages and to want to add dynamic content to your pages. To create a common foundation for all readers, the book starts out with a quick review of creating static web pages by using HTML (Hypertext Markup Language) and then looks at the added rigor and good practices provided by XML (Extensible Markup Language) to implement XHTML (Extensible HTML). The book then takes you through the use of CSS (Cascading Style Sheets) and templates to apply common features and formatting across a series of web pages.

Dynamic Web Programming: A Beginner's Guide starts the discussion of dynamic elements with an overview of JavaScript and how it is used to implement such client-side elements as changing an image when the mouse rolls over it, implementing a pop-up window, positioning the cursor in a form, and validating form entries. Next we provide an overview of PHP, along with how it is used to implement server-side elements such as using cookies and server variables to authenticate a user. Finally, the book will introduce MySQL and how it is used to store, select, and update information on a web page in combination with PHP.

Dynamic Web Programming: A Beginner's Guide is a solutions-oriented book organized around a set of detailed examples that demonstrate the full capability of common dynamic web elements. It is meant for you to use directly as a template for building web pages that have dynamic content, including fully using a MySQL/PHP database.

Listings Online

All of the listings in this book, including the complete User Authentication and Class Registration systems, are available for download from www.mhprofessional.com/computingdownload or www.matthewstechnology.com/.

Conventions Used in This Book

Dynamic Web Programming: A Beginner's Guide uses several conventions designed to make the book easier for you to follow:

- **Bold type** is used for headings, for keywords within a code listing, and for words on the screen that you are to do something with, such as "...and click **Run**."

- *Italic type* is used for a word or phrase that is being defined or otherwise deserves special emphasis.

- A monospaced typeface is used for code snippets and listings.

- Bold SMALL CAPITAL LETTERS are used for keys on the keyboard such as ENTER and SHIFT.

- When you are expected to enter a command, you are instructed to *press* the key(s). If you are to enter text or numbers, you are instructed to *type* them.

Part I

Getting Ready

Although the focus of this book is dynamic web programming with JavaScript, PHP, and MySQL, it is important that we have a common foundation with HTML, CSS, and the programming tools to create dynamic web pages. This part of the book is therefore dedicated to establishing that foundation. In this Part Introduction we'll talk about the tools needed to create and test dynamic web pages. In Chapter 1 we'll review HTML and XHTML, while Chapter 2 will cover CSS.

Setting Up Your Workstation

As you get into dynamic web programming, you will be doing extensive coding, and wanting all the support you can get to produce clean, error-free code. You will need to test not only how your code looks, as you would with static web pages, but also how it runs, and not just on one browser, but on several. You therefore want a text editor, or its more advanced form, which is more of an integrated development tool with which to write the code that will provide support for not only HTML, but also JavaScript and PHP. You also want a test server environment running on your computer that supports all the languages, especially PHP and MySQL. Finally, you will need access to several popular browsers.

NOTE

This book is written for users of Microsoft Windows, Windows XP, Windows Vista, or Windows 7. While most of the discussion in the book is also applicable for Mac and Linux users, this particular section is dedicated to Windows. Mac and Linux have their own set of editors, servers, and browsers.

Picking a Development Tool

The most important item that you need for dynamic web programming is a very capable text editor or development tool that supports you in writing code without trying to do it for you. A number of such tools are available ranging from Windows Notepad, which comes free with Windows and allows you to type in and save code to a file, to Adobe Dreamweaver ($399), which creates dynamic web code for you in a quasi-WYSIWYG (what you see is what you get) environment. Windows Notepad, shown next, might do to enter a little code in a pinch, but when you see the level of features and support that is available with free downloadable editors, you'll relegate Windows Notepad to the software dustbin.

```
Sample.html - Notepad
File  Edit  Format  View  Help
<!DOCTYPE html PUBLIC "-//W3C//DTD XHTML 1.0 Strict//EN"
"http://www.w3.org/TR/xhtml1/DTD/xhtml1-strict.dtd">
<html xmlns="http://www.w3.org/1999/xhtml" lang="en" xml:lang="en">
    <head>
        <meta http-equiv="Content-Type" content="text/html; charset=iso
-8859-1">
            <title>Sample HTML</title>
    </head>
    <body>
        <h1>Sample HTML Code Page</h1>
        <p>
            This is a standard paragraph without formatting.
        </p>
        <img src="rodie.jpg" alt="Beautiful Rodie" />
    </body>
</html>
```

NOTE
Someone may tell you that Microsoft Word will produce an HTML file from text and
graphics that you lay out on a page in the word processor. While this is true, the code
that is produced is neither very efficient nor easy to change or customize. Also Word
does not offer any web programming support. We therefore, strongly recommend
against using Word for web site development.

Full-Featured Development Packages
At the other end of the spectrum from Windows Notepad are Adobe Dreamweaver (see
Figure P1-1) and Microsoft Expression Web (Microsoft's $299 replacement for FrontPage).
Both of these offer a great deal more than an editor and are meant to tie into the other tools
offered by either Adobe or Microsoft. Other than the cost, and you can get them discounted
at Amazon and other locations, there are two major problems with these packages that prevent
us from recommending their use:

- **WYSIWYG isn't**   The display of a web page depends on the browser that is used.
  The attempts of both of these packages to show you what the final displayed page will
  look like can significantly differ from the actual display and can lead you to lay out a
  page differently than you would otherwise.

- **Unmanageable and inefficient code**   The code that is generated by the WYSIWYG
  page layout, and especially with the dynamic web features, is very complex, inefficient,
  and difficult to change and customize. If you want to do anything in PHP on your own,
  with a page in which Dreamweaver has created PHP code, it is extremely difficult.

Powerful Alternatives
In the large spectrum between Windows Notepad and Adobe Dreamweaver are a number
of noteworthy web development tools that offer a lot more than Windows Notepad and

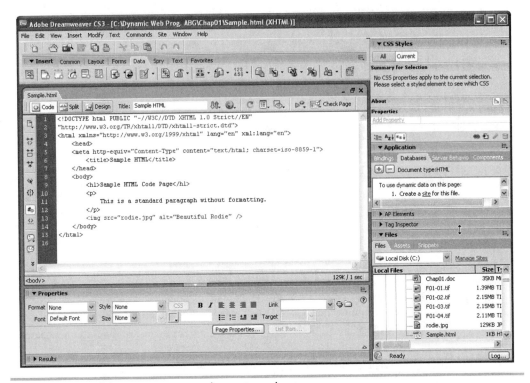

Figure P1-1 Adobe Dreamweaver shown in code view

are either free to download or relatively low cost. You can find comparisons of web development packages on a number of web sites, including http://sixrevisions.com/tools/the-15-most-popular-text-editors-for-developers/ (this site has many helpful articles on web development) and http://en.wikipedia.org/wiki/Comparison_of_html_editors.

In reviewing web development tools, you may want to consider the availability of a number of features in the tool you choose. Among these are

- **Code assistance** Provides context-sensitive assistance as you are entering code, as shown here:

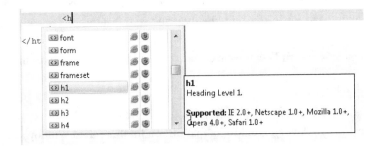

- **Code completion**   Automatically provides the ending tag for the opening tag you typed.

- **Code highlighting**   Provides color coding for various parts of the code so you can easily recognize it.

- **Code validation**   Reviews your code and tells you if it finds something that does not look correct.

- **Browser view**   Displays your code as it would appear in a browser within the development tool.

- **Outline view**   Provides an outline of your code, like this:

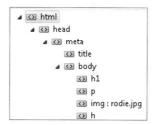

- **Line numbers**   Numbers each line of your code, so that you can quickly find the line referred to in an error message.

- **Search and replace**   Allows the changing of several instances of the same item in one operation.

- **Macro capability**   Allows the recording of a set of steps so they can be repeated.

- **Multiple open files**   Allows you to have several code pages open at the same time to compare and copy code among them.

- **Multiple language support**   Provides support for multiple programming languages, such as HTML, CSS, JavaScript, PHP, MySQL, and Ajax. For this book, the first five are most important.

- **File management**   Provides the capabilities of Windows Explorer from within the development tool.

- **FTP transfer**   Allows you to upload and download your web pages and applications to a hosting server.

- **Version control**   Provides the ability to keep track of your site versions: which one is on the server, which is the most recent on the development computer, and which versions are archive copies.

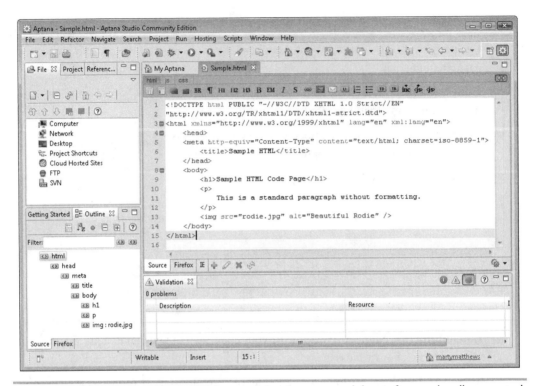

Figure P1-2 Aptana Studio is a full-featured development tool that is free and well supported.

Aptana Studio, shown in Figure P1-2, is our choice for web development, and you'll see many screenshots of it in this book. Aptana Studio is a fully integrated development environment (IDE) that combines text editing with visual browser displays of a web page, while offering a number of tools to help you produce clean code. Aptana has most of the features mentioned earlier (the illustrations were from Aptana), is free, and is supported by a large user community, as well as by its creators. Of particular importance to me is Aptana's ability to provide code assistance, code completion, and code colorization or syntax highlighting for all the languages discussed in this book, plus Ajax and Ruby on Rails. Aptana also can open a browser pane (see Figure P1-3), as well as do code validation and file management, within its window. You can download Aptana Studio for free from www.aptana.com. You can also purchase a Professional version, but for what we are doing in this book, the free package (Community Edition) is all you'll need.

Choosing a Testing Server

Static web pages and even some dynamic web pages that use JavaScript are displayed and run totally in a browser and are called *client-side* applications. All you need to test these pages is a browser. Dynamic web pages that use *server-side* features that run in the server

Figure P1-3   Aptana Studio allows both the Internet Explorer and Firefox browsers to be opened with its window.

instead of in the client's browser, such as those written in PHP and MySQL, require that you have a server on your development computer if you want to test your pages there. The two popular alternatives for a local web server are Microsoft Internet Information Server (IIS) and Apache. IIS is included with some versions of Windows, especially Windows server 2003 and 2008, so you may already have it. Apache is free to download as a part of an integrated package called XAMPP (X for cross-platform servers for Apache, MySQL, PHP, and Perl) that includes both PHP and MySQL.

Since XAMPP includes all the server and developmental tools you need and is readily available to everybody using Windows XP, Vista, or Windows 7, this book assumes that is what you are using, and we recommend that you download and install it now if needed.

NOTE
While there is a version of XAMPP for Mac OS X, you might want to investigate MAMP (Macintosh servers for Apache, MySQL, and PHP) at www.mamp.info/en/download .html. MAMP is generally thought to be superior to XAMPP on the Mac.

Getting and Installing XAMPP

XAMPP uses standard Windows installer techniques to download and install Apache, PHP, and MySQL:

1. On the computer where you want to have your testing server, open the web site www.apachefriends.org/en/xampp-windows.html. Scroll down to approximately the bottom of the second page, and under the latest version of XAMPP for Windows, click **Installer**. Skip over the advertiser's pages, and you will be taken to a download site where, depending on your version of Windows, the download will start; or you may have to right-click the message at the top of the browser and click **Download File**.

2. Click either **Run** to do that directly, or **Save** to save the file to your disk (our preference so we don't have to download again in case of a problem).

3. When the download is complete, you can click either **Run** or **Go to Folder**. If you go to the folder, double-click **xampp-win32-1-7-1-installer.exe** (depending on when you do this, the last two digits may be different), if you have User Account Control (UAC) turned on, click **Yes** to allow the program to run, and click **Run**.

4. Select the language you want to use and click **OK**. If you are on Vista or Windows 7, you may be reminded that you need to deactivate UAC and recommended to keep it deactivated. Again, click **OK**, and then click **Next**.

5. Select the destination (C:\xampp is recommended) and click **Next**. Click **Install**. The installation will commence.

6. When the installation is completed, click **Finish**, and click **Yes** to open the XAMPP Control Panel.

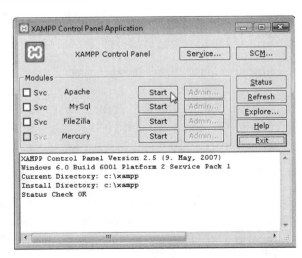

7. Click **Start** opposite Apache and MySQL to load both of those services, and click **Close** (the *X* in the upper-right corner) to close the Control Panel.

8. To see if XAMPP is running, open a web browser (Internet Explorer or Firefox), and type localhost in the address bar. XAMPP should open. Select the language you want to use, and XAMPP will open in your browser as shown in Figure P1-4.

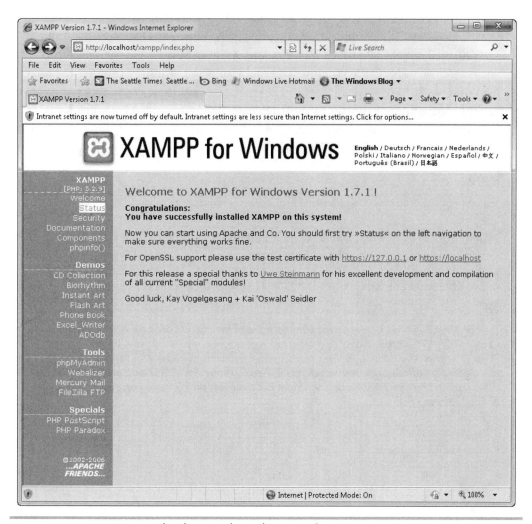

Figure P1-4   XAMPP provides the Apache web server, the PHP programming environment, and the MySQL relational database program, among other programs.

Testing Browsers

The majority of personal computer users access the Web using one of the four browsers: Microsoft Internet Explorer 6 (IE 6), which came with Windows XP; Microsoft Internet Explorer 7 (IE 7), which came with Windows Vista; Internet Explorer 8 (IE 8), which will come with Windows 7; and Mozilla Firefox, which is available for free download. At the time this was written (May 2009), the distribution of browser users from www.w3schools .com was Firefox, 47.7 percent; IE 8, 5.2 percent; IE 7, 21.3 percent; IE 6, 14.5 percent; Google Chrome, 5.5 percent; and Others (principally Safari and Opera), 5.2 percent.

You can download Internet IE 7 for Windows XP from Microsoft at www.microsoft.com/ windows/downloads/. Click **Windows Internet Explorer | Windows Internet Explorer 7 for Windows XP**.

The same web page (www.microsoft.com/windows/downloads/) has a link for IE 8; click **Download Now**. If you want it for Vista, click **Download Now** again. If you want it for XP, click **Other Locales and Versions**. In either case, follow the instructions that appear.

NOTE
You can have only one version of Internet Explorer on a computer at a time.

Firefox can be downloaded from www.mozilla.com/en-US/. Click **Download Firefox**. We recommend that you download both Firefox and IE 7 or 8 and do your testing on those plus IE 6.

TIP
You can't install IE 6 on Vista, but you can make use of the Internet Explorer Application Compatibility VPC Images that allow you to test web pages on IE 6, IE 7, and IE 8 on either Windows XP or Windows Vista. You can download this from www.microsoft.com/ downloads/en/details.aspx and search for "IE App Compat VHD." You must also download and run the latest version of Virtual PC, available on the same page as IE App Compat VHD.

Chapter 1
XHTML and HTML
Refresher

Key Skills & Concepts

- Understanding X/HTML
- Reviewing Basic HTML Tags
- Setting Paragraph Styles
- Applying Character Styles
- Displaying Special Characters
- Working with Images and Image Maps
- Adding Hyperlinks and Bookmarks
- Creating Forms and Tables

HTML (Hypertext Markup Language) is the foundation programming language of the Web and provides the backbone of all web pages. You may add JavaScript and PHP to your pages, but the structure around that code is HTML. While HTML provides the critical infrastructure on a web page, it also has been around for a while; it has not kept up with the demands of new web sites, especially those on smart phones and PDAs (personal digital assistants). For that reason, two supplements have been created:

- **CSS (Cascading Style Sheets)** was developed to substantially enhance the layout and formatting of a web page. CSS is covered in Chapter 2.
- **XML (Extensible Markup Language)** is a *meta* language, a language in which you develop other languages, where markup tags as well as many other elements can be defined. Using XML, HTML was rewritten, creating XHTML (Extensible HTML). XHTML is further discussed in this chapter and used throughout this book.

This first part of the book provides a robust and up-to-date foundation with XHTML and CSS upon which you can build dynamic web sites with JavaScript and PHP and MySQL. Where applicable throughout the book, CSS and XHTML replace the equivalent HTML.

HTML, XML, XHTML, and CSS are controlled by recommended standards set by the World Wide Web Consortium (W3C—www.w3c.org/). As of this writing, the latest recommendations are CSS 2 (4/11/2008), XML 1.1 second edition (2/4/2004, revised 8/16/2006), XHTML 1.0 second edition (1/26/2000, revised 8/1/2002), and HTML 4.01 (12/24/1999). You can see that HTML is pretty old, and XHTML is not much younger. Newer standards are in the works (HTML 5 had a working draft published 6/10/2008), but the process is very slow, in part because the consortium is very large, including most organizations, academics, and individuals who are active on the Web.

CAUTION

To be sure that your web sites are viewable in the maximum number of browsers, use only the recommended standards for HTML, CSS, and XHTML.

XHTML vs. HTML

Remember that XHTML is just HTML written in XML. It's HTML written under a set of rules that standardize it more, so that it's easier for a browser to interpret what it is you want to do. This takes away some of the flexibility or looseness in the way that HTML can be written, but it also means that the browser software can be simpler. The latter is very important when you are trying to fit a browser into a smart phone or a PDA. Also, plain HTML can create some significant problems in your scripts, such as mismatched tags and missing closing tags.

So why even talk about HTML, as ancient and limited as it is? First, because XHTML is just HTML with a set of rules. Second, billions of web pages are written using HTML, and millions of people know how to use it. Also, it is easy to use, one of the major reasons for the phenomenal growth of the Web. So it is still very important to have a strong knowledge of HTML; you just want to use it according to the XHTML rules and to ignore the older formatting and layout tags that have been replaced with CSS. This book assumes that is what you want to do, and the examples reflect that.

XHTML Rules

XHTML rules all deal with *how* HTML is written, not *what* is written. XHTML uses the same tags, attributes, and values (see "Reviewing HTML" later in this chapter) as HTML.

The difference is in the *syntax,* the way the parts of code are put together. Generally speaking, XHTML is just a stricter form of HTML.

- A full set of heading tags, DOCTYPE, html, head, and body, must be included. If you use Aptana and its standard template (shown next), you will do this automatically.

```
<!DOCTYPE html PUBLIC "-//W3C//DTD XHTML 1.0 Strict//EN"
"http://www.w3.org/TR/xhtml1/DTD/xhtml1-strict.dtd">
<html xmlns="http://www.w3.org/1999/xhtml" lang="en" xml:lang="en">
    <head>
    <meta http-equiv="Content-Type" content="text/html; charset=iso-8859-1">
        <title>Untitled Documentt</title>
    </head>
    <body>

    </body>
</html>
```

- All opening tags must have a closing tag. Again, Aptana will fill in the closing tag for you.

- All tags, attributes, and predefined attribute values must be in lowercase.

- All attribute values must be in quotation marks.

- All attribute values must be stated and cannot be assumed, even if they are the same as the attribute.

- An inner tag must be closed before closing an outer tag.

All of these rules are just a strict interpretation of the original definition of HTML and make common sense. Aptana helps you follow the rules, and it is not hard to get in the practice of it. When you do, you buy yourself greater assurance that your code will be properly supported by a broad range of browsers.

Deprecated HTML Tags

With the increased use and desirability of CSS, a number of formatting and layout tags have been identified to be removed from the recommended HTML standard. These tags are called *deprecated tags,* meaning they have fallen out of favor. Currently W3C deprecated tags are

- **applet** (a Java applet)
- **basefont** (font characteristics)
- **center** (a center-aligned div)
- **dir** (directory list)

- **font** (font change)
- **frame** (create a frame)
- **frameset** (define a frameset)
- **iframe** (create a floating frame)
- **isindex** (single-line prompt)
- **menu** (menu list)
- **noframe** (alternative to a frame)
- **s** (strikethrough style)
- **strike** (strikethrough text)
- **u** (underlined style)

NOTE

Frame-related tags are not officially deprecated by the W3C, but they are discouraged because frame pages can foul up search engines.

In addition to the tags, several attributes of acceptable tags have been deprecated. These include

- **align** (align left, right, center)
- **alink**, **link**, **vlink** (link color)
- **background** (background image)
- **bgcolor** (background color)
- **compact** (reduce interim spacing)
- **target** (specify a frame)
- **text** (text color)
- **type** (type style)

There are three levels of implementing XHTML: *strict, transitional,* and *frameset.* The level is identified in the DOCTYPE line of a web page, as shown earlier in the Aptana template. "Strict" means that you have followed all the XHTML rules and have not used any of the deprecated or frame-related tags. "Transitional" means that you have followed the rules, but you want to use some of the deprecated tags. "Frameset" means that you have followed the rules, but you want to use the frame-related tags. This book assumes that you want to use the strict level of XHTML and does not include a discussion of any of the deprecated tags.

NOTE

Even though there is a standards body for the Web (W3C), compliance with its standards is voluntary. As a result, you cannot count on all web browsers to interpret your HTML code identically. Some differences are relatively minor, while others are not. It's always best to test your work in the major browsers (IE 6, IE 7, and Firefox) before publishing it.

Reviewing HTML

HTML is a series of tags that identify the elements in a web page. *Tags* or *markup tags* consist of a tag name enclosed in angle brackets (< >) and normally come in pairs. Tags are placed at the beginning and end of an element, generally text, that you want to identify; the ending tag name is preceded by a slash. For example,

```
<title>This is a title</title>
```

uses the Title tag to identify text that will be placed in the title bar of the browser window. With XHTML, tags should be lowercase. Tags are placed around text to identify it and how it is handled.

NOTE

This chapter will not provide exhaustive coverage of HTML, nor will it cover every nuance of every HTML tag. Both areas are fully covered by sites on the Web, most particularly www.w3c.org.

In addition to a tag name, a tag may contain one or more *attributes* that modify what the tag does. For example, if you want to display an image on your web page, you could use this tag:

```
<img src="rodie.jpg" />
```

An *attribute* of the **img** tag is src, and the *value* of the src attribute is rodie.jpg.

NOTE

In the listings and HTML examples in this chapter, tags are shown in bold, while attributes and their values are not. Also, continuation lines are indented from their parents. These conventions are used solely for readability. Aptana, by default, color-codes and indents HTML for readability. Dark red is used for tags, bright red is used for attribute names, blue is used for attribute values, and black is used for plain text. You can change colors used by Aptana by clicking **Windows | Preferences** and selecting **Aptana | Editors | HTML | Colors**.

Using Basic Tags

All web pages must contain a basic set of tags. These tags identify the document as being an HTML or XHTML document and identify the major parts of the document. With XHTML these tags must be included in a web page to conform to the standard. The basic tags, which are automatically placed on a page with the Aptana template, are shown in Listing 1-1 and are described with their attributes in Table 1-1.

TIP

The listings here and in the rest of the book are available online at www.matthewstechnology.com/. See the book's Introduction on how best to access the online listings.

Listing 1-1   Basic set of tags

```
<!DOCTYPE html PUBLIC "-//W3C//DTD XHTML 1.0 Strict//EN"
"http://www.w3.org/TR/xhtml1/DTD/xhtml1-strict.dtd">
<html xmlns="http://www.w3.org/1999/xhtml" lang="en" xml:lang="en">
   <head>
   <meta http-equiv="Content-Type" content="text/html; charset=iso-8859-1">
      <title>Untitled Document</title>
   </head>
   <body>

   </body>
</html>
```

Tag or Attribute	Description
`<!DOCTYPE ...>`	Identifies the document as adhering to the given HTML or XHTML version.
`<html> </html>`	Identifies the intervening text as being HTML.
`<head> </head>`	Contains the title and document identifying information. The `<title>` tag is required in the `<head>` tag.
`<title> </title>`	Identifies the title that is placed in the browser's title bar.
`<meta ...>`	Assigns content to an element that can be used by a server or browser and that cannot otherwise be assigned in HTML; "Content-Type" is assigned to http-equiv in Listing 1-1 and placed within the `<head>` tag.
content	Identifies information about the page.
http-equiv	Identifies how the meta tag is used.
name	Provides information that can be used by search engines.
`<body> </body>`	Specifies the part of the page that is shown to the user and defines overall page properties.

Table 1-1   Basic Set of HTML Tags

NOTE

In the tables of tags and attributes in this chapter, tags are shown with their angle brackets, and attributes are indented from the left.

Setting Paragraph Styles

Paragraph styles include basic paragraph definition and headings; the line break; bulleted, numbered, and definition lists; preformatted paragraphs; comments; and horizontal lines or rules. Unless the preformatted style is used, normal line endings, extra spaces of more than one, and tabs are ignored in HTML. Lines simply wrap to fit the space allotted for them unless you use the Paragraph tag. Listing 1-2 shows examples of paragraph styles. This listing is combined with the tags in Listing 1-1 to produce the web page shown in Figure 1-1. Paragraph styles are described in Table 1-2.

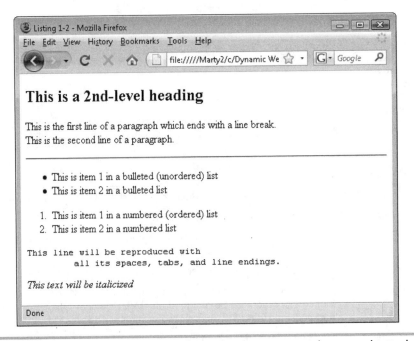

Figure 1-1   The web page listing resulting from placing Listing 1-2 between the Body tags of Listing 1-1

Listing 1-2   Example of using paragraph style tags

```
<h2>This is a 2nd-level heading</h2>
<p>This is the first line of a paragraph which ends with a line break.<br />
This is the second line of a paragraph.</p>
<hr>
<ul>
  <li>This is item 1 in a bulleted (unordered) list</li>
  <li>This is item 2 in a bulleted list</li>
</ul>
<ol>
  <li>This is item 1 in a numbered (ordered) list</li>
  <li>This is item 2 in a numbered list</li>
</ol>
<!-- This is a comment, it is ignored by a browser and not displayed -->
<pre>This line will be reproduced with
 all its spaces, tabs, and line endings.</pre>
<address>This text will be italicized</address>
```

Tags or Attributes	Description
`<p> </p>`	Identifies the start and end of a paragraph
`<hn> </hn>`	Identifies a heading in one of six heading styles (n = 1 to 6)
` `	Forces a line break similar to pressing SHIFT-ENTER in Microsoft Word
`<hr>`	Creates a horizontal rule or line
`<ol> </ol>`	Contains an ordered (numbered) list
`<ul> </ul>`	Contains an unordered (bulleted) list
`<li> </li>`	Identifies an item in a numbered or bulleted list
`<dl> </dl>`	Contains a definition list
`<dt> </dt>`	Identifies a term to be defined, displayed on the left of a window
`<dd> </dd>`	Identifies the definition of the term that immediately precedes it, indented from the left
`<address> </address>`	Identifies a paragraph of italicized text
`<blockquote> </blockquote>`	Identifies a paragraph that is indented on both the left and right, as you might do with a quotation
cite	Identifies a URL for the `blockquote`
`<!-- -->`	Identifies a comment that the browser will ignore and not display

Table 1-2   Paragraph Style HTML Tags *(continued)*

Tags or Attributes	Description
`<div> </div>`	Identifies a division of a page
class	Identifies a class of `divs` for applying styles
id	Attaches a name for linking
`<pre> </pre>`	Identifies preformatted text in which all spaces, tabs, and line endings are preserved

Table 1-2 Paragraph Style HTML Tags *(continued)*

NOTE

You can nest lists within lists and get automatic indenting.

Applying Character Styles

Character styles, which determine how one or more characters will look or behave, come in two forms. *Logical* character styles are defined by the browser and may be displayed in any way that the browser has established. *Physical* character styles have a strict definition that will be the same in all browsers. Examples of character style tags are shown in Listing 1-3, while Figure 1-2 shows how Microsoft Internet Explorer 7 and Mozilla Firefox 3 display them. Note the lack of differences. Table 1-3 describes most character styles.

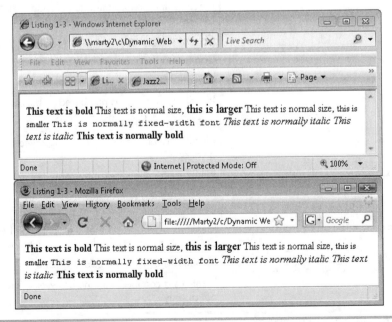

Figure 1-2 Character style tags displayed in Microsoft Internet Explorer 7 and Mozilla Firefox 3

NOTE

Figure 1-2 demonstrates that browsers ignore line endings unless they are marked with
`<p>`, `<br>`, or other paragraph styles.

Listing 1-3 Examples of using character style tags

```
<b>This text is bold</b>
This text is normal size, <big>this is larger</big>
This text is normal size, <small>this is smaller</small>
<code>This is normally fixed-width font</code>
<em>This text is normally italic</em>
<i>This text is italic</i>
<strong>This text is normally bold</strong>
```

NOTE

Character styles and formatting once had a number of deprecated tags, such as `font`,
`strike`, and `u`.

Tag	Description
`<b> </b>`	Applies the Bold physical character style to the enclosed characters
`<big> </big>`	Makes the enclosed characters one size larger
`<cite> </cite>`	Applies the Citation logical character style to the enclosed characters; normally italic
`<code> </code>`	Applies the Code logical character style to the enclosed characters; normally a fixed-width font
`<dfn> </dfn>`	Applies the Definition logical character style to the enclosed characters; normally italic
`<em> </em>`	Applies the Emphasis logical character style to the enclosed characters; normally italic
`<i> </i>`	Applies the Italic physical character style to the enclosed characters
`<kbd> </kbd>`	Applies the Keyboard logical character style to the enclosed characters; normally a fixed-width font
`<samp> </samp>`	Applies the Sample logical character style to the enclosed characters; normally a fixed-width font
`<small> </small>`	Makes the enclosed characters one size smaller
`<strong> </strong>`	Applies the Strong logical character style to the enclosed characters; normally bold
`<sub> </sub>`	Applies the Subscript physical character style to the enclosed characters
`<sup> </sup>`	Applies the Superscript physical character style to the enclosed characters
`<tt> </tt>`	Applies the Typewriter Text physical character style to the enclosed characters; a fixed-width font

Table 1-3 Character Style HTML Tags

Displaying Special Characters

HTML defines the less-than, greater-than, and ampersand characters as having special meanings, and therefore they cannot be used as normal text. To use these characters normally, replace them as follows:

To Display	Type
Less-than (<)	< or <
Greater-than (>)	> or >
Ampersand (&)	& or &

All other characters that you can type on your keyboard will be displayed as they are typed. In addition, HTML has defined a number of other characters that can be displayed based on entering an *escape sequence* where you want the character displayed. The escape sequence can take either a numeric or a textual format, as was shown with the three special characters just mentioned. In either case, the escape sequence begins with an ampersand (&) and ends with a semicolon (;). In the numeric format, the ampersand is followed by a number symbol (#) and a number that represents the character. All characters, whether they are on the keyboard or not, can be represented with a numeric escape sequence. The textual format has been defined only for some characters and excludes most characters on the keyboard. Additional examples of the two formats are shown in Table 1-4.

NOTE

Unlike the rest of HTML, escape sequences are case-sensitive—for example, you cannot use < for the less-than symbol.

Character	Name	Numeric Sequence	Text Sequence
…	Horizontal ellipsis	&#133;	&hellip;
•	Bullet	&#149;	&bull;
™	Trademark	&#153;	&trade;
©	Copyright	&#169;	&copy;
Æ	AE ligature	&#198;	&aelig;
Ä	A umlaut	&#228;	&auml;
É	E acute accent	&#233;	&eacute;
Õ	O tilde	&#245;	&otilde;

Table 1-4   Samples of Character Escape Sequences

TIP

For the complete list of character escape sequences, open www.w3c.org/markup/html-spec/html-spec_13.html.

Working with Images and Image Maps

Images are added to a web by use of the Image (`<img />`) tag, which specifies the path and filename of the image as well as a number of attributes such as size, positioning, margins, and border. One of the attributes, `ismap`, identifies the image as having an image map attached to it. The image map is a separate MAP file used by the server to relate areas of the image to URLs. To use `ismap`, you must include the Image tag in an Anchor tag (see the next section, "Adding Hyperlinks and Bookmarks"). A couple of examples are given in Listing 1-4 and shown in Figure 1-3. Many of the Image attributes are described in Table 1-5.

Figure 1-3 Example using the Image tag in Listing 1-4

NOTE

The   (which can also be) in Listing 1-4 is a non-breaking space and is used to add space or with the Paragraph tags to create a blank line (paragraph) that HTML will retain.

Listing 1-4   Examples of using the Image tag

```
<p><img src="hibiscus.jpg" alt="A picture of a hibiscus"
  width="166" height="190" /> This is a picture of a hibiscus...</p>
<p> </p>
<p><img src="undercon.gif" alt="Under
  Construction" width="40" height="38" />
  This is the Under Construction symbol...</p>
```

TIP

Specifying the `height` and the `width` speeds up loading, because a quick placeholder will be drawn for the image, allowing the text to continue to be loaded while the image is drawn. Without these dimensions, the loading of the text must wait for the image to be drawn and thereby determine where the remaining text will go. Current browsers will automatically scale the other dimension based on the current aspect ratio of the image if just one of the dimensions (`height` or `width`) is given.

Adding Hyperlinks and Bookmarks

Hyperlinks provide the ability to click an object and transfer what is displayed by the browser (the *focus*) to an address associated with the object. HTML implements hyperlinks with the Anchor tag (**`<a> </a>`**), which specifies that the text or graphic that it contains is a hyperlink or a bookmark or both. If the tag is a *hyperlink* and the contents are selected, then the focus is moved either to another location in the current page or web, or to another web. If the tag is a *bookmark,* then another Anchor tag may reference it and potentially transfer the focus to it.

An image used as just described assumes that the entire image is the hyperlink. An image may also be broken into sections, where each section is a link or a *hotspot*. To break an image into multiple links requires an *image map* that is implemented with the Map tag. The Map tag contains Area tags that define the shape of a specific area of the image and the link that it is pointing to.

Listing 1-5 provides some examples of the Anchor, Map, and Area tags, which are shown in Figure 1-4. Table 1-6 describes these tags and their attributes.

Attribute	Description
alt	Identifies alternative text that is displayed when the mouse pointer is placed on the image or if the image cannot be displayed
height	Specifies the height, in pixels, of the image
ismap	Specifies a server-side image map
src	Identifies the path and filename or URL of the image
usemap	Specifies a client-side image map
width	Specifies the width, in pixels, of the image

Table 1-5   Image Tag Attributes

NOTE

The finger in Figure 1-4 is pointing to the hotspot labeled "screen," as shown at the bottom of the window ("…/Listing 1-5.html#screen").

Figure 1-4   Hyperlinks and bookmarks defined in Listing 1-5, including a hotspot link. (Lenovo IdeaCentre K220 desktop computer, photo courtesy of Lenovo, used by permission.)

Listing 1-5   Examples of hyperlinks and bookmarks

```
<p>This is a link to the <a href="default.html">Home
  Page.</a></p>
<p><a name="This ">This </a>is a bookmark.</p>
<p>This <a href="#This ">link </a>takes you to the bookmark.</p>
<p><map name="ComputerMap">
  <area shape="polygon" coords="163, 121, 197, 145, 91, 183, 55,
    157" href="#keyboard">
  <area shape="polygon" coords="6, 90, 147, 87, 148, 115, 46, 145,
    2, 124" href="#processor">
  <area shape="rect" coords="30, 6, 124, 70" href="#screen"></map>
  <a href="computer.map" />
    <img align="bottom" src="Lenovo K220.jpg" width="200" ismap
      usemap="#computermap" height="186" /></a></p>
```

NOTE

The `shape` attribute of the Area tag may be left out, and a rectangular shape will be assumed.

Tag or Attribute	Description
`<a> </a>`	Specifies the definition of a hyperlink
`accesskey`	Specifies a shortcut key to the link
`href`	Identifies the destination URL, which can be a bookmark, page, or web
`name`	Identifies the bookmark at this location
`tabindex`	Identifies this link's position in the tabbing order
`<map> </map>`	Specifies the definition of an image map
`name`	Identifies the name of the image map
`<area> </area>`	Specifies the definition of one image area
`accesskey`	Specifies a shortcut key to the link
`coords`	Identifies the coordinates of the shape being defined using x and y positions in terms of image pixels for each point
`href`	Identifies the bookmark or URL to which the focus is transferred
`nohref`	Indicates that a given area causes no action to take place
`shape`	Specifies the type of shape being defined to be `circ`, `circle`, `poly`, `polygon`, `rect`, or `rectangle`
`tabindex`	Identifies this link's position in the tabbing order

Table 1-6   Anchor, Map, and Area Tags and Their Attributes

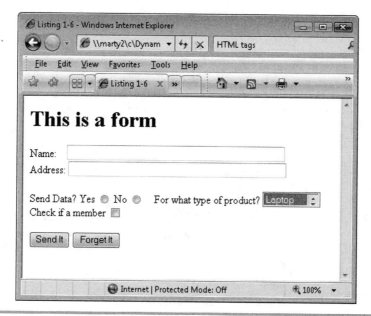

Figure 1-5   Form created with Listing 1-6

Defining Forms

A form in HTML is defined by the input fields that it contains. Each input field is defined by its type, name, and potentially a default value. There are a number of field types around which you can wrap text and formatting to get virtually any form you want to define. One example is shown in Listing 1-6 and displayed in Figure 1-5. Table 1-7 describes the tags and attributes related to forms.

Listing 1-6   Example of a form

```
<h1>This is a form</h1>
<form action="saveresults" METHOD="post">
    Name:     <input type="text" size="50" maxlength="256"
    name="name"><br />
    Address: <input type="text" size="50" maxlength="256"
    name="address"><br /><br />
    Send Data? Yes <input type="radio" name="Send" value="Yes">
    No <input type="radio" name="Send" value="No">   
    For what type of product? <select name="Product" multiple
    size="1">
    <option selected value="Laptop">Laptop
    <option value="Desktop">Desk Top
        </select><br />
```

```
Check if a member <input type="checkbox" name="Member"
  Value="true">
<br /><br />
<input type="submit" value="Send It"> <input type="reset"
  value="Forget It">
</form>
```

Tag or Attribute	Description
`<form> </form>`	Specifies the definition of a form
`action`	Specifies the URL with code to process the form upon submittal
`method`	Specifies how the form is sent to the server: `get` transmits the data as part of the URL; `post` transmits the data only when queried by the processing code and is more secure
`<input>`	Identifies one input field
`accesskey`	Specifies a shortcut key to the field
`checked`	If `type=checkbox` or `radio`, determines if by default they are selected (`true`) or not (`false`)
`disabled`	Specifies that the field cannot be used
`maxlength`	Specifies the maximum number of characters that can be entered in a text field
`name`	Specifies the name of the field
`readonly`	Specifies that the field contents cannot be changed
`size`	Specifies the width of a text field in characters, or the width and height in characters and lines of a text area
`src`	Specifies the URL of an image if `type=image`
`tabindex`	Identifies this field's position in the tabbing order
`type`	Specifies the field type as `checkbox`, `hidden`, `image`, `password`, `radio`, `reset`, `submit`, `text`, or `textarea`
`value`	Specifies the default value of the field
`<select> </select>`	Specifies the definition of a drop-down menu
`disabled`	Specifies that the definition cannot be used
`multiple`	Specifies that multiple items can be selected in a menu
`name`	Specifies the name of a menu
`size`	Specifies the height of the menu

Table 1-7   Form Tags and Attributes

Tag or Attribute	Description
`<option>`	Identifies one option in a menu
`disabled`	Specifies that the option cannot be used
`label`	Specifies the label of the option
`selected`	Specifies that this option is the default
`value`	Specifies the value if the option is selected

Table 1-7 Form Tags and Attributes *(continued)*

Creating Tables

HTML provides a very rich set of tags to define a table, its cells, borders, and other properties. As rich as the original HTML table specification was, many extensions to it have been made by both Microsoft and Netscape. Since these extensions are not consistent between the two companies, they need to be used with caution. Listing 1-7 provides an example of the HTML for creating the simple table shown in Figure 1-6. Table 1-8 shows the principal table tags and their attributes.

Listing 1-7   Table example

```
<h2>A New Table</h2>
<table border="2" cellpadding="3" cellspacing="4" width="100%" >
  <caption>This Is The Table Caption</caption>
  <tr valign="bottom">
    <th align="left" width="25%">Cell 1, a header</th>
    <td colspan="2" width="25%">Cell 2, This cell spans two
      columns</td>
    <td width="10%">Cell 3</td>
    <td width="10%">Cell 4</td>
  </tr>
  <tr>
    <td width="25%">Cell 5, 25%</td>
    <td width="25%">Cell 6, 25%</td>
    <td width="25%">Cell 7, 25%</td>
    <td width="10%">10%</td>
  </tr>
  <tr>
    <td rowspan="2" width="25%">Cells 9/13, These cells were
    merged</td>
    <td width="25%">Cell 10</td>
    <td width="25%">Cell 11</td>
    <td width="10%">Cell 12</td>
  </tr>
```

```
<tr>
  <td width="25%">Cell 14</td>
  <td width="25%">Cell 15</td>
  <td width="10%">Cell 16</td>
</tr>
</table>
```

TIP

There is no rule that the `<tr> </tr>` tags must be on separate lines, as shown in Listing 1-7, but doing so makes it much easier to distinguish rows (`<tr> </tr>`) and cells (`<td> </td>`).

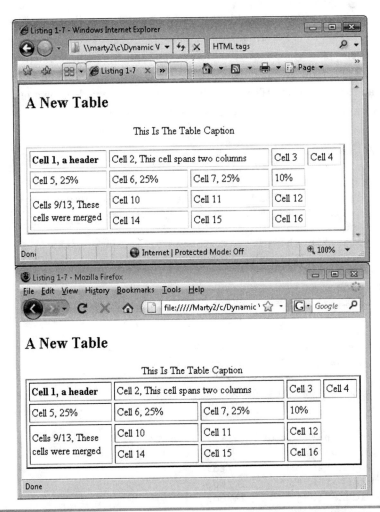

Figure 1-6 Table created with Listing 1-7. Notice some differences between IE 7 and Firefox 3.

Tag or Attribute	Description
`<table> </table>`	Specifies the definition of a table
`border`	Specifies the size, in pixels, of a border to be drawn around all cells in a table
`cellspacing`	Specifies the amount of space, in pixels, between cells; a default of 0 is used when not specified
`cellpadding`	Specifies the amount of space, in pixels, between the cell wall and its contents on all sides; a default of 0 is used when not specified
`frame`	Specifies which of the outside borders of a table are displayed—`void` (none), `above` (only the top), `below` (only the bottom), `hsides` (horizontal sides), `vsides` (vertical sides), `lhs` (left-hand side), `rhs` (right-hand side), `box` or `border` (all)
`rules`	Specifies which of the inside borders of a table are displayed—`none`, `basic` (horizontal rules between the heading, body, and footer sections), `rows`, `cols`, `all`
`summary`	Specifies the purpose of the table
`width`	Specifies the width of a table as either a certain number of pixels or a percentage of the window
`<tr> </tr>`	Identifies the cells in a single row of a table
`align`	Specifies that the text in the cells of this row is aligned on the `left`, `center`, or `right` of each cell
`valign`	Specifies that the text in the row can be aligned with the `top`, `center`, `baseline`, or `bottom` of the cells; if not specified, text is center-aligned
`<td> </td>` `<th> </th>`	Identifies a single data cell in a table (`<td>`) or a header cell in the table (`<th>`)
`align`	Specifies that the text in this cell is aligned on the `left`, `center`, or `right` of the cell
`colspan`	Specifies the number of columns a cell should span
`rowspan`	Specifies the number of rows a cell should span
`nowrap`	Specifies that the text in the table cannot be wrapped to fit a smaller cell, forcing the cell to enlarge
`<caption> </caption>`	Identifies the caption for a table
`<col> </col>`	Identifies a group of columns
`align`	Specifies the horizontal alignment to the `left`, `center`, or `right` of the column group
`span`	Specifies the number of columns in the column group
`valign`	Specifies that the vertical alignment at the `top` or `bottom` of the column group
`width`	Specifies the column width

Table 1-8 Table Tags and Attributes

TIP
A table without the `border` attribute will not have a border, but will take up the same space as if it had a border of 1. Therefore, specifying a border of zero (0) will take up less space.

HTML Authoring Resources

A number of excellent resources on HTML authoring are available on the Web. The following is a list of the ones that are most important. Some of these documents are ancient by Internet standards (several years old), but the basic information is still valid. It is important to understand that HTML has become a mature web language. Nonetheless, a solid understanding of HTML, which these documents will provide, will give you a firm foundation for dynamic web programming.

NOTE
URLs change very quickly. While every effort was made to get the following URLs correct when this book went to print, some probably will have changed by the time this book reaches the bookstores. If you are having trouble with a URL, drop off right-hand segments, delineated by slashes, until it works. Microsoft's site changes faster than anybody's, so if one of their URLs isn't working, don't be surprised. The best work-around is to go to **www.microsoft.com/** and work forward.

The following is a list of resources available online:

- "Getting Started with HTML," "More Advanced Features," and "Adding a Touch of Style" by Dave Raggett of W3C provide a foundation understanding of HTML and CSS from the organization that sets the standards. Last updated May 24, 2005. The "Getting Started" document has links to the other two, and is available at **www.w3c.org/Markup/Guide/Overview.html**.

- **W3 Schools** is a major resource for HTML, XHTML, CSS, JavaScript, and PHP. It has tutorials, references, examples, and forums on all subjects for free. You can access it at **www.w3schools.com/**.

- **HTML Goodies** provides a good HTML primer and a number of advanced resources for HTML, CSS, JavaScript, and PHP at **www.htmlgoodies.com/**.

- **HTML Code Tutorial** has tutorials, forums, and other resources at **www.htmltutorial.com/**.

- "Composing Good HTML" by James "Eric" Tilton (last updated July 13, 1998). Available at **www.ology.org/tilt/cgh/**.

- "HTML Tags," a free online cheat sheet by VisiBone at **html-tags.info**.
- "Style Guide for Online Hypertext" by Tim Berners-Lee (the originator of the World Wide Web). Last updated May 1995. Available at **www.w3.org/Provider/Style/**.
- "A Basic HTML Style Guide" by Alan Richmond (NASA GSFC). Last updated July 11, 2001. Available at **heasarc.gsfc.nasa.gov/docs/heasarc/Style_Guide/ styleguide.html**.

Among a number of other good books on the Web and HTML authoring are

- *HTML and XHTML: The Complete Reference, Fourth Edition* by Thomas A. Powell (McGraw-Hill/Professional, 2003).
- *Web Design: The Complete Reference, Second Edition* by Thomas A. Powell (McGraw-Hill/Professional, 2002).
- *HTML, XHTML, and CSS QuickSteps, Second Edition* by Guy Hart-Davis (McGraw-Hill/Professional, 2009).

Chapter 2
Styling with CSS

Key Skills & Concepts

- Attaching CSS

- Understanding CSS Rules

- Selecting What to Format

- Applying CSS Concepts

- Using Text Properties

- Implementing Page Properties

- Laying Out with CSS

With XHTML you can build the structure of a web page, but if you follow the strict definition of XHTML and don't use any of the deprecated HTML tags, you can't make the page look very good, and it may look different in different browsers. Making a page consistently look good in many browsers is the job of *CSS* (Cascading Style Sheets). CSS is a collection of rules for specifying the colors, fonts, and layout of a web page. Today it is not only the primary way of formatting a web page, but it is also the most efficient.

In this chapter we'll look at the structure of CSS rules, how style sheets are added to a web page, how rules are applied, what the more common rules are, and examples of their use.

NOTE

In hopes of simplifying the discussion in this chapter, several terms are meant in their generic sense. These include the following:
Page or "web page" is the original area or "canvas" on which the web designer lays out the elements to be displayed.
Browser is any software that can render the page so it can be read.
Screen is any device that can display the page, including hand-held devices and printers.

Creating CSS

CSS is simply lines of text (the rules) embedded in either an XHTML or an HTML (from here on referred to as *X/HTML*) page, or, more commonly, in a separate CSS file, where it can be applied to a number of X/HTML pages. CSS is designed to be very compact, with many features that keep it from being verbose, as shown in Listing 2-1.

Listing 2-1   CSS example

```
body {
        background:yellow;
        color:red;
        font: 12pt Arial;
     }
h1, h2 {
        color:blue;
        font: 24pt "Comic Sans MS";
     }
```

In the CSS listing shown in Listing 2-1, the X/HTML **<body>** tag on the web page to which this CSS is attached is assigned a background color of yellow, a text color of red, and a font of 12-point Arial. Additionally, both the **<h1>** and **<h2>** heading tags are assigned a text color of blue and a font of 24-point Comic Sans. This also shows how CSS cascades: the **body** attributes are assigned to the elements on the page, except the **h1** and **h2** elements, which have their own attribute assignments.

Attaching CSS

A CSS is attached to X/HTML pages or files in one or both of two primary ways:

- **Embedded** in the X/HTML file using the **<style>** tag.
- **Linked** as an external CSS file using the **<link>** tag.

Listing 2-2 shows how the **<style>** tag is used. Note that the CSS is embedded in the **<style>** tag. Listing 2-3 shows the **<link>** tag. Both of these tags only appear in the **<head>** section of an X/HTML document, but you can have multiple **<link>** tags if needed. Figure 2-1 shows that the two methods of attaching a CSS produce exactly the same result (you have to use your imagination for the color, but it is as stated), while Table 2-1 shows the tags and their attributes.

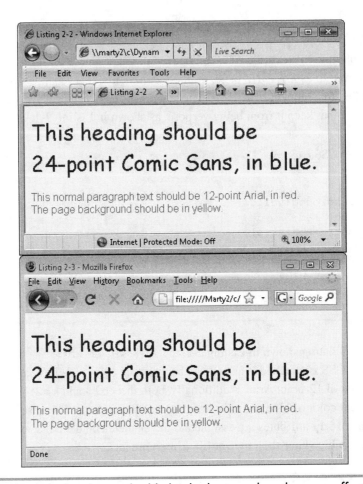

Figure 2-1   Both a linked and an embedded style sheet produce the same effect, but a linked one can be used on multiple pages.

Listing 2-2   X/HTML page with `<style>` tag

```
<!DOCTYPE html PUBLIC "-//W3C//DTD XHTML 1.0 Strict//EN"
"http://www.w3.org/TR/xhtml1/DTD/xhtml1-strict.dtd">
<html xmlns="http://www.w3.org/1999/xhtml" lang="en" xml:lang="en">
   <head>
   <meta http-equiv="Content-Type" content="text/html; charset=iso-8859-1">
      <title>Listing 2-2</title>
      <style type="text/css">
```

```
body {
        background:yellow;
        color:red;
        font: 12pt Arial;
        }
h1, h2 {
        color:blue;
        font: 24pt "Comic Sans MS";
        }
    </style>
  </head>
  <body>
    <h1>This heading should be<br />24-point Comic Sans, in blue.</h1>
    <p>
        This normal paragraph text should be 12-point Arial, in red.<br />
        The page background should be in yellow.
    </p>
  </body>
</html>
```

Tag or Attribute	Description
`<style> </style>`	Allows the embedding of CSS rules in an X/HTML document.
`type`	Specifies the style sheet content type, normally `text/css`. This attribute must be supplied.
`media`	Specifies the intended medium for the styles. The default is `screen`.
`<link />`	Attaches an external CSS to an X/HTML document.
`rel`	Specifies the relationship between the X/HTML document and the style sheet. It is most commonly `stylesheet`, but it can also be `alternate` to specify an alternative style sheet with a name.
`href`	Specifies the URL or filename of the style sheet.
`type`	Specifies the style sheet content type, normally `text/css`. This must be supplied.
`media`	Specifies the intended medium for the styles. The default is `screen`; an alternative is `printer`.
`title`	Specifies the name of an alternative style sheet.

Table 2-1   Style and Link Tags

Listing 2-3 X/HTML page with `<link>` tag

```
<!DOCTYPE html PUBLIC "-//W3C//DTD XHTML 1.0 Strict//EN"
"http://www.w3.org/TR/xhtml1/DTD/xhtml1-strict.dtd">
<html xmlns="http://www.w3.org/1999/xhtml" lang="en" xml:lang="en">
   <head>
   <meta http-equiv="Content-Type" content="text/html; charset=iso-8859-1">
      <title>Listing 2-3</title>
      <link rel="stylesheet" type="text/css" href="listing 2-1.css" />
   </head>
   <body>
      <h1>This heading should be<br />24-point Comic Sans, in blue.</h1>
      <p>
         This normal paragraph text should be 12-point Arial, in red.<br />
         The page background should be in yellow.
      </p>
   </body>
</html>
```

TIP

A practice that you might see in older code samples is to put `<!-- -->` comment tags inside style tags enclosing all of the styles to prevent them from displaying in old browsers. While this works, very few people use older browsers, and this practice with the comment tags isn't XHTML compliant.

CSS Rules

A CSS rule in its simplest form is a line of text with three components: a selector, a property, and a value. For example:

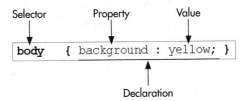

where the *selector* is **body**, the *property* is background, and the *value* is yellow. The property and value are separated by a colon, and together they form the *declaration,* which is enclosed in curly braces ({}). A single selector can have multiple property/value pairs, as shown in Listing 2-1, which are separated by a semicolon. With only a single property/value pair or for the last property/value pair, a semicolon is not necessary, but it is suggested simply for consistency and to promote good habits.

CSS rules are case sensitive and must be in lowercase. You can add as many spaces, tabs, and new-lines as you want to make a CSS easy to read. It is recommended that you spread out the rules so that you can easily see what is affecting the various parts of your web pages.

You can both help your own memory of what you did in a style sheet and tell others about it by adding comments, either after completing a rule on the same line, or on a separate line. To do this, enclose the text comment within a /* */ pair, as shown here:

```
body { background : yellow; }  /* Makes the background yellow */
```

Types of Selectors

The selector part of a CSS rule identifies the element of a web page that will be affected by the rule. You can have selectors that cover the entire page, such as **body**, or a single type of tag, such as **h1**, as you have seen in Listings 2-1 and 2-2. You can also have selectors that identify parts of a page, or just some of a particular tag, some **h1**s, for example. So a selector can be a tag name, a tag name modified by a class, an ID, an attribute, an event or its context, or parts of an element identified by a tag.

Class and ID Selectors

You can add class names and/or IDs to most tags to identify just the ones that you want affected by a style, by adding the class or ID to the selector. A class is added to a selector by following the tag name with a period (.) and the class name. An ID is added to a selector by following the tag name with a pound sign (#) and the ID. For example, Listing 2-4 and Figure 2-2 show the selectors needed to specifically format a class of paragraphs and a particular heading with an ID when headings and paragraphs not so identified are formatted differently.

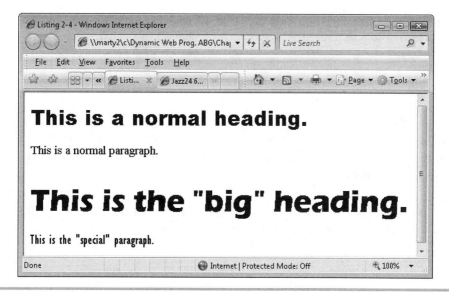

Figure 2-2 ID and class attributes let you style particular elements.

NOTE

In Listing 2-4, and in the remaining listings in this chapter, the `<!DOCTYPE>` and `<meta>` tags, as well as the `<html>` attributes have been left out for compactness.

Listing 2-4   Class and ID selectors

```html
<html>
   <head>
      <title>Listing 2-4</title>
      <style type="text/css">
         h1 {font : 24pt "Arial Black";   }
         p { font : 14pt "Times New Roman"; }
         h1.big { font : 36pt "Eras Bold ITC"; }
         p#special { font : 16pt "Gill Sans MT Condensed"; }
      </style>
   </head>
   <body>
      <h1>This is a normal heading.</h1>
      <p>This is a normal paragraph.</p><br />
      <h1 class="big">This is the "big" heading.</h1>
      <p id="special">This is the "special" paragraph.</p>
   </body>
</html>
```

TIP

A CSS selector can be just a class or an ID, with its identifier (`.` or `#`) and without a tag name. For example, `.legal { font : 16pt "Franklin Gothic Book"; }` would apply to all tags with the `legal` class. While you can do the same thing with an ID (`#note { font : 16pt "Franklin Gothic Book"; }`), only one element in an X/HTML document can have a particular ID.

Other Selectors

The most often used selectors are tag names followed by a tag name with class or ID. However, five other types of selectors use events, attributes, context, location, or groups to identify what is to be styled:

- **Events** consider the interactive events affecting a tag and are generally used with a hyperlink in the `<a>` (anchor) tag. For example:

  ```css
  a:link  { color : green; }
  ```

colors the link green if it has not been visited. Five possible events can be styled; all are preceded by a colon (:) immediately following a tag:

- **link**, for hyperlinks that have not been clicked

- **visited**, for hyperlinks that have been clicked

- **active**, for elements that are in the process of being clicked

- **hover**, for elements on which the mouse is pointing

- **focus**, for elements selected but not activated, like with the TAB key

- **Attributes** of a tag, where the attribute is enclosed in brackets (**[]**). For example:

  `input[readonly]   { background : gray; }`

  applies a gray background to form fields that have a `readonly` attribute. You can also style just those tags with an attribute that has a particular value. For example:

  `table[border="2"]   { border-color : blue; }`

  sets only the table borders of tables with an attribute of `border="2"` to blue. Additionally, a tag with an attribute value that is one of a list of values can be styled with

  `area[coords~="147"]   { background-color : yellow; }`

  which places a yellow background behind the area(s), one of whose coordinates is 147. Finally, a tag with an attribute value that is the first value in a list of values can be styled with

  `area[coords|="60"]   { background-color : fuchsia; }`

  which places a fuchsia background behind the area(s), whose first coordinate is 60.

- **Context** of a tag considers where a tag is in relationship to another tag and has three possibilities (see Listing 2-5):

  - **Descendant** selectors, where the tag to be styled, called a *descendant* tag, is contained any place in another tag, called the *ancestor,* including inside a third tag. As a selector, the descendant follows the ancestor, with a space separating them. For example:

    `div em { font-family : "Comic Sans MS" }`

    makes the contents of any **<em>** within a **<div>** Comic Sans, like this:

Listing 2-5	Example of context modified selector

```html
<html>
   <head>
      <title>Listing 2-5</title>
      <style type="text/css">
         div em { font-family : "Comic Sans MS"; }
      </style>
   </head>
   <body>
      <div>
         <ul>
            <li>This line is <em>FUNNY!</em></li>
            <li>This line is <em>FUNNIER!!</em></li>
         </ul>
      </div>
   </body>
</html>
```

- **Child** selectors, where the tag to be styled (called a *child* tag) is contained immediately within its *parent* tag. It cannot be within a third tag. As a selector, the child follows the parent, with a **>** (greater-than) separating them. For example:

  `ul > li { font-family : "Comic Sans MS" }`

  makes the contents of both **<li>** Comic Sans, like this:

  > • This line is *FUNNY!*
  > • This line is *FUNNIER!!*

- **First Child** selectors, where the tag to be styled is a child tag and immediately follows its *parent* tag. As a selector, `:first child` follows the parent. For example:

  `ul :first-child { font-family : "Comic Sans MS" }`

  makes the contents of the first **<li>** Comic Sans, like this:

  > • This line is *FUNNY!*
  > • This line is FUNNIER!!

- **Adjacent** selectors, where the tag to be styled is immediately preceded by its *sibling* tag at the same level. As a selector, the tag to be styled follows the sibling, with a plus (**+**) separating them. For example:

  `li + li { font-family : "Comic Sans MS" }`

makes the contents of the second `<li>` Comic Sans, like this:

> - This line is *FUNNY!*
> - **This line is *FUNNIER!!***

- **Location** within an element, where either the *first letter* or *first line* of an element is to be styled. For example:

  `p:first-letter` { font : 18pt "Copperplate Gothic Bold" }

  will make the first letter enclosed in a `<p>` tag 18pt Copperplate Gothic Bold, as you can see next, where each paragraph is in separate `<p> </p>` tags.

  > Four score and seven years ago our fathers brought forth on this continent, a new nation, conceived in Liberty, and dedicated to the proposition that all men are created equal.
  >
  > Now we are engaged in a great civil war, testing whether that nation, or any nation so conceived and so dedicated, can long endure. We are met on a great battle-field of that war. We have come to dedicate a

- **Groups** of tags that have the same declaration can be listed as a common selector, separated by commas. For example:

  `h1, h2, h3` { font-family : "Copperplate Gothic Bold" }

  will set the first three heading levels to use the Copperplate Gothic Bold font.

TIP

You can combine many of the methods of specifying a selector to refine what is to be styled. For example:
`p#first span` { font : 18pt "Copperplate Gothic Bold" ; }
will make the text in the `<span>` tag(s) that are a descendant of the `<p>` tag with an ID `first`, 18pt Copperplate Gothic Bold.

CSS Properties and Values

The properties and values that you can use in a CSS rule are many and varied, but roughly fall into three groups: text properties, page properties, and layout properties, which are each discussed in their own section, later in this chapter. To understand and appropriately use these properties and values requires an initial understanding of the fundamental concepts upon which CSS is built.

CSS Concepts

Seven fundamental concepts underlie CSS: cascading and inheritance, the box and visual models of page layout, element positioning, units of measure, use of color, text and fonts, and tables and lists. Text and fonts are discussed with the text properties. The box and visual models of page layout, as well as positioning and tables and lists, are discussed with layout properties. The rest are discussed here.

Cascading and Inheritance

In CSS every property must have a value. That value can be specific, computed, or inherited. To arrive at the actual or final value that will be used with a property, a browser must go through three sets of processes. The first of these is the *cascade,* which determines the order of precedence of various factors that can influence the final property value. The second is *inheritance,* which considers the influence of values determined for elements that are parents to the current element. The third process is the *calculation* of the final value.

Cascading Order   In a cascading order, a value is determined by the influence that is found to be most important in a given hierarchy. For CSS, the cascading order of precedence, in ascending order where 1 is least important and 5 is most important, is

1. Conventions and settings in the browser or viewing software.

2. Default settings made by the user or viewer of the web page.

3. Imported or linked style sheet property values.

4. Embedded style sheet property values.

5. Settings made by the user or viewer as the page is being viewed.

In other words, the browser begins with its own settings, which may be changed by the user, replaced by first an external style sheet, and then by an embedded style sheet, and finally is adjusted in the viewing program by the user.

If you want a particular style to override what would otherwise occur with the cascade, you can give that style an !important declaration and it will do so. An example of such a declaration is

```
h1 { font : 24pt "Arial Black" !important ; }
```

Inheritance   Through inheritance, an element's value can be determined by the values of elements that are earlier in the document tree. For example, Listing 2-6 shows a simple web page with the document tree as displayed by Aptana's Outline view, shown next:

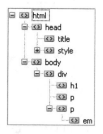

| **Listing 2-6**   Document tree example |

```html
<html>
    <head>
        <title>Listing 2-6</title>
        <style type="text/css">
            div.main { font : 12pt "Bodoni MT"; }
            em { font : 14pt "Script MT Bold"; }
        </style>
    </head>
    <body>
        <div class="main">
            <h1>The main heading.</h1>
            <p>The first paragraph.</p>
            <p>The second, <em>yes, second</em> paragraph.</p>
        </div>
    </body>
</html>
```

In this document tree, as in most, **<body>** is the root of the tree, the first child is **<div class="main">**, which in turn has three children **<h1>**, **<p>**, and **<p>**. The second **<p>** has one child, **<em>**. Without a style sheet, or the users making changes in their browser, the default style settings in the browser would flow through the entire tree based on the cascade. When a style sheet is introduced with a font style for **<div class="main">**, this style will flow to its children and its children's children unless interrupted by another style. This is the fundamental principle of inheritance. As you can see next, the font set for **<div class="main">** appears in the **<h1>** and two **<p>**s, except for the text enclosed in **<em>**, which has its own style.

The main heading.

The first paragraph.

The second, *yes, second,* paragraph.

Inheritance works for those properties, such as font, which allow it. In the lists in later sections of this chapter, you'll see a column labeled "Inherited?," which shows the properties that can be inherited. If you want a property that isn't normally inherited to be inherited, you can create a style for the element, and use inherit for its value.

Units of Measure

Horizontal and vertical measurement values in CSS are used with a number of properties including border-width, font, line-height, margin, and text-indent. Units of horizontal and vertical measurement can be in two forms: relative to some other measure, and absolute.

Relative units scale the current element to the element's font size, to the element's font "*x*-height" (the size of the lowercase *x*), or relative to the output device's resolution. The relative units of measure are

- **em**, which scales the element to its font size. 1em is the same size as the font or equal to 100 percent. So 1.4em is 140 percent of the font, and .6em is 60 percent of the font size.

- **ex**, which scales the element to its "*x*-height," is similar to em, 1ex is the same size as the "*x*-height" or 100 percent of the size of the current font's letter "*x*." As a default, 1ex is considered equivalent to .5em.

- **px** or pixel, which scales the element to the viewed resolution. On a computer screen at 96dpi (dots per inch), viewed at arm's length, or about 28 inches, 1px is approximately 0.01 inch or 0.26 mm, and is slightly smaller (72 percent) than a point (pt, see next list), which is 0.01389 inch.

NOTE

When **em** is used with a font, it is relative to or a percent of the parent element's font.

Absolute units of measurement are specific measurements in any of the following units:

- **cm**, centimeters, 0.3937 inch

- **in**, inches, 2.54 centimeters

- **mm**, millimeters, 0.1 centimeter, 0.03937 inch

- **pc**, picas, 1/6 of an inch, 12 points

- **pt**, points, 1/72 of an inch, 1/12 pica

TIP

When you use absolute units, you should be pretty certain of the dimensions of the displaying device. As hand-held devices become more common, using relative units become more important.

Listing 2-7 and Figure 2-3 show examples of the application of various units of measure.

Listing 2-7   Units of measure

```html
<html>
    <head>
        <title>Listing 2-7</title>
        <style type="text/css">
            body {
                    margin : .5in ;
                    font : 14px "Arial";
                }
            h1    {
                    font : 2em "Arial Black"; /* twice the body font */
                    line-height : 1.5em ; /* 150% of font or 36 points */
                    margin : -.32cm ; /* outdented about a third of the margin */
                }
            p     {
                    margin : 25mm ; /* about twice the body margin */
                    font : 1.1em; /* 110% of the body font*/
                    border : .25ex dashed; /* 25% of the font's x-height */
                }
        </style>
    </head>
    <body>
        <h1>This is approximately a 20pt heading that is outdented.</h1>
        <p>
            This a paragraph with approximately 11pt type, indented and
                with a dashed border.
        </p>
    </body>
</html>
```

This is approximately a 20pt heading that is outdented.

This a paragraph with approximately 11pt type, indented and with a dashed border.

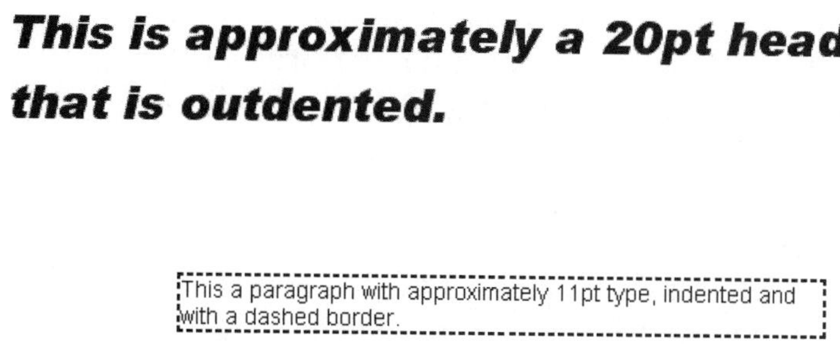

Figure 2-3   Web-based documents will scale much better with relative units of measure.

Use of Color

In CSS you can add color to the background of a page with the `background-color` property or to one of three foreground elements: text, with the `color` property; borders, with the `border-color` property; and outlines, with the `outline-color` property. The value for each of these properties is a specific color identifier, plus, in the case of `border-` and `outline-color`, you have the option of `transparent`.

The color identifier can be a color name or a numerical representation of a color using the RGB (Red, Green, Blue) color specification. The color name can be one of the classic color names: `aqua`, `black`, `blue`, `fuchsia`, `gray`, `green`, `lime`, `maroon`, `navy`, `olive`, `orange`, `purple`, `red`, `silver`, `teal`, `white`, or `yellow`, or it can be one of the over 140 extended color names implemented in most browsers and shown at www.w3.org/TR/css3-color/.

The RGB color can be specified in four ways (shown in examples for making paragraph text the color Cyan):

- As a six-digit hexadecimal (hex) number preceded by #, for example:

  `p`.cyan { color: #00ffff }.

- As a three-digit hex number preceded by #, for example:

  `p`.cyan { color: #0ff }.

  The three-digit hex number only works when each of the three colors, normally represented by two digits, has two digits of the same character. The three digits are expanded to six digits by doubling each of the original digits.

- As a set of three percentages, separated by commas, enclosed in parentheses, and preceded by `rgb`, where hex 00 is 0% and hex FF is 100%, for example:

  `p`.cyan { color: rgb(0%,100%,100%) }.

- As a set of three decimal numbers, separated by commas, enclosed in parentheses, and preceded by `rgb`, where hex 00 is 0 and hex FF is 255, for example:

  `p`.cyan { color: rgb(0,255,255) }.

The two-digit hexadecimal number used to represent the Red, Green, or Blue color component can have 256 values (ranging from 0 to 255 decimal or 00 to FF hexadecimal). The combination of the three colors or six hex digits, allows a total of over 16 million colors, compared with the 140 named colors. The colors range from Black at decimal 0,0,0 or hex #000000 (the absence of any color) to White at decimal 255,255,255 or hex #ffffff (the sum of all color). Red is 255,0,0 or #ff0000, Lime (not Green) is 0,255,0 or #00ff00, and Blue is 0,0,255 or #0000ff.

TIP

An easy way to convert between decimal and hexadecimal notation is to use the Windows Calculator in Scientific mode. Open the calculator from **Start | All Programs | Accessories | Calculator**, and then select **View | Scientific**. Click either the **Hex** or **Dec** option, enter a hexadecimal or decimal number, and click the opposite option (**Hex** or **Dec**).

In the past, any discussion of color on the Web focused on the Web Safe palette—216 colors that would display correctly on virtually any monitor. One reason the earliest browsers had only 16 named colors was that many systems wouldn't support more than 16 colors. Today, this situation, like everything else connected with the Web, is vastly different. At this point, it makes little sense to adhere to a standard that has been made obsolete by advanced technology. This doesn't mean that named colors should not be used when they fit the application, only that the importance of adhering to this standard has greatly diminished.

A number of color charts are available on the Internet in addition to the one at W3C mentioned earlier. Do a search on "Internet Color Chart." One of the best, and our favorite, is at http://html-color-codes.com, is produced by Bob Stein of VisiBone (www.visibone.com, which has many other charts and guides, a number of which are mentioned in this book).

Text Properties

CSS provides a wide variety properties and values to facilitate the styling of text, as set out in Table 2-2, and as shown in many of the listings, figures, and illustrations in this chapter. Text styling has two major components: the application of fonts and font characteristics, and the alignment and spacing of text.

Application of Fonts

The key ingredient in the application of fonts is for the browser to present to the user the font that the web designer specified in the correct size, weight, variant, and style. Most browsers have an algorithm for choosing a substitute font if the specified one with its attributes is not available. The W3C provides a model for such substitution at http://w3.org/TR/CSS21/fonts.html. As a designer you can do several things to assist this process: choose common fonts, add alternative fonts, and add a generic font.

For example, if you wanted to specify Garamond as the font family for the main division of your page, you might use the following rule:

```
div.main { font-family : "Garamond", "Palatino Linotype", "Times", serif }
```

The fonts are listed in priority order from left to right, so Garamond is used first if it is available, and the generic serif font is only used if all three of the named fonts cannot be found.

Property	Allowed Values	Inherited?
color	The color of text. See "Use of Color" earlier in this chapter.	Yes
font	A combination of font size and font family, but can include `font-variant`, `-weight`, `-style`, and `line-height`, which must be preceded by a slash (/).	Yes
font-family	One or more font names in quotation marks and separated by commas, and optionally a generic font type (`serif`, `sans-serif`, `cursive`, `fantasy`, and `monospace`) as a fallback if the specified font is unavailable.	Yes
font-size	A font size as an absolute value (`xx-small`, `x-small`, `small`, `medium`, `large`, `x-large`, `xx-large`); a specific numeric value in one of the units of measure; a relative size (`larger`, `smaller`); or a percentage (120%).	Yes
font-style	`normal`, `italic`, `oblique`.	Yes
font-variant	`normal`, `small-caps`.	Yes
font-weight	`normal`, `bold`, `bolder`, `lighter`, `100-900`.	Yes
letter-spacing	`normal` or a specified added space between letters in one of the units of measure.	Yes
line-height	`normal` or a specified height in one of the units of measure, a number to multiply by the font size, or a percentage multiplied by the font size.	Yes
text-align	`left`, `right`, `center`, `justify`.	Yes
text-decoration	`none`, `underline`, `overline`, `line-through`, `blink`.	No
text-indent	A specified amount in one of the units of measure for indenting the first line of text.	Yes
text transform	`capitalize`, `uppercase`, `lowercase`, `none`.	Yes
vertical-align	Align text relative to the line containing it: `baseline`, `sub` (subscript), `super` (superscript), `top`, `text-top`, `middle`, `bottom`, `text-bottom`, a positive or negative percentage, or a specific amount relative to the baseline. The default is `baseline`.	No
white-space	`normal` (collapse any white space and allow all line breaks), `pre` (prevent collapsing white space and allow some line breaks), `nowrap` (collapse white space and ignore line breaks), `pre-wrap` (prevent collapsing white space and allow all line breaks), `pre-line` (collapse white space and allow some line breaks).	Yes
word-spacing	`normal` or a specified added space between words in one of the units of measure.	Yes

Table 2-2 Text Properties

NOTE

Font names do not need to be in quotes if they do not contain a space or a special character. Nevertheless, it's a good practice to put all font names in quotes.

Considerations to keep in mind with the various font properties include

- A value of `italic` for the `font-style` will select both italic and oblique font names, while a value of `oblique` will only select oblique font names.

- The numeric values for `font-weight`, such as 200 and 600, are names, and you *cannot* interpolate between them, for example, by using "250." The value 400 is the same as `normal`, and 700 is the same as `bold`. Fonts with "light" in their name are 300, "book," "regular," and "roman" are all normal or 400, "medium" or "demi" is 500, "heavy" is 800, and "black" is 900.

- The `font` property allows you to combine in one property the values for the other five font properties, plus `line-height`, as you can see in Listing 2-8 where the individual properties listed in the first rule, are combined into one at the end. In the `font` property, you must have a font size and a font family, and the size must precede the family. You can have zero to three of the other font properties, among themselves they can be in any order, but they all must precede the font size. The line height must be between the size and the family and when combined it must be preceded by a slash.

Listing 2-8   The same rule

```
P  {
   font-style : italic;
   font-variant : small-caps;
   font-weight : 800;     /* 25% bolder than "bold" */
   font-size : 16px;
   line-height : 1.5em;
   font-family : "Garamond", "Palatino Linotype", "Times", serif;
   }
p  { font : italic small-caps 800 16px /1.5em "Garamond"; }
```

Alignment of Text

The properties for the alignment of text are reasonably self-explanatory, but several of the less obvious features include

- The text-indent property applies only to the first line of a block of text and can be negative, to move the line of text to the left, as shown next and in Listing 2-9, but if you don't have a margin to contain the outdented text, it will be cut off.

> **FOUR SCORE AND SEVEN YEARS AGO** our fathers brought forth on this continent, a new nation, conceived in Liberty, and dedicated to the proposition that all men are created equal.

Listing 2-9   Using text-indent

```html
<html>
    <head>
        <title>Listing 2-9</title>
        <style>
            p#first {
                margin : .5in ;
                text-indent : -.25in ;
                }
            p#first span { font : 18pt "Copperplate Gothic Bold" ; }
        </style>
    </head>
    <body>
        <p id="first">
            <span>Four score and seven years ago</span> our fathers brought
forth on this continent, a new nation, conceived in Liberty, and dedicated
to the proposition that all men are created equal.
        </p>
    </body>
</html>
```

- The algorithm used with text-align : justify is unique to each browser, and therefore may produce different results, and may conflict with rules incorporating word and letter spacing.

- The text-decoration property is applied to text within an element, including the white space between characters, words, and sentences, using the same text color as that specified for the element.

- The blink value for the text-decoration property is an optional value and does not work in IE 6, IE 7, and IE 8. It does work in Firefox 3.0 and 3.5.

- The letter-spacing and word-spacing property values are in addition to the normal spacing between characters, words, and sentences. When the spacing is changed with these properties, the text-align : justify value cannot further adjust the spacing to justify lines of text.

- The vertical-align property aligns text relative to the line of text (called a *line-box*) it is in. It does *not* do vertical alignment with a paragraph or other containing block.

- The white-space property determines how a browser treats the space at the beginning and end of lines of text. Spaces, tabs, and carriage returns are all considered "white space," which is eliminated by use of the normal, nowrap, and pre-line values, but not with the pre and pre-wrap values.

NOTE
Where applicable, most properties default to values of auto, normal, medium, or none, as appropriate unless otherwise specified.

Page Properties

Page properties, shown in Table 2-3, when used with the **<body>** tag, are applied to the entire page, but you can also apply them to segments of a page using **<div>**, **<h1...>**, **<p>**, **<table>**, and other elements that define space on a page.

Property	Allowed Values	Inherited?
background	Any combination of background-attachment, background-color, background-image, background-position, background-repeat.	No
background-attachment	scroll or fixed with regard to the viewer, with scroll the default.	No
background-color	A color (see "Use of Color" earlier in this chapter) or transparent, with transparent the default.	No
background-image	The filename or URL of the image, or none.	No
background-position	A horizontal percentage or absolute distance, left, center, or right; and/or a vertical percentage or absolute distance, top, center, or bottom. The default is 0%, 0%, the top left corner.	No
background-repeat	repeat (both horizontally and vertically), no-repeat, repeat-x (horizontally), or repeat-y (vertically), with repeat the default.	No
border; border-top, -right, -left, -bottom	Any combination of border-width, border-style, and border-top-color.	No

Table 2-3   Page Properties *(continued)*

Property	Allowed Values	Inherited?
`border-color;` `border-top-color` `-right-, -left-,` `-bottom-`	A specific color (see "Use of Color" earlier in this chapter) or `transparent`, with `transparent` the default.	No
`border-style;` `border-top-style` `-right-, -left-,` `-bottom-`	Up to four (one per side) of `dashed`, `dotted`, `double`, `groove`, `hidden`, `inset`, `outset`, `ridge`, and `none`. The default is `none`.	No
`border-width;` `border-top-width,` `-right-, -left-,` `-bottom-`	Up to four (one per side) of `thin`, `medium`, `thick`, or a specific value in one of the units of measure. The default is `medium`.	No
`cursor`	A type of cursor: `auto`, `crosshair`, `default`, `pointer`, `move` (four-headed arrow), `text` (I-beam), `wait` (hourglass), `progress` (spinning beach ball); or moving one of the sides of the cursor, where a side is specified by `n-resize` (north side), `ne-resize` (north-east side), `e-resize`, `se-resize`, `s-resize`, `sw-resize`, `w-resize`, and `nw-resize`; or the filename of an image to use for the cursor.	Yes
`orphans`	The minimum number of lines that must be left at the bottom of the page. The default is 2.	Yes
`outline`	Any combination of `outline-color`, `outline-style`, and `outline-width`.	No
`outline-color`	A specific color (see "Use of Color" earlier in this chapter) or `invert` (an inversion of the element color), with `invert` the default.	No
`outline-style`	Up to four (one per side) of `dashed`, `dotted`, `double`, `groove`, `inset`, `outset`, `ridge`, and `none`.	No
`outline-width`	Up to four (one per side) of `thin`, `medium`, `thick`, or a specific value in one of the units of measure.	No
`overflow`	`visible` (content flows out of the box), `hidden` (content clipped at the edge of the box), `scroll` (scroll bar added to see content), `auto` (normally the same as `scroll`).	No
`page-break-after` `page-break-before`	`auto` (neither force nor forbid a page break), `always` (force a page break before/after a box), `avoid` (forbid a page break before/after a box), `left` (force one or two page breaks so the page is a left-hand, even-numbered, page), `right` (force one or two page breaks so the page is a right-hand, odd-numbered, page).	No
`page-break-inside`	`auto` (neither force nor forbid a page break), `avoid` (forbid a page break before/after a box).	Yes
`widows`	The minimum number of lines that must be left at the top of the page. The default is 2.	Yes

Table 2-3 Page Properties *(continued)*

NOTE

While you can apply many of the page properties to the `<html>` tag, the effect is almost always the same as applying them to the `<body>` tag.

Considerations to keep in mind with the page properties include (see Listing 2-10 and Figure 2-4 for examples of applying the `background` and `border` properties):

- The `background` property can be a color, an image, or both. If you have both, the color will be displayed until the image is generated. The color will also show though any transparent areas of the image. The background covers the content, padding, and border of the element to which it is assigned.

- Backgrounds, colors, or images, are at the "bottom" (furthest away from the viewer) of the stack of elements on the screen and can be covered up by other elements. This can be controlled by the `z-index` property, discussed with "Layout Properties" later in this chapter.

- If you use the `background` property with, for example, the `<p>` tag, you will want to add some padding around the `<p>` to allow the background to extend slightly beyond the text.

- If you use an image as the background, you normally want to use a small image so that it will download quickly. To have the image cover the element, it will probably have to be repeated, which is the default of the `background-repeat` property, so it does not need to be stated.

- If you want a single image centered both horizontally and vertically on a page, you need to use the `no-repeat` value, but only one `center` value.

- Borders produced with the `border` property are placed on the outside of the element's content plus any padding that has been added, but on the inside of the margin. See "The Box and Visual Models of Page Layout" in the "Layout Properties" section later in this chapter.

- Similar to the `background` property, if you add a border, you will want to add some padding around the `<p>` and other content areas to place the border slightly outside the text.

- With `border-style` and `border-width` properties, if there is one value, it applies to all sides; if two values, the first refers to the top and bottom, and the second refers to the left and right; if three values, the first is the top, the second is the left and right sides, and the third is the bottom; if four values, the order is top, right, bottom, and left.

- The `outline` property draws lines on top of objects, not outside, like borders, and therefore the lines do not take space. They take the shape of the object, which may be nonrectangular, such as a button. The outline is the same on all sides.

- The `orphan` and `widow` properties are only considered if there is not enough room on the first page for a block of text. Also, if there is not enough text to satisfy both an `orphan` and `widow` property, and there is not enough room on the first page for the full block of text, then the full block of text is moved to the second page.

- The three `page-break` properties control whether page breaks can occur before, after, or within a an element block, such as a paragraph, an image, or a table. The default is that all three are allowed but not forced. If page breaks are allowed, then the widow and orphan properties control how that is done.

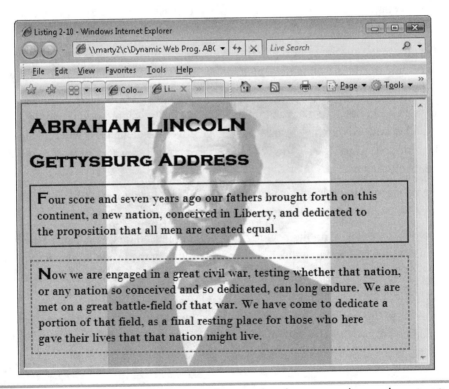

Figure 2-4 If you use a background image, be sure that the text can be read against it.

Listing 2-10   Page properties

```html
<html>
    <head>
        <title>Listing 2-10</title>
        <style type="text/css">
            body {
                    background : #dcdcdc url(alincoln-transparent.jpg)
                    no-repeat center;
                    }
            h1, h2 {font-family : "Copperplate Gothic Bold"; }
            h1 { font-size : 24pt; }
            h2 { font-size : 20pt; }
            p {
                font : 14pt "Bodoni MT";
                padding : .5em;
                }
            p:first-letter  { font : 18pt "Copperplate Gothic Bold" ; }
            p#one { border : thin double blue}
            p#two { border : .1em dashed red}
        </style>
    </head>
    <body>
        <h1>Abraham Lincoln</h1>
        <h2>Gettysburg Address</h2>
        <p id="one">
            Four score and seven years ago our fathers brought forth on ...
        </p>
        <p id="two">
            Now we are engaged in a great civil war, testing whether that ...
        </p>
    </body>
</html>
```

Layout Properties

While CSS is often thought of for formatting and styling a web page, it is at least equally useful for laying out a web page. With CSS' layout properties, shown in Table 2-4, you can position an element on a page in a number of different ways: you can determine how elements interact with each other and the amount of separation between them, how lists and tables are formed, and the characteristics and behavior of a page. As mentioned earlier in this chapter, several basic concepts are important to the layout properties, including the box and visual models, positioning, and tables and lists.

Property	Allowed Values	Inherited?
border-collapse	collapse or separate for tables, with separate the default.	Yes
border-spacing	One or two absolute distances between table and cell borders. One value specifies both the horizontal and vertical distances. With two values, the first is the horizontal distance, and the second is the vertical distance. 0 is the default.	Yes
bottom, left, top, right	A specific distance in one of the units of measure that an element side is separated from its containing block, a percentage of the containing block's height (bottom or top) or width (left or right) or auto.	No
caption-side	top (position the caption above the table), bottom, with top being the default.	
clear	The top border of the current box is placed beneath both, left, or right, border of another floating box, or none.	No
clip	auto (the element is not clipped), or rect (*top, right, bottom, left*), where *top, right, bottom*, and *left* are specific distances in one of the units of measure, separated by commas, that the side of an absolutely positioned element is clipped or offset from its upper-left corner (may be negative).	No
display	block (displays the element as an independent block), inline (displays the element within the block of another element), inline-block (displays the element as an independent block within the block of another element), list-item (displays a set of elements as a parent block with a set of inline children), run-in (displays an element as an independent block that adjoins another independent block), table, inline-table, table-*element* (displays elements as tables or table elements, independently or inline), none (causes the element and its descendants to have no effect on the layout).	No
float	Positions a block box to the left or right of other elements, closest to the left or right of the containing box, or none.	No
height, width	A specific distance in one of the units of measure of an element's height or width, a percentage of the containing block's height or width or auto. Excludes padding, borders, and margins.	No
list-style	Set any of the properties for list-style-type, list-style-position, and/or list-style-image, in that order.	Yes
list-style-image	Filename of the image to be used for the list item marker, or none. Replaces list-style-type marker.	Yes
list-style-position	Positions the list-item marker inside or outside (as in a hanging indent) the list-item box, with outside the default.	Yes

Table 2-4 Layout Properties

Property	Allowed Values	Inherited?
list-style-type	Specifies the list-item marker as disc, circle, square, decimal, decimal-leading-zero, lower-roman, upper-roman, lower-alpha, upper-alpha, lower-greek, or none.	Yes
margin; margin-top, -right, -left, -bottom	A specific distance in one of the units of measure that an element side is separated from its containing block, a percentage of the containing block's height (bottom or top) or width (left or right), or auto. The default is 0. If one value, it applies to all sides. If two values, the first refers to the top and bottom, and the second refers to the left and right. If three values, the first is the top, the second is the left and right sides, and the third is the bottom. If four values, the order is top, right, bottom, and left.	No
max-height max-width min-height min-width	A specific minimum or maximum length in one of the units of measure of an element's height or width, a percentage of the containing block's height or width, or none.	No
padding; padding-top, -right, -left, -bottom	A specific distance in one of the units of measure that an element's side is separated from its containing block, a percentage of the containing block's height (bottom or top) or width (left or right) or auto. Default is 0. If one value, it applies to all sides. If two values, the first refers to the top and bottom, and the second refers to the left and right. If three values, the first is the top, the second is the left and right sides, and the third is the bottom. If four values, the order is top, right, bottom, and left.	No
position	absolute (a box is removed from the normal flow and positioned and sized relative to the containing block's upper-left corner by the top, right, bottom, left properties), fixed (a box is positioned as in the absolute value, but then fixed in that position when the page is scrolled), relative (a box's position is offset relative to its normal position, determined by the normal flow, using the top, right, bottom, left properties), and static (a normal box that behaves in the normal flow of elements, it is the default).	No
table-layout	fixed (uses the specified table, column, cell, and border widths), or auto (reflects the data in the table and doesn't require specific widths).	No
visibility	visible (box is visible), hidden (box is invisible, but affects layout), collapse (in tables, collapses rows and/or columns; otherwise the same as hidden).	Yes
z-index	An integer, representing the stacking level from the viewpoint of the screen with what the viewer sees being "on top," or the highest stacking level; or auto.	No

Table 2-4   Layout Properties *(continued)*

The Box and Visual Models of Page Layout

In the simplest sense, a web page is a series of boxes within boxes, next to other boxes, and above and below still other boxes. The process of laying out a web page can be thought of as sizing and arranging the boxes so they all fit in the order you want, like this:

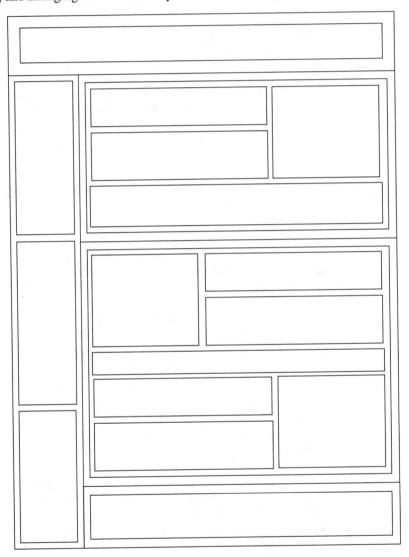

Elements on a web page are in one of two classes:

- **Block-level elements** take a specific, unique area of the screen and generate a block that is a containing block for its descendants. This is called a *block-level box,* or just a "block box." Block-level elements include `<body>`, `<div>`, `<h1...>`, and `<p>`.

- **Inline-level elements** do not take a unique area of the screen, nor do they, by default, form a unique block. Inline-level elements are inside (inline with) the blocks created by block-level elements. Inline-level elements include `<em>`, `<cite>`, and `<kbd>`. For the sake of layout, inline-level elements can be thought of as being contained in an "inline box."

The `display` property can make block-level elements inline-level, and make inline-level elements block-level.

Block-level elements not only have an invisible box that contains them, but also that box can be contained in up to three additional boxes associated with the element:

- **Padding**, the area separating the content from the border.

- **Border**, the normally visible line or decoration that surrounds the padding.

- **Margin**, the area separating the border from its containing block, such as a page or a parent block.

The total size of a block-level element is the sum of the content, padding, border, and margin, as shown next. If the padding, border, and margin are all 0, which is the default, the content immediately abuts its containing block.

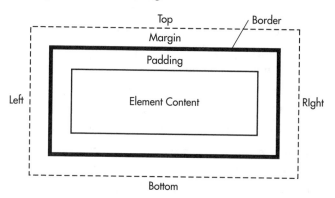

As a web page is rendered on a screen or other device, it flows on in a specific order, and later elements can both affect and be affected by earlier elements. As each element comes in, it generates none, one, or more boxes. How these boxes appear on the screen and affect other boxes is called the *visual formatting model,* or just "visual model." Components of the visual model affect how the final page appears on the screen and include

- **Viewpoint**, the area that the user sees; we have called this the *screen.* This may be larger or smaller than the designer's page or canvas, and has to be considered by both the browser and the designer.

- **Containing block** is a block created by an element higher in the hierarchy, either a parent or an ancestor, which contains the current element, which itself may be a containing block for its children and descendants. For example, as shown next, the **<body>** element contains a **<div>** element, which contains **<h1>** and **<p>** elements. The **<body>** element containing block holds the other three elements as either a child or descendants. The **<h1>** and **<p>** elements are in the containing blocks of both the **<div>** and **<body>** elements, which are parent and ancestor respectively.

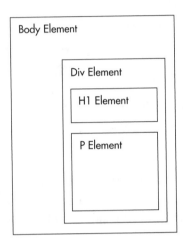

- **Box generation** occurs as elements are flowed onto a page. Depending on the type of element and the `display` property, the element generates a *block box,* which is displayed in a separate area of the page, or an *inline box,* which is displayed within another element's block box. In the example shown next, the **<p>** tag generates a block box that contains the **<span>** inline box.

  ```
  <p> <span>Four score and seven years ago</span> our fathers brought...</p>
  ```

- **Run-in box**, created with the `display` property `run-in` value, allows a block-level element to share the same block with a sibling (at the same level) block-level element. For example, a heading that runs into a following paragraph, as shown in Listing 2-11, with the result shown next:

> **The first heading.** The first paragraph into which the first heading is run-in.
>
> **The second heading.** The second paragraph into which the second heading is run-in.

Listing 2-11   Run-in example

```html
<html>
   <head>
      <title>Listing 2-11</title>
      <style type="text/css">
         h4 { display : run-in; }
      </style>
   </head>
   <body>
      <h4>The first heading.</h4>
      <p>The first paragraph into which the first heading is run-in.</p>
      <h4>The second heading.</h4>
      <p>The second paragraph into which the second heading is run-in.</p>
   </body>
</html>
```

NOTE

Listing 2-11 only produces the desired results just shown in IE 8, which comes with Windows 7. In IE 7 and Firefox 3.0 and 3.5, the `run-in` value does not work and produces the results shown here:

> **The first heading.**
>
> The first paragraph into which the first heading is run-in.
>
> **The second heading.**
>
> The second paragraph into which the second heading is run-in.

Positioning

Positioning determines how element boxes are sized and aligned relative to each other as the elements flow onto a page. The positioning is done using one of five methods that are determined by the `position`, `top`, `right`, `bottom`, `left`, `float`, `clear`, and `z-index` properties. The five positioning methods are

- **Normal flow** is the default flow of elements and their boxes onto a page with all of the positioning properties set to their default or initial values; in particular, `position` is set to `static`, which negates the other positioning properties.

- **Relative positioning** starts with the normal flow and then offsets the element's box relative to its "normal" position by the values of the top, right, bottom, and left properties. Boxes that follow a relative-positioned box are positioned as though the box were normally positioned.

- **Float positioning** also starts with the normal flow and then offsets the element's box to the left or right as far the containing box allows.

- **Absolute positioning** determines an element's position and possibly its size relative to the sides of the containing block by using the values of the top, right, bottom, and left properties. An absolute-positioned element has no impact on the layout of other elements, and its margins do not collapse with other margins.

- **Fixed positioning** is the same as absolute positioning, and additionally the element remains at a fixed position (its original position) on the screen as a page is scrolled.

Normal Flow   In the normal flow, block boxes flow onto the page, starting at the top, and are positioned vertically one after the other, separated by their margins. The left edge of a block box is positioned against the left edge of the containing block. Inline boxes flow onto the page starting at the top left and are positioned horizontally across the containing block to the right edge, where they then move down and start another horizontal set of boxes. Such a set of inline boxes that stretch across the width of a containing block is called a *line box*. A set of inline boxes may be aligned within the line box horizontally with the vertical-align property and aligned vertically with the text-align property.

Float Positioning   Float positioning allows you to pull a block box out of its normal flow's vertical position and attach it to the left or right side of the containing block. Once attached, the floated block will allow other blocks on its unattached side. This is the primary and recommended way of producing multiple columns. That said, it is not always the easiest way to do that. Tables, discussed later in this chapter, can produce sure placement of information on a page if your only audience is a 1024×786-pixel computer screen. The beauty of a floated block is that it is flexible and can look good on many different viewing devices, *if* you can get all the pieces to "float" where you want them.

In Listing 2-12 you'll see a CSS and the related XHTML used to create a common three-column page with header and footer blocks, as shown in Figure 2-5.

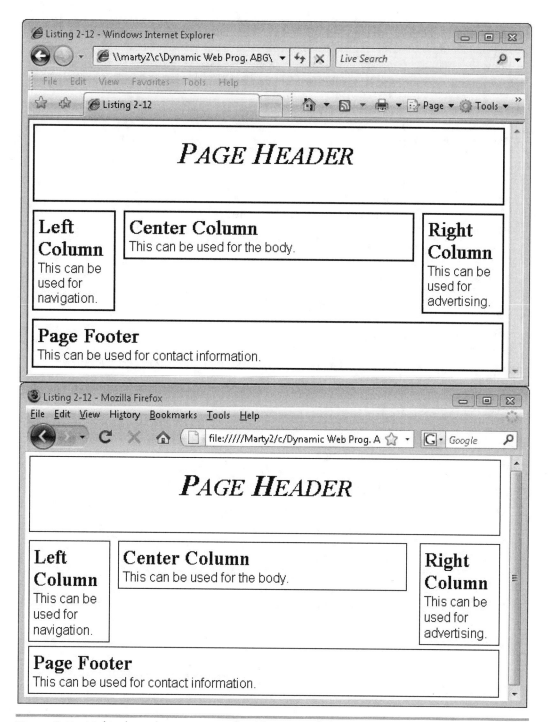

Figure 2-5   Multicolumn layout is most flexibly accomplished with floating blocks.

Listing 2-12 Floating columns—CSS

```
body            {
                 width : 600px;
                 margin : 0;
                 padding : 0;
                }
div, h1, h2, p  {
                 margin : 0;
                 padding : 0;
                }
h2              {font : 600 24px "Futura" ; }
p               {font : 16px "Arial", "Helvetica", sans-serif ; }
div#header      {
                 top : 0px;
                 left : 0px;
                 height : 80px;
                 margin : 5px;
                 border : thin solid;
                 padding : 5px;
                }
h1#title        {
                 font : italic small-caps 600 36px /1.5em "Futura" ;
                 text-align : center;
                }
div#left        {
                 float : left;
                 width : 15%;
                 margin : 5px;
                 border : thin solid;
                 padding : 5px;
                }
div#main        {
                 position : relative ;
                 float : left;
                 width : 58%;
                 margin : 5px;
                 border : thin solid;
                 padding : 5px;
                }
```

```
div#right        {
                 position : relative ;
                 float : right;
                 width : 15%;
                 margin : 5px;
                 border : thin solid;
                 padding : 5px;
                 }
div#footer       {
                 clear: both ;
                 margin : 5px;
                 border : thin solid;
                 padding : 5px;
                 }
```

Floating columns—HTML

```
<html>
   <head>                   <title>Listing 2-12</title>
         <link rel="stylesheet" type="text/css" href="Listing 2-12.css" />
   </head>
   <body>
      <div id="header">
         <h1 id="title">Page Header</h1>
      </div>
      <div id="left">
         <h2> Left Column </h2>
         <p> This can be used for navigation.</p>
      </div>
      <div id="main">
         <h2> Center Column </h2>
         <p> This can be used for the body.</p>
      </div>
      <div id="right">
         <h2> Right Column </h2>
         <p> This can be used for advertising.</p>
      </div>
      <div id="footer">
         <h2> Page Footer </h2>
         <p> This can be used for contact information.</p>
      </div>
   </body>
</html>
```

In the CSS portion of Listing 2-12, much is obvious, but several areas are not:

● It makes sense to float left the left column and float right the right column, but you might not guess that *you also need to float left the middle column.* If you don't do this, the right column does not know that it can scoot up beside the middle column, and the middle column shifts to the left, like this:

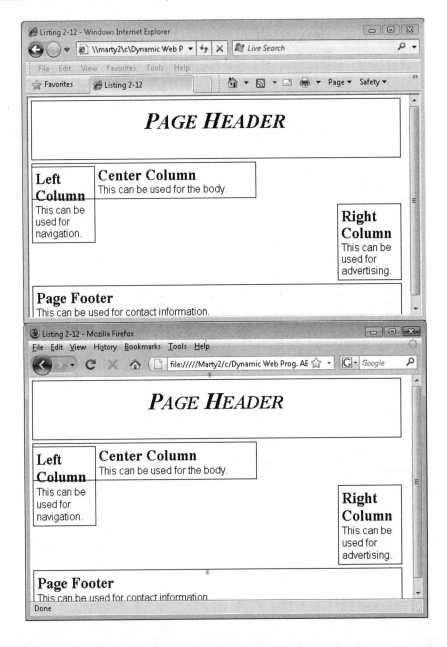

NOTE

This code falls victim to the IE 6 "float bug," which doubles the left margin on `float:left` blocks that start a row. This makes everything else shift right, so the right box still gets shifted down in IE 6. This can be fixed by adding the `display:inline` style to `div#left`. For further information, see www.positioniseverything.net/explorer/doubled-margin.html.

- If you give each of the two outer columns 15 percent of the space, you should be able to give the middle column 70 percent and have it all fit. But if you do that, you will find it doesn't fit, as shown next. As you can see in the listing, the middle column had to be reduced to 58 percent to get it to fit. The reason for this is that the height and width properties set the *content height or width, and exclude the padding, border, and margin,* which must be added to the height or width values. You can see this best by looking at the absolute number instead of percentages (although using percentages is preferred for their flexibility).

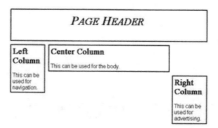

- The body width = 600 pixels.

- Left and right columns, both: `margin` = 5 pixels × 2, `border` = 2 pixels (in IE 7, Firefox = 1 pixel) × 2, `padding` = 5 pixels × 2, a total of 24 additional pixels in each column, plus the 90-pixel content width, for a total of 114 pixels.

- The middle column also has 24 pixels in the margins, border, and padding.

- If the two columns and the 24 added pixels in the middle are subtracted from the 600-pixel body width, it leaves 348 pixels for the content of the middle column, or 58 percent.

- You'll notice that at the top of the CSS part of Listing 2-12, we zero-out the `padding` and the `margin` for all basic elements. The reason for this is that all browsers set a default value for these elements (and apply the default differently from browser to browser). When you set your own values, it becomes additive to the browser set values and makes the elements look different than what you want. The next illustration shows how the three-column-float example looks without zeroing the basic elements. Compare this illustration with Figure 2-5, which includes the zeroing of the elements:

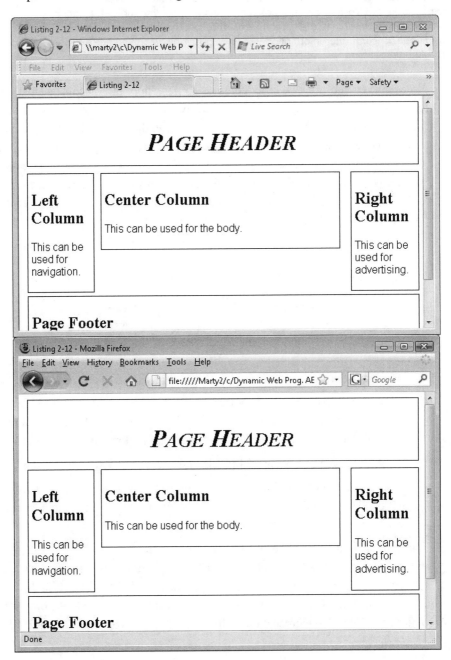

NOTE

IE 8 displays the three-column-float example without zeroing the basic elements in the same way as Firefox 3.0.5, *not* the way IE 7 does it.

Tables and Lists

Tables and lists are a powerful set of X/HTML elements for handling tabular information. Tables can also be used for laying out a web page, but that is discouraged because of the limited flexibility it provides, as well as the difficulty of maintenance. Tables divide an area of a web page, or the whole page, into rows and columns, creating *cells* where the two intersect. *Lists* are an indented set of items, which can be automatically numbered or have a small image at the beginning of each line, called a *bullet*. As shown in Chapter 1, there is an extensive set of X/HTML tags for making tables and lists, but there is an equally extensive set of CSS properties and values that can be applied for formatting and laying out tables and lists.

NOTE

The table values in the `display` property (`table`, `table-row`, `table-row-group`, `table-column`, `table-column-group`, `table-cell`, `table-caption`, `table-header-group`, `table-footer-group`), which are meant for creating table elements, are for languages other than X/HTML, like XML, that do not define table elements. In X/HTML this function is performed with the table tags, and the display properties are ignored when applied to X/HTML table elements.

Table Layout and Formatting   A table's formatting is the sum of the formatting applied to the various table elements based on a hierarchy that can be thought of as a set of layers. For formatting—for example, a border or a background—to appear to the viewer, it must be applied on either the top layer, or the layers above it must be transparent, which is the default. The layers, from top (closest to the viewer) to bottom are

1. Cells (`<td>` or `<th>`)

2. Rows (`<tr>`)

3. Row groups (`<tbody>`)

4. Columns (`<col>`)

5. Column groups (`<colgroup>`)

6. Table (`<table>`)

TIP

You can see all the defaults that Firefox uses in displaying a web page because it uses a CSS file to do it. You will find this CSS file on Windows computers in c:\program files\ mozilla firefox\res\html.css.

Listing 2-13 is a simple table with a number of styles applied to it. Look at how the application of styles affects the table:

1. Start with just the table and no styling or formatting, except the default for the various elements, and you get the table shown next. Notice how the header rows are bold and centered, while the body rows are normal weight and left aligned. Also, there are no borders.

UR 771 Part Cost		
Name	**Annual**	**Hours**
of Part	**Cost**	**to Repair**
Gauge	$425	12
Switch	$158	8
Control	$218	10

2. Give the **<table>** tag `background`, `width`, and `border` properties, and get the table shown next. (In IE 6 through 8 the border comes in lighter than in Firefox.)

UR 771 Part Cost		
Name	**Annual**	**Hours**
of Part	**Cost**	**to Repair**
Gauge	$425	12
Switch	$158	8
Control	$218	10

3. Add a background to the **<thead>** tag. This background overlays the table background except for where cell borders would be.

UR 771 Part Cost		
Name	**Annual**	**Hours**
of Part	**Cost**	**to Repair**
Gauge	$425	12
Switch	$158	8
Control	$218	10

4. Add the **<table>** tag attribute `cellspacing="0"` to eliminate the space between the cells. Also, give the `<colgroup id="part">` the same background as the heading, and give the cell class `<td class="name">` the `font-weight : bold`.

UR 771 Part Cost		
Name of Part	**Annual Cost**	**Hours to Repair**
Gauge	$425	12
Switch	$158	8
Control	$218	10

5. Finally, spruce up the formatting of the caption, add some padding beneath it, add a bottom border under the heading, right-align the numbers with some padding on the right so they are not hard against the right edge of the cells, and right-align the part names, again with some padding on the right. The result is shown here—quite a change from the unformatted table.

UR 771 Part Cost		
Name of Part	**Annual Cost**	**Hours to Repair**
Gauge	$425	12
Switch	$158	8
Control	$218	10

NOTE

Table grouping elements such as <thead> and <colgroup> have limitations on the style properties that can be used with them. For example, the bottom border does not show up if it is added to <thead>, and the font bolding does not work with <colgroup>.

Listing 2-13 Table example

```
<html>
  <head>
    <title>Listing 2-13</title>
    <style type="text/css">
      table {
            background : #dcdcdc;
            border : thin solid;
            width : 240px;
          }
```

```
        thead, #part { background : #fffacd; }
        .name {
                font-weight : bold;
                text-align : right;
                padding-right : 12px;
                }
        caption {
                font : bold 14px "arial";
                padding-bottom : 5px;
                }
        .line { border-bottom : medium solid #00008b }
        .data {
                text-align : right;
                padding-right : 12px;
                }
    </style>
</head>
<body>
    <table cellspacing="0">
        <caption>UR 771 Part Cost</caption>
        <colgroup id="part" />
        <colgroup span="2" id="costs" />
        <thead>
          <tr>
              <th>
                 Name
              </th>
              <th>
                 Annual
              </th>
              <th>
                 Hours
              </th>
          </tr>
          <tr>
              <th class="line">
                 of Part
              </th>
              <th class="line">
                 Cost
              </th>
              <th class="line">
                 to Repair
              </th>
          </tr>
        </thead>
```

```
<tbody>
  <tr>
    <td class="name">
      Gauge
    </td>
    <td class="data">
      $425
    </td>
    <td class="data">
      12
    </td>
  </tr>
  <tr>
    <td class="name">
      Switch
    </td>
    <td class="data">
      $158
    </td>
    <td class="data">
      8
    </td>
  </tr>
  <tr>
    <td class="name">
      Control
    </td>
    <td class="data">
      $218
    </td>
    <td class="data">
      10
    </td>
  </tr>
</tbody>
</table>
</body>
</html>
```

Styling Lists   X/HTML contain several ways of displaying lists, including ordered (numbered) lists, unordered (bulleted) lists, and definition (indented) lists. CSS adds to this several properties for styling, positioning, and replacing the marker (the number, letter, or bullet at the head of each list item). Listing 2-14 produces a list of lists—a definition list that contains first an unordered and then an ordered list. Figure 2-6 shows these lists without either CSS or HTML styling.

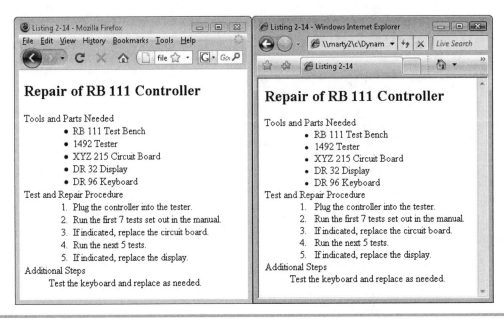

Figure 2-6 Initial list of lists without any styling or a CSS

Listing 2-14 List of lists

```html
<html>
   <head>
      <title>Listing 2-14</title>
      <style type="text/css">
         body { background : #dcdcdc; }
         dl {
             background : #fafad2;
             padding : 5px;
         }
         dt { font : bold 12pt arial; }
         ul { list-style-type : square; }
         ol { list-style-type : lower-alpha; }
      </style>
   </head>
   <body>
      <h2>Repair of RB 111 Controller </h2>
      <dl>
         <dt> Tools and Parts Needed </dt>
         <dd>
            <ul>
               <li>RB 111 Test Bench </li>
               <li>1492 Tester </li>
               <li>XYZ 215 Circuit Board </li>
```

```
         <li>DR 32 Display</li>
         <li>DR 96 Keyboard </li>
      </ul>
   </dd>
   <dt> Test and Repair Procedure </dt>
   <dd>
      <ol>
         <li>Plug the controller into the tester. </li>
         <li>Run the first 7 tests set out in the manual. </li>
         <li>If indicated, replace the circuit board. </li>
         <li>Run the next 5 tests. </li>
         <li>If indicated, replace the display. </li>
      </ol>
   </dd>
   <dt> Additional Steps  </dt>
   <dd> Test the keyboard and replace as needed.  </dd>
   </dl>
   </body>
</html>
```

To the basic X/HTML code, add CSS styles to **<body>** and **<dl>** elements for contrasting backgrounds; add padding to **<dl>** so the text is not on the edge of the background; format the **<dt>** elements so they are more like headings; and then change the **<ul>** marker to a square, and the **<ol>** marker to lowercase letters. The result is shown in Figure 2-7.

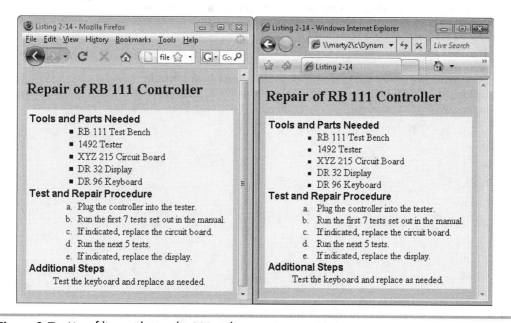

Figure 2-7   List of lists with simple CSS styling

TIP

Not all properties and values work in all browsers, for example, in IE- 6, and you need to test any code in the browsers that you think will be viewing your pages.

Here are some notes on using the CSS list properties:

- If you apply a background to a list item, the marker will not share that background (it is transparent) if the marker is positioned "outside."

- If you have both `list-style-image` and `list-style-type` properties, the `list-style-image` will be used.

- The types of numbering and alphabetic systems that are available are

  - `decimal`: 1, 2,...9

  - `decimal-leading-zero`: 01, 02,...99

  - `lower-roman`: i, ii, iii, iv...

  - `upper-roman`: I, II, III, IV...

  - `lower-latin` or `lower-alpha`: a, b, c,...z

  - `upper-latin` or `upper-alpha`: A, B, C,...Z

  - `lower-greek`: α, β, γ,...ω

- The HTML and CSS specifications do not state what happens when a list has run though an alphabet, so you should use numbering for long lists.

TIP

Go to W3C (www.w3.org/style/css/) for the latest and most detailed explanation of CSS, and test your CSS code with the W3C CSS Validator (jigsaw.w3.org/css-validator).

Part II

Adding JavaScript Dynamic Elements

Part I of this book provided the elements of layout and consistent styling through the application of XHTML and CSS. Part II introduces JavaScript, a programming language that can be used to make dynamic elements for a web page. Chapter 3 describes the various components JavaScript uses, and then Chapters 4 and 5 show how JavaScript is used to create a number of dynamic elements on a web page. This Part introduction provides general information on programming and JavaScript.

NOTE
There are many similarities between JavaScript and PHP (described in Part III). To provide a consistent feel and format to the information, some duplication occurs between the two parts.

Understanding Programming and JavaScript

JavaScript, despite a name that implies otherwise, is a programming language designed for web computing. It provides new users an opportunity to learn about the mechanics and elements of programming without some of the overhead required of more robust and verbose languages. JavaScript has no direct connection with Java, except that they both come from Sun Microsystems and share some common syntax and keywords.

NOTE
Primarily thought of as a programming tool for web pages, JavaScript finds its way into several computing tools, such as in Adobe Acrobat and Adobe Reader support of JavaScript in PDF files.

Delving into JavaScript

A programming language is simply a set of rules, called *syntax,* that govern how you communicate with a computer using various elements of the language. JavaScript uses a model called *OOP* (object-oriented programming). You have *objects* (for example, a window) that have *properties* (for example, length) and *methods,* or actions, that the object can perform (such as open), while responding to *events,* or actions performed upon the objects (for example, a click). Once you are familiar with the basic terminology and syntax, JavaScript programming is only a matter of writing a sequential set of *commands,* or *statements,* for the computer and its software to understand and act upon. (Chapter 3 describes the elements and syntax of JavaScript in detail.) How and where this interaction takes place between the computer and the user is what differentiates JavaScript (and other scripting languages) from conventional languages, such as C or Java.

NOTE

Many programmers scoff at the notion that JavaScript uses the object-oriented model of programming. We will leave the discussion to the purists, but for the purposes of an introduction to JavaScript, the model is close enough to be of value in explaining the workings of the language.

Compiled vs. Interpreted Programming Languages

Though it's often easy to forget, it helps to remember that a computer's ability to perform the numerous and complex tasks we ask of it is solely based on whether a gazillion silicon-based, electronic switches are turned on (1) or off (0). To shield us from the tediousness of a binary life, we use programming languages, written in some semblance of a written and spoken language, which are then translated into a form the computer can understand. Programming languages that create applications (for example, the Word.exe file that is the core of Microsoft Word) require special software to create the code and then must be run through a *compiler* in order to become computer readable. A compiler is software that checks the code for errors and then translates the written code into computer code. While this method allows for very serious computing, it takes time and resources to accomplish.

In contrast, JavaScript is referred to as an *interpreted* language, which means its code is run on the fly, without the need to compile it. All that is needed is a text editor to create the files that contain the code, and a web browser that provides the underlying interpretation of the code (which are the same requirements to create and display an XHTML page, described in Part I of this book, or a PHP page, described in Part III). While interpreted code like JavaScript tends to not perform as efficiently or quickly as compiled code, its performance for the sorts of tasks used in creating dynamic web pages is good enough, and its advantages of being easy to edit and embed on a page more than make up for its shortcomings. Also, compiled code tends to be platform specific (Windows versus Mac), while interpreted JavaScript is not.

Client-Side vs. Server-Side Computing

As the names imply, client-side and server-side computing refer to where the programming code is being executed. With server-side programming such as PHP, a request from a user's web page is sent to the hosting web server, is executed, and then the results are sent back to a web page in the user's browser. While having a server and its available networked resources and databases provides almost unlimited access to information and computing power, it requires a round-trip of information to pass from client to the server and back. Additionally, its services are shared among other users, thus opportunities exist for delays. Client-side computing performs the code execution on the client's computer, freeing the server to perform more intensive tasks and providing the user a faster experience. (Many web applications use both server-side and client-side computing to split the workload and take advantage of the benefits offered by each.) JavaScript is a client-side program, which allows for faster execution of code and more responsive feedback to the user.

Introducing JavaScript

JavaScript was created by the team of Sun Microsystems and Netscape in the mid-1990s to allow more simplified web programming than the client-side, compiled Java language previously used in Netscape browsers. Over time JavaScript has been morphed through updated versions (the latest version as of spring 2009 is 1.8) and complementary products (JScript is Microsoft Internet Explorer's version). Mozilla's Firefox, having its roots in Netscape, should provide you with the most accurate interpretation of your code. This is all to say that, as with working with web pages in general, you need to be using the latest browsers (which will include the latest respective versions of their JavaScript incarnation) and to test your work using different popular browsers (Firefox, IE, and Apple's Safari) to ensure your code functions as you designed it.

Tools Needed for JavaScript

To effectively work with JavaScript, you need to have a development environment that supports both the writing and the testing of JavaScript scripts. You'll need tools for

- **JavaScript script writing**, with code assistance and validation as you write the script.
- **JavaScript script testing** on your development computer.
- **Developmental support** in a browser, to help debug.

The Part I introduction describes and recommends packages that you can download for these tools, including

- **Aptana Studio**, an integrated development environment that provides powerful authoring for HTML, CSS, and JavaScript by default.
- **XAMPP**, a combination of the Apache web server, the MySQL database server, and the PHP server that runs on your computer and duplicates what you will see when you upload your web site to a commercial web host.

- **IE 6**, **IE 7**, and **Firefox** browsers, all needed to test and debug your scripts. Since large percentages of the web browsing population are using these browsers, it is important to try your web pages in all of them. IE 8, which is in final testing as this is written, is also a strong candidate for you to use for testing. It is available for both Windows XP and Windows Vista, as well as for the latest version, Windows 7. In addition to simply trying out your pages on these browsers, we recommend a Web Developer's Toolbar available for Firefox.

If you do not already have Aptana Studio, XAMPP, IE 6, IE 7, Firefox, and the Firefox Web Developer's Toolbar, return to the Part I introduction, and follow the instructions to download and install them. They are recommended for the discussion in the remaining chapters of this book.

Chapter 3
Fundamentals of JavaScript

Key Skills & Concepts

- Using JavaScript with X/HTML Pages

- Introducing JavaScript Basics

- Writing and Testing JavaScript

- Using Variables, Constants, and Operators

- Incorporating Statements and Expressions

- Building Functions and Objects

- Applying Conditional Statements

Chapter 3 discusses the basic constructs used by JavaScript and how JavaScript is tied into an HTML code page. This chapter describes variables, operators, and functions, and shows examples of their use. The `if/else` statements and the conditions that control them are demonstrated along with `for`, `while`, and `do` loops. The chapter also reviews objects, including their constituent components of properties, methods, and event handlers. You'll see examples of their more common uses.

JavaScript Introduction

The elements of any language only work together in an understandable form if they all operate in concert, according to a set of rules and a given format. This section describes the basic techniques and conventions used in JavaScript to get you started, and offers you shortcuts and suggestions to make working with scripts easier and more efficient.

Using JavaScript with X/HTML Pages

You can use JavaScript code on X/HTML pages in one of two ways: directly on the X/HTML page where it's being used, or in a separate file. Scripts that you write for singular uses are most easily written directly on the affected page (which is the manner used predominantly in this book). As you become better acquainted with JavaScript and develop more advanced uses, you will find saving your longer scripts to separate JS pages provides for cleaner web pages and the ability to use the same code on several pages within your web site.

NOTE

The terms *code* and *script* are used interchangeably for describing the various elements of the JavaScript language found within the `<script>` tag found on X/HTML pages and in separate JS files.

Entering JavaScript Directly on an X/HTML Page

The easiest way to start coding JavaScript is to enter the script directly on the X/HTML page within the JavaScript tag set `<script></script>`. The `<script>` tag is placed either in the `<head>` or `<body>` section of the page. Typically, code that writes output directly to the page is placed within the X/HMTL in the `<body>` section. Scripts placed in the `<head>` section are generally called for use by code placed elsewhere in the `<body>` section. Listing 3-1 shows these two techniques in use.

Listing 3-1   Example script placement

```
<!DOCTYPE html PUBLIC "-//W3C//DTD XHTML 1.0 Strict//EN"
"http://www.w3.org/TR/xhtml1/DTD/xhtml1-strict.dtd">
<html xmlns="http://www.w3.org/1999/xhtml" lang="en" xml:lang="en">
    <head>
        <meta http-equiv="Content-Type" content="text/html;
            charset=iso-8859-1">
        <title>Listing 3-1</title>
        <script language="javascript" type= "text/javascript">
            //<![CDATA [
            //The bgColor property of the document object is set to
                Dodger Blue;
            document.bgColor="dodgerblue"
            //]]>
        </script>
    </head>
    <body>
        <script language="javascript" type= "text/javascript">
        //<![CDATA [
            //The document.bgColor property is used to display the
                hexadecimal of the background color set in the header;
                document.write("The hexadecimal value of Dodger Blue
                is "+ document.bgColor)
        //]]>
        </script>
    </body>
</html>
```

NOTE

The purpose of Listing 3-1 is to provide an example of how script can be placed and effectively used in both the header and body of a script. Firefox has a problem with the code in the header because it comes before and yet refers to the `<body>` tag. Since the `<body>` tag hadn't been defined, the JavaScript returns #ffffff, or white. IE 6–8 handle this just fine. Also, `document.bgColor` is considered obsolete and is deprecated. It is used here to get a simple example.

Using JavaScript Files

As your scripting becomes more complex and you find repetitive uses within your web site for your code, you can minimize the size of your X/HTML pages and reuse the same code by outsourcing much of the code to a separate text file with the .js file extension. Whenever you want to employ the code in the JS file (for example, myjavascript.js), you can request its action by adding an attribute to the `<script>` tag, such as `<script type = "text/ javascript" src = myjavascript.js>`.

JavaScript Basics

Before you start trying to create scripts, you will want to become familiar with several general aspects of JavaScript syntax.

Commenting Your Script

JavaScript allows you to add comments to your script in two ways:

- On a single line starting with //

  ```
  //This is a comment
  ```

- On multiple lines enclosed with /* */

  ```
  /* This is a comment that can
  be on several lines. */
  ```

TIP

It is strongly recommended that you comment your scripts to help you in deciphering and debugging your work.

Coding Conventions

JavaScript is fairly easygoing as far as conventions are concerned. Here are the most common conventions:

- JavaScript contains some elements that are case sensitive. JavaScript commands and variable names are case sensitive. For example, if you define **person** as a variable name and later use the word **Person**, JavaScript will not recognize the second instance as the original variable. The best rule of thumb is to use all lowercase. When employing other JavaScript elements such as objects, properties, methods, and event handlers from other sources, use the case referenced in the book, web page, or other example you are using to assist you.

- Each *statement* (or command) in JavaScript typically ends with a semicolon. (A statement is a line of code that is complete and correct in its syntax to perform a task.) While it is not required for you do this, it will prevent errors, make debugging easier, and it gets you in the habit of doing it for use in other languages that do insist upon it (for example, PHP, described in Part III).

- You can encapsulate your scripts within tags to identify it as character data so your scripts are not misinterpreted. The predominant concern is that older browsers will not recognize the JavaScript and will return errors. To protect your code from possible problems (at least problems of this nature), contain your scripts within an HTML comment `<!-- //-->`. Moving forward, the greater concern is that the X/HMTL validator will consider something in the script to be in its purview and will produce an error. To avoid this, we suggest preceding your scripts with `//<! [CDATA [` and terminating them with `//]]>`. This marker is shown in JavaScript examples in this book and is included in the suggested template for creating new HTML pages that contain JavaScript.

- Text, any combination of letters and numbers, also called a *string,* needs to be enclosed in quotation marks, either single (`' '`) or double (`" "`)—differences in their use are explained in a following Note. Quotation marks must be in like pairs.

- Legitimate numbers, which can have a decimal point, do not have to be in quotation marks.

- Multiple arguments are separated by commas (`,`).

- Most functions require that their arguments be enclosed in parentheses.

Special Characters and Escape Sequences

You may have wondered since quotation marks are used to identify a string, how you display a quotation mark that is part of the string to be displayed on an X/HTML page. For this purpose JavaScript uses the backslash (\) in what is called an *escape sequence,* which tells JavaScript to treat the following character not as part of the scripting syntax but as a *literal,* or part of the text string. For example:

```
document.write("My name is \"Marty\"");
```

The two double quotes on either side of *Marty* within the outer pair would produce an error if they weren't "escaped" by preceding each with the backslash.

Another way of looking at this is that you want to add a literal character, in this case, double quotes. In this usage, we typically say we are adding a JavaScript *special character*. Actually, both escape sequences and special characters share the same codes and accomplish the same result. The only difference between the two is whether you're calling the glass half full or half empty.

Most of the characters that JavaScript assigns a special use for or as an escape sequence are preceded with a backslash. Here are some of the more common escape sequences / special characters:

- \" produces a double quotation mark.

- \' produces a single quotation mark.

- \\ produces a backslash.

- \b produces a backspace.

- \r produces a carriage return.

- \n produces a linefeed.

- \t produces a tab.

NOTE

While either single or double quotation marks can be used to enclose a string, in some circumstances, one or the other is preferable. With single quotation marks enclosing the string, you can use literal double quotation marks without the backslash in the string, as shown next. With single quotation marks, though, escape sequences other than \' or \\ will display the backslash and not perform their function. With double quotation marks, all escape sequences work.

```
document.write('My name is "Marty"');
```

Avoiding Reserved Words

Several words, called *reserved* words or *keywords* (see Table 3-1), should not be used to name elements in JavaScript, as they are a part of the language and have special meaning to the JavaScript interpreter.

abstract	boolean	break	byte	case
catch	char	class	const	continue
debugger	default	delete	do	double
else	enum	export	extends	false
final	finally	float	for	function
goto	if	implements	import	in
instanceof	int	interface	label	long
native	new	null	package	private
protected	public	return	short	static
super	switch	synchronized	this	throw
throws	transient	true	try	typeof
var	void	volatile	while	with

Table 3-1   Reserved Words in JavaScript

Writing and Testing JavaScript

As an interpreted language, JavaScript doesn't require any ancillary software (such as a software development kit, or SDK), to be written, checked for errors, or tested. You can start writing JavaScript using any text editor you would otherwise use to write X/HTML; however, we strongly recommend Aptana Studio, described in the introduction to Part I. To simplify your work in JavaScript, we further suggest you create a basic template to start any of your scripting projects.

Modifying the Default HTML Page in Aptana

When you create a new HTML file in Aptana, it adds the requisite HTML header data and tags to display the page in a browser. With a few easy modifications, you can modify this default file to include the X/HTML doctype (to ensure your files are compliant with future web specifications), and you can add the `<script>` tag, an attribute, and an optional comment to accommodate JavaScript (described earlier in the chapter). To modify the default HTML file in Aptana, do the following:

TIP

To create an X/HTML file in Aptana that doesn't include the `<script>` tag after modifying the default new HTML page text, simply delete the added text in the Aptana editor.

1. Open **Aptana Studio** (see Chapter 1 for information on installing Aptana Studio).

2. Click **File** on the menu bar, and click **New | Untitled HTML File**.

3. In the Aptana editor (right pane), modify the text as shown next and in Listing 3-2.

```
1   <!DOCTYPE html PUBLIC "-//W3C//DTD XHTML 1.0 Strict//EN"
2       "http://www.w3.org/TR/xhtml1/DTD/xhtml1-strict.dtd">
3   <html xmlns="http://www.w3.org/1999/xhtml" lang="en" xml:lang="en">
4       <head>
5           <meta http-equiv="Content-Type" content="text/html;
6               charset=iso-8859-1">
7           <title>Untitled Document</title>
8           <script language="javascript" type= "text/javascript">
9               //<![CDATA [
10              //]]>
11          </script>
12      </head>
13      <body>
14          <script language="javascript" type= "text/javascript">
15              //<![CDATA [
16              //]]>
17          </script>
18      </body>
19  </html>
```

4. Select the modified text and press CTRL-C to copy the text to the Clipboard.

5. Click **Window** on the menu bar and click **Preferences**.

6. In the Preferences dialog box, click the plus sign next to Aptana to expand its list.

7. Expand Editors and click **HTML**.

8. In the HTML pane, under Initial HTML File Contents toward the bottom of the pane, select the default text and press CTRL-V to paste the modified text in its place, as shown in Figure 3-1.

9. Click **Apply** and then click **OK** to close the Preferences dialog box.

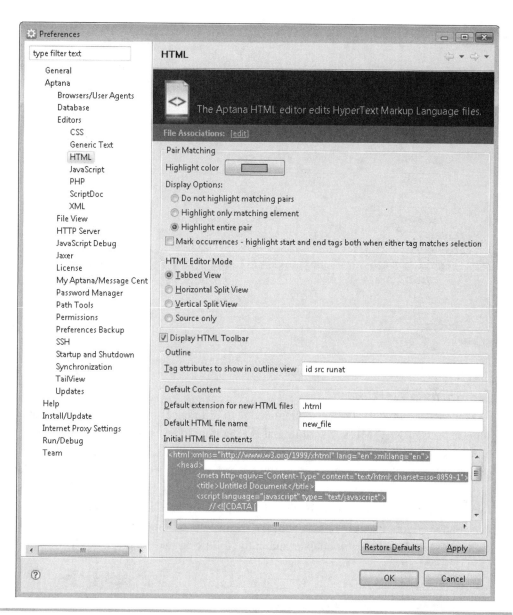

Figure 3-1   Change the default code for new X/HTML pages created in Aptana to add tags to support XML and JavaScript.

Listing 3-2   Changed default X/HTML code for Aptana pages

```
<!DOCTYPE html PUBLIC "-//W3C//DTD XHTML 1.0 Strict//EN"
"http://www.w3.org/TR/xhtml1/DTD/xhtml1-strict.dtd">
<html xmlns="http://www.w3.org/1999/xhtml" lang="en" xml:lang="en">
   <head>
      <meta http-equiv="Content-Type" content="text/html;
         charset=iso-8859-1">
      <title>Untitled Document</title>
      <script language="javascript" type= "text/javascript">
         //<![CDATA [
         //]]>
      </script>
   </head>
   <body>
      <script language="javascript" type= "text/javascript">
         //<![CDATA [
         //]]>
      </script>
   </body>
</html>
```

Testing Your Work

As was mentioned in the Part introduction, due to differences in how browsers interpret some aspects of X/HTML and scripting, it is important to test your work with popular browsers to determine if the differences affect your intent. A sample of JavaScript code shown in Listing 3-3 is used to display a message box slightly differently in two popular browsers (see Figure 3-2). In this case, the differences are slight and cosmetic, not a cause for concern. However, that will not always be the case. Don't be concerned about the appearance or your lack of understanding of the code in Listing 3-3 at this point. All will make sense in the rest of this chapter and in the following two chapters.

Figure 3-2   Firefox (left) and IE (right) use similar but slightly different interpretations to display message boxes.

NOTE

The listings shown in the rest of the chapter have omitted some default X/HTML code found in web pages, such as the DOCTYPE declaration, to provide a more concise example.

Listing 3-3   Browser differences example

```
<html>
   <head>
      <title>Listing 3-3</title>
      <script language="javascript" type= "text/javascript">
         //<![CDATA [
         // This code produces the classic Hello World! message
            box window.alert("Hello, World!");
         //]]>
      </script>
   </head>
   <body>
   </body>
</html>
```

Parts of JavaScript

Much as a spoken language comprises elements of speech such as nouns, verbs, adverbs, adjectives, and other parts of speech, programming languages have their own set of components. In this part, we'll cover the more common elements of JavaScript, providing the groundwork for constructing working scripts in Chapters 4 and 5. In this section, we explore JavaScript information types, variables, operators, statements, and functions. In the following part, we explore statements that act as control structures.

NOTE

As with any language, JavaScript contains many elements in each part of the language, far more than can be covered here. To look at a comprehensive list, go to www.javascriptkit.com/jsref/ or www/webreferemce.com/javascript/ reference/core_ref/contents.html.

Variables and Constants

Information (or data) used in JavaScript falls into one of two categories. In either case, it is defined by a name you assign to it and its category of data, or *data type*.

- **Variables**, which are items that can contain different values at different times during script execution, start with the keyword **var** and are followed by a name that you give it.

- **Constants** contain the same value throughout the execution of your script.

TIP

Variables may have different values at different times during the execution of a script, while constants have a single value throughout execution.

Types of Data

JavaScript will generally recognize the data type you are using by its context within your scripts, shielding you from assigning a specific type. However, in instances where JavaScript misinterpreted your intent, it's helpful to have an understanding of the available data types and some of their characteristics. The more common data types are shown in Table 3-2.

- The Boolean FALSE is equivalent to the integer 0, the floating point number 0.0, an empty string or a string of "0", an array of zero elements, or NULL. Everything else is TRUE.

- Integers are by default decimal (base 10) numbers. To make a number octal (base 8), precede it with 0 (zero). To make a number hexadecimal (base 16), precede it with 0x.

- Very large integers (larger than 2,147,483,647) are considered floating point numbers.

- If you divide two integers, you get a floating point number unless the numbers are evenly divisible.

- Floating point numbers are not accurate to the last digit because of the infinite progression of fractions like one-third. Therefore, you should not compare two floating point numbers for equality.

- A string containing a number (either integer or floating point) immediately following the left quote can be used as a number. For example **"18.2"** and **"4 cars"** can both be used as numbers, while **"his 4 cars"** cannot.

Data Type/ Subtype	Name	Description	Examples
Boolean	bool	Either TRUE or FALSE and is not case sensitive, but commonly uppercase	TRUE, FALSE
Numeric/Floating point numbers	float	A fractional number with a decimal; may be negative, and may use scientific notation	7.34, −21.89, 2.31e3
Numeric/Integers	int	A whole number without a decimal; may be negative	43, 928, −4
Numeric/Null	null	The absence of any value	NULL
String	string	A series of characters (one of 256 letters, numbers, and special characters) enclosed in either single or double quotation marks	"Mike", 'Seattle', "1495 W. 18th St"
Undefined		A named variable that has not been assigned a value	

Table 3-2   JavaScript Data Types

NOTE
In this book two additional pseudo-types are used for discussion purposes only: "mixed" is used for any combination of other types, and "numbers" is used for a combination of integers and floating point numbers.

Naming Conventions

The name that you give to either variables or constants (or any other label in JavaScript) is case sensitive (see "JavaScript Basics" earlier in the chapter), can begin with either the letters *a–z* (or *A–Z,* though not recommended) or an underscore (_), can be of any length, and can contain letters, numbers, underscores, and the characters in western European alphabets. While you may find that some special characters will be allowed, the best practice is to not use them. Blank spaces are not allowed.

A good practice is to make variable and constant names more self-descriptive, and in the process to stay away from any possibility of conflict with a predefined name. For example, if you are collecting a buyer's name and address, you might be tempted to use name, street, and city. While there is nothing wrong with those names, it is better to get in the habit of using compound names both that are more descriptive and that stay away from common names, for example, buyer_name, buyer_street, and buyer_city. It may take a couple of seconds more to type these names, but they won't be confused with other names. Also, most programmers get really good at cutting and pasting to reduce typing.

TIP

If you are having trouble finding a problem, or bug, in a program, look at the names you have assigned to variables and constants; try changing any that could possibly have a conflict with predefined or reserved names, such as changing `name` to `buyer_name`, or `private` to `my_own`.

Operators

Having created a variable or a constant, you are going to want to give it a value through assignment, calculation, or comparison. JavaScript has defined a number of operators of various types, as shown in Table 3-3, to do this.

Type Operator	Name	Example	Explanation
Arithmetic			Performs arithmetic calculations on two operands which can be variables, numbers, or a number and a variable.
+	Add	`a + b`	Sums two operands.
-	Subtract	`a - b`	Returns the difference between two operands.
*	Multiply	`a * b`	Multiplies two operands.
/	Divide	`a / b`	Divides two operands.
--	Decrement	`--a` `a--`	Subtracts 1 from a and returns a. Returns a, then subtracts 1 from it.
++	Increment	`++a` `a++`	Adds 1 to a and returns a. Returns a, then adds 1 to it.
%	Modulus	`a % b`	Returns the remainder from a Divide operation.
=	Unary negation	`=a`	Converts a negative to a positive, or a positive to a negative.
Assignment			Replaces a value with another.
=	Assign	`a = 7`	a is set to 7.
+=	Add and assign	`a += 2`	a is incremented by 2 and assigned the new value.
-=	Subtract and assign	`a -= 2`	a is decremented by 2 and assigned the new value.
*=	Multiply and assign	`a *= 2`	a is multiplied by 2 and assigned the new value.
/=	Divide and assign	`a /= 2`	a is divided by 2 and assigned the new value.
%=	Modulus and assign	`a %= 2`	a is divided by 2 and assigned the remainder.

Table 3-3 JavaScript Operators

Type Operator	Name	Example	Explanation
Bitwise			Logical consequences turn specific bits in an integer on or off.
&	And	a & b	Bits set in both a and b are set.
|	Or	a | b	Bits set in either a or b are set.
^	Xor	a ^ b	Bits set in a or b but not both are set.
~	Not	~a	Bits set in a are not set.
<<	Shift left	a << b	Shift bits in a by b steps to the left (each step is multiplying by 2).
>>	Shift right	a >> b	Shift bits in a by b steps to the right (each step is dividing by 2).
Comparison			Compares two values and returns TRUE or FALSE.
==	Equal	a == b	TRUE if a equals b.
===	Identical	a === b	TRUE if a is identical to b.
!=	Not equal	a != b	TRUE if a is not equal to b.
!==	Not identical	a !== b	TRUE if a is not identical to b.
<	Less than	a < b	TRUE if a is less than b.
>	Greater than	a > b	TRUE if a greater than b.
<=	Less than or equal to	a <= b	TRUE if a is less than or equal to b.
>=	Greater than or equal to	a >= b	TRUE if a is greater than or equal to b.
Logical			Logical consequence.
&&	And	a && b	TRUE if both a and b are TRUE.
||	Or	a || b	TRUE if either a or b is TRUE.
!	Not	!a	TRUE if a is not TRUE.
Other			
?:	Conditional	Condition ? value : value	An if-then-else statement where a condition is set to the left of the ? and values are placed on either side of the :.
delete	Delete	delete window2	Deletes an object, a property, or an array element.

Table 3-3   JavaScript Operators *(continued)*

If you combine several operators in a single expression, the order of precedence is as follows, beginning with the highest or first executed: `++`, `--`, `!`, `delete`, `*`, `/`, `%`, `+`, `-`, `.`, `<<`, `>>`, `<`, `<=`, `>`, `>=`, `==`, `!=`, `===`, `!==`, `&`, `^`, `|`, `&&`, `||`, `?:`, `=`, `+=`, `-=`, `*=`, `/=`, `&=`, and, `xor`, `or`. You can use parentheses to get around the order of precedence. Other notes about the JavaScript operators are

- When the arithmetic (+) operator is used to combine text (for example, `window.alert ("Marty" + "Matthews")` to display "Marty Matthews" in a dialog box) or text with numbers (for example, `window.alert (1234 + "Broadway, " + "Anytown")` to display "1234 Broadway, Anytown"), the operation is referred to as *concatenation*.

- The modulus (`%`) does not yield a percentage; rather it gives the remainder, the part that is left after whole division.

- The equal sign (`=`) does not mean "equal," it means "assign" or "replace."

- To compare two variables, you can use equality (`==`) or identical (`===`). The difference is that `==` tests if two values are equal, independent of the type of value, while `===` tests if two values are not only equal in value, but also of the same type.

- If `a = "2"` and `b = 2.0`, they are not identical, because one is a string and the other is a floating point number, but they are equal in value.

Listing 3-4 shows examples of the use of JavaScript variables and operators. The results that this script returns are shown here:

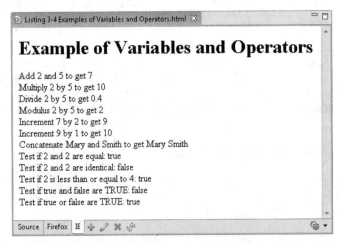

Listing 3-4   Examples of variables and operators

```html
<html>
    <head>
        <title>Listing 3-4</title>
    </head>
    <body>
        <h1>Example of Variables and Operators</h1>
        <script language="javascript" type= "text/javascript">
        //<![CDATA [
        //Math
        var a = 2;
        var b = 5;
        document.write("Add ", a, " and ", b, " to get   ",
            a+b, "<br>");
        document.write("Multiply ", a, " by ", b, " to get   ",
            a*b, "<br>");
        document.write("Divide ", a, " by ", b, " to get   ",
            a/b, "<br>");
        document.write("Modulus ", a, " by ", b, " to get   ",
             a%b, "<br>");
        //Assign, Increment and Concatenate
        var a = 7;
        document.write("Increment ", a, " by 2 to get ", a+=2,
            "<br>");
        document.write("Increment ", a, " by 1 to get ", ++a,
            "<br>");
        first_name = "Mary "; last_name = "Smith";
        document.write("Concatenate ", first_name, " and ",
            last_name, " to get  ", first_name + last_name,
            "<br>");
        //Comparison
        a = "2"; b = 2.0; c = 4; d = a == b; e = a === b;
        document.write("Test if ", a, " and ", b,
            " are equal: ", a==b, "<br>");
        document.write("Test if ", a, " and ", b,
            " are identical: ", a===b, "<br>");
        document.write("Test if ", a, " is less than or equal
            to ", c, ": ",   a<=c, "<br>");
        //Logical
        document.write("Test if ", d, " and ", e, " are TRUE: ",
            d&&e, "<br>");
        document.write("Test if ", d, " or ", e, " are TRUE:  ",
            d||e, "<br>");
        //]]>
        </script>
    </body>
</html>
```

Statements and Expressions

JavaScript scripts contain either comments or statements. A *statement* is a line of code that is complete and correct in its syntax to perform a task, typically anything that is in between semicolons and the opening and closing JavaScript tags. Often a statement is a single line of code ending in a semicolon, but you can have several statements on a single line, and you can have statements that take several lines. Statements contain one or more expressions.

Expressions are anything that has a value. *Values* are anything that can be assigned to a variable, so values can be any of the data types: integer, floating point, string, or Boolean. While the NULL data type is the absence of a value, it is still considered a value for this discussion.

Expressions can contain expressions, or said another way, expressions are building blocks that can be used to build other expressions. For example, a = 2 is three expressions: 2, a, and a = 2.

Functions

A function is a piece of script (a *snippet*) that does something and can be repeatedly called within a larger script. Global functions already exist, and you write user-defined functions. Some functions require that you pass them values or *arguments,* which the function uses to return a value to you. Other functions simply return a value when they are called.

Global Functions

Unlike other languages and programs such as PHP or Microsoft Excel, JavaScript does not have a large library of internal, global functions to perform day-to-day tasks that are not *object*-specific. On the other hand, JavaScript contains a full complement of *methods,* which are function calls that are related to objects. (Methods and objects are described later in the chapter.) In this manner, you can achieve essentially the same results using JavaScript methods as you can by using internal functions found in other languages and programs. The more commonly used JavaScript global functions are listed in Table 3-4.

NOTE
A *constructor* function is used to create objects. The function is not a particular global function, but rather it's a way to use the standard syntax of a user function to structure an object by naming it, declaring its parameters, and assigning the parameter values to the properties of the object.

Function	Description
escape( )	Returns the hexadecimal code of a string
eval( )	Evaluates a string of JavaScript code without reference to a specific object
isFinite( )	Evaluates an argument to determine if it's a finite number
isNaN( )	Evaluates an argument to determine if it's not a number (NaN)
parseFloat( )	Parses a string argument and returns a floating point number
parseInt( )	Parses a string argument and returns an integer
unescape( )	Returns an ASCII string for hexadecimal code

Table 3-4 Global Functions

User-Defined Functions

As you write JavaScript scripts, you'll often find that you want to repeatedly use the same code. You could simply copy the code to all the places you want to use it, but if you want to change that code, you would have to change it everywhere it was copied. The solution for this is to create a function containing the code you want to repeat, and to simply call that function everywhere you want to use it. Functions also let you segment or compartmentalize your code, making it easier to debug and maintain.

There is even a bigger reason for using functions. Up to now, all the JavaScript code in this chapter is meant to run when the page is loaded. But if you don't want that, you can create a function, place it in the X/HTML header, and it won't be run until it is called.

Like predefined or global functions, user-defined (just "user" from here on) functions may optionally have arguments that are passed to them, and return a value after they are executed. Once a user function has been defined, it is *called,* that is, a statement in the script requests the function perform the action it is designed to do. The function itself can do anything you can do with JavaScript using all of the features of JavaScript, including calling other functions, or even calling itself to create a recursive function (this should not be done over a 100 times or errors may occur).

User functions are defined with the `function` keyword using this form:

```
function name(argument1, argument2,...)
{
     [any JavaScript statements];
     return returnValue;
}
```

Functions are called to perform their actions in a script in this form:

```
name(argument1, argument2,...)
```

NOTE

Functions without arguments are defined by providing a *name* and an empty set of parentheses, for example:

```
function calrate()
```

The name that you give to a function uses the same naming rules as variables, constants, and other labels. It is case sensitive, can begin with either the letters *a–z* or *A–Z,* or an underscore (_), can be of any length, and can contain letters, numbers, underscores, and the characters in western European alphabets.

Listing 3-5 shows an example of a user function with the result shown next.

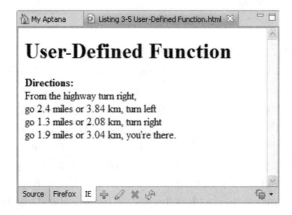

Listing 3-5   User-defined function

```html
<html>
    <head>
        <title>Listing 3-5</title>
    </head>
    <body>
        <h1>User-Defined Function</h1>
        <script language="javascript" type= "text/javascript">
            //<![CDATA [
            function tokm(miles)
            {
                var km = miles * 1.6;
                return km;
            }
            document.write("<b>Directions:</b><br>");
            document.write("From the highway turn right,<br>");
            " ("go 2.4 miles or " + tokm(2.4) + " km, turn left<br>");
```

```
        document.write("go 1.3 miles or " + tokm(1.3) +
            " km, turn right<br>");
        document.write("go 1.9 miles or " + tokm(1.9) + " km,
            you're there.<br>");
        //]]>
    </script>
  </body>
</html>
```

Objects

As mentioned in the Part II introduction, JavaScript is an object-based programming language. Objects are the visual elements of a web page such as windows, buttons, check boxes, and dates. Objects are also more abstract elements such as math calculations and arrays. You will probably find that the predefined objects in JavaScript are all you will need for your basic programming work, but you can also create your own objects. And to make things even more interesting, objects can have child-objects, which can begin to resemble a family-tree hierarchy of the elements that constitute a web page.

TIP

There are dozens of predefined JavaScript objects, many associated with several properties and methods, far too many to list in this book. We suggest you obtain both online and hardcopy reference charts that list objects with their constituents. References I've found useful are www.javascriptkit.com and *JavaScript: The Complete Reference* by Thomas Powell and Fritz Schneider, published by McGraw-Hill/Professional, 2004.

Predefined objects are identified by a keyword name, and custom objects are given a unique name, using the same naming rules as described earlier in the chapter for naming variables. You can have several instances of an object in a web page. Take, for example, the window object. Each window or frame in a web page is uniquely identified by name, is further defined by its characteristics, or *properties*; by the things it can do, called *methods*; and by which user *events* (for example, a mouse click) affect it. The relationship of an object to its constituents is shown through the use of the *dot syntax,* whereby the object name is separated from its constituent by a period. At the beginning of this chapter (see Listing 3-3) you saw the use of the alert method being applied to the window object to produce an alert dialog box (Hello World!):

```
window.alert("Hello, World!");
```

where **window** is the predefined object, **alert** is a method that displays an Alert message box, and **"Hello, World!"** is the method value that displays text in the message box.

Another example of the dot syntax you've seen so far in this chapter is the commonly used statement that displays scripting results to the browser:

```
document.write("From the highway turn right,<br>");
```

Custom Objects

You can create your own objects, such as furniture items for sale on a store's web site. You can use either of two ways to create the objects:

- **Use a constructor function** to first create the structure of the object, and then use the new keyword to create an instance of the object.
- **Use an object initializer** to name the object and to assign property values in one statement.

Using the constructor function, you first name an object, and then its parameter values are assigned to the properties of the object. For example:

```
function furniture()
{
this.era=era
this.wood=wood
}
```

NOTE
The JavaScript keyword this is used in the sense this *object*, that is, the parameter is assigned to *this object* being defined:

Next, you have to create an instance of the object as a variable, using the keyword new, and assign it values. For example:

```
var buffet = new furniture("Eastlake", "Oak");
```

The object initializer method accomplishes the same result, but in a more shorthand fashion, directly creating an object instance:

```
buffet = {era: "Eastlake", wood: "Oak")
```

Using objects in scripting will be covered in greater depth in Chapters 4 and 5.

NOTE
One of the more useful objects you can create is an *array*, a data storage mechanism that provides for easy and efficient use of data in scripts. As with other objects, arrays have associated properties and methods that offer a lot of flexibility in how you store and call your data. Arrays are used in examples in the remaining chapters.

Properties

Objects have properties that allow you to describe an object, distinguishing different variations of the same object from one another, as well as to customize an object to fit your needs. For example, you can modify a window by its outer height and width dimensions (outerHeight/outerWidth), as well as its inner, or display area, dimensions (innerHeight/innerWidth). Some objects have several properties (such as a window), while others have few (the string object has only one property, length). Also, different types of objects can have the same property (but they would be unlikely to share the same values of those properties).

Properties are applied to an object by using the dot statement syntax in the form objectname.propertyname="value"; Listing 3-6 illustrates two uses of a property using JavaScript. First, in the head section, the background color of the web page is set using its name. Then, in the body section of the page, the background color is called, and its hexadecimal code is returned.

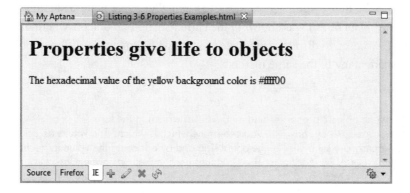

Listing 3-6   Properties examples

```
<html>
   <head>
      <title>Listing 3-6</title>
      <script language="javascript" type= "text/javascript">
         //<![CDATA [
         document.bgColor="yellow"
         //]]>
      </script>
   </head>
```

```
<body>
  <h1>Properties give life to objects</h1>
  <script language="javascript" type= "text/javascript">
    //<![CDATA [
  document.write("The hexadecimal value of the yellow
    background color is " + document.bgColor);
    //]]>
  </script>
</body>
</html>
```

Methods

The actions that objects can perform are called *methods*. In many cases, you can think of methods as being predefined functions for an object. For example, to return the square root of three, you would use the math object's square root method. Using the dot syntax, this would be in the form: math.sqrt(3). Another example of using methods to elicit actions from an object was shown in the earlier section on objects where the alert() method was used to display a message box. As with properties, different object and object types share many of the same methods.

TIP

Since both an object's properties and methods are written in the form object.method or object.property, how can you determine which is which? The values associated with a property are set by use of the equal sign and by enclosing the value in quotes (document.bgColor="dodgerblue"). Values used in methods are enclosed in parentheses (Math.sqrt(3)).

Event Handlers

JavaScript allows you to easily take advantage of events, or *triggers*, such as mouse clicks and page openings performed by a user on your web page, through the use of predefined *event handlers*. The event handlers recognize the event taking place and then perform one or more tasks, adding an ease-of-coding level of interactivity between the web page and the user. For example, when a user hovers the mouse pointer over a button, an alert dialog box opens, warning of the consequences of clicking the button (the clicking action being directed to another action by a second event handler). Chapter 4 provides several examples of event handlers being employed to spice up web pages.

Table 3-5 lists the JavaScript event handlers and the triggers needed to perform their assigned tasks.

Event Handler	Event Trigger
onAbort	An image's loading is interrupted.
onBlur	Focus is removed from an element.
onChange	Contents of a form are changed.
onClick	An element is single-clicked.
onDblClick	An element is double-clicked.
onDragDrop	An object is dragged-and-dropped into a window.
onError	An error occurs when loading a web page or picture.
onFocus	The user places the focus on an element.
onKeyDown	The user presses a defined key.
onKeyPress	The user presses and holds down a defined key.
onKeyUp	The user releases a defined pressed key.
onLoad	A web page completes loading in a browser.
onMouseDown	The user presses a mouse button.
onMouseMove	The user moves the mouse pointer.
onMouseOut	The user moves the mouse pointer from a link.
onMouseOver	The user moves the mouse pointer to a link.
onMouseUp	The user releases a mouse button.
onMove	A window or frame is moved.
onOpen	A web page opens in a browser.
onReset	A form is reset.
onResize	A window or frame is resized.
onSelect	A field in a form is selected.
onSubmit	A user submits a form.
onUnload	A user opens another web page.

Table 3-5 JavaScript Event Handlers

Control Structures

Simple scripts are executed from the first statement to the last statement without interruption or change of direction. Often you will want to ask if the script should go one way or another, or go back and reexecute a particular piece of code. That is the purpose of control structures, which include if/else statements; while, do-while, and for statements; and switch statements, among others.

If/Else Statements

The `if/else` statement is the primary decision-making construct in JavaScript. It allows you to specify that `if` some expression is TRUE, then a group of statements will be executed, `else` a different group of statements will be executed. It takes this form:

```
if (conditional expression) {
   statements executed if TRUE;
   }
else   {
   statements executed if FALSE;
   }
```

The `else` statements are optional and are needed only if you want to do something other than continue with the script if the conditional expression is FALSE. Also, you can nest `if/else` statements, like this:

```
if (outer conditional expression) {
   statements executed if first conditional is TRUE;
   if (inner/nested conditional expression){
      statements executed if second conditional is TRUE;
   }
   else {
      statements executed if second conditional is FALSE;
   }
}
else {
   statements executed if first conditional is FALSE;
}
```

In all cases the conditional expression must result in a Boolean TRUE or FALSE (1 or 0). If a variable simply exists, that is, it has been defined as containing something other than NULL, FALSE, or 0, then it is TRUE.

TIP

If you define a variable as containing a constant like NULL, TRUE, or FALSE, you must remember *not* to put the constant in quotation marks.

Many conditional expressions are comparisons that test if two elements are equal, greater than, or less than. Remember that when you test for equality in JavaScript, you must use a double equal sign (`==`), not a single one, which means assignment.

Listing 3-7 shows several examples of `if/else` statements, the results of which are shown next. A number of examples will be shown in the following chapters.

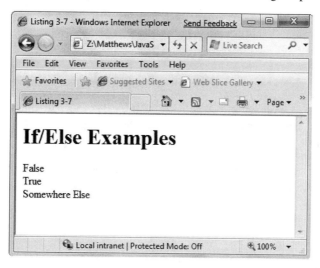

Listing 3-7   If/Else statements

```html
<html>
   <head>
      <title>Listing 3-7</title>
   </head>
   <body>
      <h1>If/Else Examples</h1>
      <script language="javascript" type= "text/javascript">
         //<![CDATA [
         //if the variable "a" is declared, return True/write
            True; else return False/write False. Since no variable
            "a" declared, expect False;
         if (a){
         document.write("True <br>");
         }
         else {
            document.write("False <br>");
         }
         //If the variable "a" is declared, return True/write
            True; else return False/write False. Since variable
            "a" is declared, expect True;
         var a = "Something";
         if (a){
```

```
         document.write("True <br>");
         }
         else {
           document.write("False <br>");
         }
         //If variable "state" equals "WA", return True/write
            "Pacific Northwest;" else return False/write Somewhere
            Else. Since variable "a" equals "CA", expect False;
         var state="CA";
         if (state=="WA"){
           document.write("Pacific Northwest <br>");
         }
         else {
           document.write("Somewhere Else <br>");
         }
         //]]>
      </script>
   </body>
</html>
```

Ternary Operator

A shorthand method of doing if/else decision making in JavaScript scripts uses
the ternary operator (? :), where ? replaces the if test and follows the conditional
expression, and the : replaces else. For example, (a==3) ? "True" : "False";

While and Do-While Statements

The while and do-while statements are looping constructs that allow you to repeatedly
execute a piece of code until a conditional expression is no longer TRUE. The while
statement is the foundation of this set of statements and takes the following form:

```
while (conditional expression) {
      statements executed while TRUE;
      }
```

The do-while statement is similar to the while statement, except that the conditional
expression is at the end of the statement instead of at the beginning, allowing the do portion
to execute even if the while statement is FALSE. The do-while statement takes this form:

```
do {
    statements executed while TRUE;
    }
while (conditional expression);
```

The most common conditional expression is to compare a counter with some end value—in other words, to initialize a counter, and then to loop though some statements, incrementing the counter with each loop, until the counter exceeds the end value. Listing 3-8 shows examples of this for both `while` and `do-while`, with the results shown next. You can see that the `while` statement runs until the counter ends. In the case of the `do-while` statements, the `do` statement is TRUE and executes once, but the `while` statement is FALSE, doesn't loop, and doesn't execute the `write` statement.

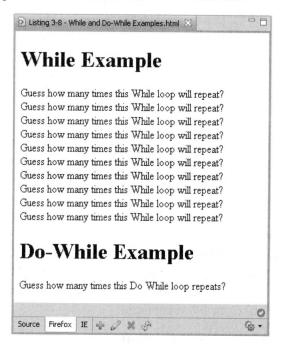

Listing 3-8   While and do-while examples

```
<html>
   <head>
      <title>Listing 3-8</title>
   </head>
   <body>
      <h1>While Example</h1>
      <script language="javascript" type= "text/javascript">
         //<![CDATA [
         var i = 1;
```

```
       while (i <= 10) {
           document.write("Guess how many times this
               While loop will repeat?<br>");
           i += 1;
       }
       //]]>
   </script>
   <h1>Do-While Example</h1>
   <script language="javascript" type= "text/javascript">
       //<![CDATA [
       var i = 10;
       do {
       document.write("Guess how many times this Do While loop
           repeats?<br>")
       i += 1;
       } while (i < 11);
       //]]>
   </script>
   </body>
</html>
```

For Statement

The for statement is an additional looping construct. The for statement, which is similar to its counterpart in other languages, places the initialization of the counter, its conditional limit, and its incrementing all in a series of expressions immediately following the for. The for statement takes the following form:

```
for (initializing expression; conditional expression; incrementing
expression)
   {
   statements executed while TRUE;
   }
```

In its basic form, the for expression might be for (i = 1; i <= 5; i++), where i++ increments i after it is used. If any of these expressions are handled elsewhere in the script, they can be left blank in the for expression, which at its minimum is for (; ;).

Listing 3-9 shows examples of the `for` statement, with the results shown next. The `for` statement can be used in a manner very similar to `while`.

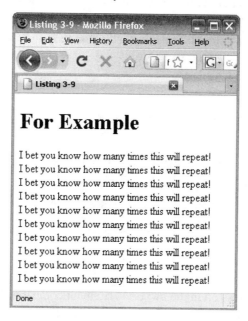

Listing 3-9   For example

```
<html>
   <head>
      <title>Listing 3-9</title>
   </head>
   <body>
      <h1>For Example</h1>
      <script language="javascript" type= "text/javascript">
         //<![CDATA [
         for (i=1; i <= 10; i++) {
         document.write("I bet you know how many times this will
repeat!<br>")
         }
         //]]>
      </script>
   </body>
</html>
```

Switch Statements

The switch statement is similar to a series of if/else statements. The switch statement is used where you want to compare a single variable with a number of different values and to do something different depending on the value. Three additional keywords are used with switch: case, break, and default, taking this form:

```
switch (avariable) {
    case "1" :
        statements executed while TRUE;
        break;
    case "2" :
        statements executed while TRUE;
        break;
    case "3" :
        statements executed while TRUE;
        break;
    default :
        statements executed when all cases are FALSE;
    }
```

Each case expression in the switch statement compares the switch variable with the case value, which can be a string. If it is equal, the statements following the case expression are executed, and then the break expression sends the script's flow to the first statement after the switch's closing curly brace. If none of the case expressions is successful, the statements following the default expression are executed, and the script's flow exits the switch statement. Listing 3-10 demonstrates how this works, which provides these results:

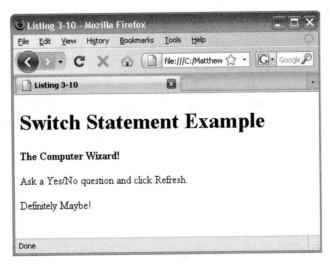

Listing 3-10   Switch statement example

```html
<html>
   <head>
      <title>Listing 3-10</title>
   </head>
   <body>
      <h1>Switch Statement Example</h1>
      <p><b>The Computer Wizard!</b></p>
      <p>Ask a Yes/No question and click Refresh.</p>
      <script language="javascript" type= "text/javascript">
         //<![CDATA [
         var randNum = Math.ceil(8*Math.random())
         switch (randNum) {
         case 1 :
            document.write("Definitely Yes!");
            break;
         case 2 :
            document.write("Probably Yes!");
            break;
         case 3 :
            document.write("Definitely Maybe!");
            break;
         case 4 :
            document.write("Probably No!");
            break;
         case 5 :
            document.write("Definitely No!");
            break;
         default :
            document.write(randNum,"<br>");
            document.write("Computer Malfunction, Try Again");
         }
         //]]>
      </script>
   </body>
</html>
```

In the following chapters, you'll see how to take the many pieces of JavaScript and weave them into a script that actually does something useful, like passing data between web pages or between sessions, or reading and writing files on the server, or authenticating a user.

An excellent book on JavaScript is *JavaScript: A Beginners Guide, Third Edition*, by John Pollock, published by McGraw-Hill/Professional, 2009.

Chapter 4
Responding to Events

Key Skills & Concepts

- Placing Event Handlers in Code

- Understanding Event Handler Syntax and Usage

- Displaying Messages When a Page Opens/Closes

- Placing and Removing Focus

- Resizing a Window

- Working with `onclick`, `ondblclick`, and Arrays

- Moving the Mouse Pointer to Trigger Events

- Using the Keyboard Event Handlers

As was introduced in Chapter 3, *events* are actions performed by a web user that affect a web page or elements on a web page.

Chapter 4 looks at various types of events that can occur on a web page, how JavaScript event handlers respond to them, and demonstrates several examples of their use. The chapter is organized around four basic categories of event handler use:

- **Window** event handlers deal with events such as opening, closing, resizing, and moving that a user does to an entire web page.

- **Mouse** event handlers work with the actions of the mouse pointer such as clicking or double-clicking an element, or moving the mouse pointer on to or off of an element.

- **Keyboard** event handlers respond to keypresses on the keyboard.

- **Form** event handlers react to the user's actions within a data collection form, such as selecting form elements, resetting the values in a form, or submitting the form to a recipient or database (covered in Chapter 5).

NOTE
Not every event handler listed in this chapter is fully described or demonstrated. Many are so closely related that to detail their use would be redundant.

Introducing Event Handlers

When a browser interprets an event as happening, it invokes, or triggers, a JavaScript object, called an *event handler,* to perform a certain action (see Chapter 3 for a list of the JavaScript event handlers). For example, when you move your mouse pointer over a link or image, often you will see a pop-up message informing you about the nature of the link or image. In this case, the *event* of placing the mouse pointer over the link *triggers* (or fires) the onmouseover *event handler* to display the message. When you move the mouse pointer away from the link or image, typically the onmouseout event handler closes the message.

If you have had experience with X/HTML event handlers, you may be wondering why you can't just continue to use them. You can, but the big advantage JavaScript event handlers have over their X/HTML brethren is that they can call other JavaScript code such as functions, opening a much broader range of interactivity to your web pages. X/HTML event handlers are limited to the values of their attributes. The following section describes how this relationship between the X/HTML and JavaScript ways of handling events are interconnected.

Placing Event Handlers in Your Code

Event handlers are a unique feature of JavaScript in that they can be used outside of the <script> tags normally used to encapsulate scripts.

You can add JavaScript event handlers to a number of X/HMTL tags as an attribute. Which tags are available depends on the particular event handler. For example, the window-type event handler onload can be used with the <body>, <frame>, <frameset>, <iframe>, <img>, <link>, and <script> tags, while a click-type event handler such as onclick is compatible with dozens of tags. However, the majority of common uses occur within the <body>, <form>, and <link> tags. An example of this usage is

```
<body onload="window.alert('Welcome to Past Times Antiques');">
```

which adds the JavaScript onload event handler to the X/HTML <body> tag as an attribute.

Understanding Event Handler Syntax and Usage

Event handlers are added to X/HTML tags in the form:

```
<X/HTML tagname eventhandlername="JavaScript Statement; JavaScript
    Statement; …;">
```

NOTE

When using JavaScript as an attribute, you need to surround the JavaScript in double quotes. Text strings within the double quotes such as message text for alert message boxes are identified by using single quotes.

where:

- `<` identifies the start of an X/HTML tag
- **X/HTML** `tagname` is one of the available tags associated with the event handler
- `eventhandlername` is the event handler you are using
- `=` assigns the JavaScript statement(s) to trigger when the event occurs
- `"` opening double quote starts the JavaScript code
- `;` ends each JavaScript statement, separating multiple statements
- `"` ending double quote completes JavaScript code
- `>` identifies the end of the X/HTML tag

As you can see, you can string together several JavaScript statements within one argument, separated by semicolons. While this is acceptable for short statements and statements that will be used only once, a much more efficient (and elegant) way to accomplish this is to create a function that contains the statements and then to call the function as needed in the body of your web page.

Working with the Window Event Handlers

In this section, we'll work with a number of the event handlers associated with the web page itself, referred to as the window events. Table 4-1 lists the related event handlers.

Event Handler	Event Trigger
onabort	An image's loading is interrupted.
onblur	Focus is removed from an element.
onerror	An error occurs when loading a web page or picture.
onfocus	The user places the focus on an element.
onload	A web page completes loading to the browser.
onmove	A window or frame is moved.
onresize	A window or frame is resized.
onunload	A user opens another web page.

Table 4-1 Window Event Handlers

Displaying Messages When a Page Opens/Closes

Very common uses for event handlers are to display messages when users first open a web page or when they leave the page.

onload Event Handler

Let's say, for example, you are building a web site that deals with animal neglect, and you have some pictures that might be offensive to some. Yes, you could use headings, banners, and other means to try and get the users' attention, but you have no way of ensuring the users acknowledge having read your warnings. A better solution would be to pop up a *modal* message box when the page finishes loading that requires the user to click OK to close the message box (presumably after reading the message). A modal window (in this case, an alert message box) is a window that requires user input to close it before the focus can change to another window or web page. The event handler that triggers the message box is onload. Some other ways to use the onload event handler with more scripting include checking to see the type and version of the user's browser and then loading pages customized to that browser, and requesting a user's name and storing that information in a cookie so that subsequent visits can greet the user by name.

Using the syntax described in the previous section, Listing 4-1 shows the code to create an alert/announcement message box using the onload event handler. Figure 4-1 displays the message box on a commercial-style web page.

NOTE

In Chapter 3, we showed an example of using the alert() method by containing it in a JavaScript statement within the <head> section of a web page. You might be wondering what the difference is between that usage and using the onload event handler in the <body>. It's all about timing the appearance of the message box. In the former usage, the message box is displayed immediately, before any page elements finish displaying (the process is so fast that some page elements such as text can load before the message box appears). In the case of the onload event handler, you can be assured that all page elements, including pictures and other media, will display before the message box appears, perhaps giving the user a better sense of the nature of the message box.

Listing 4-1   onload example

```
<html>
  <head>
    <title>Listing 4-1</title>
  </head>
  <body onload="window.alert('The next hematology class is
    scheduled for March 24th');">
  </body>
</html>
```

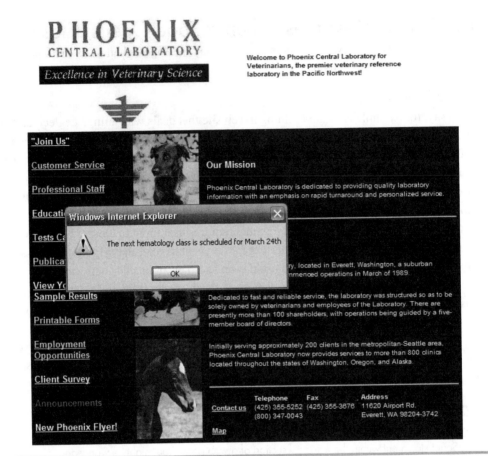

Figure 4-1 Use the `onload` event handler to display message boxes after a page loads all its elements.

onunload Event Handler

As the `onload` event handler can be used to welcome or provide announcements to a user, you can provide a farewell of sorts by displaying a message box when the user attempts to leave the page by any number of methods: clicking a link, using File | Open, closing the browser window, and so forth. An example of the `onunload` event handler being used is shown here, and the code is displayed in Listing 4-2. (Note the use of the \' escape sequence in the listing within the alert method attribute to display the single quote in the word "don't.")

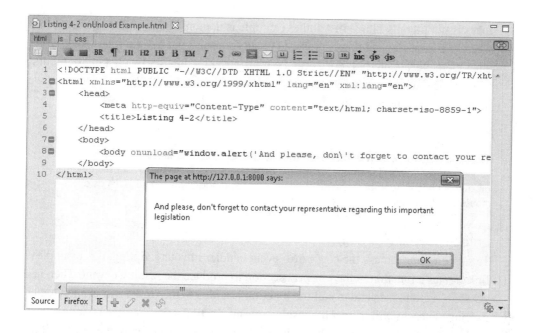

Listing 4-2   onunload example

```html
<html>
   <head>
      <title>Listing 4-2</title>
   </head>
   <body onunload="window.alert('And please, don\'t forget to contact your
         representative regarding this important legislation');">
   </body>
</html>
```

CAUTION

You can easily overuse the `onunload` event handler to the annoyance of many of your web page viewers. Think how you'd feel when your mind's eye is already visualizing the display of your next web surfing page when all comes to a halt and you have to "kill" this &^%$ message box to continue. Use it sparingly or you might alienate the users whose favor you are trying to gain.

Placing and Removing Focus

Focus is a fancy word used by programmers to describe which window, or which element in a window, has your attention. For example, in the case of windows, the active window has the focus, and the inactive window(s) don't have the focus (in Figure 4-1, the message box has the focus). That is, they are *blurred* (another programmers' term, although the focus is not literally blurred). Another example is demonstrated within data input forms, where the form element that is prepared to accept user input has the focus, and the other elements are blurred. Focus can be transferred by the user by clicking or tabbing to a different window or web page element, or programmatically by you and other web programmers by using scripts or other coding methods.

TIP

Programming terminology can be very specific and logical, or at times it can be quite vague and colloquial. To remove focus from an element, that is, to *blur* it, doesn't mean an element becomes visibly unreadable, only that some additional action (such as a mouse click) is required for it to accept user input.

onfocus Event Handler

To see how you can use the `onfocus` event handler in your scripting, this example first creates a function in the `<head>` section to produce the result we want. Then in the `<body>` section, the code to call the function is added to the `onfocus` event handler so a change in focus will trigger the result we want. Listing 4-3 shows the code to change the background color of a text box within a form (forms are covered in more detail in Chapter 5) when a user moves focus to it, as shown next.

NOTE

Focus can be applied to an element programmatically, which is shown in an example later in the chapter.

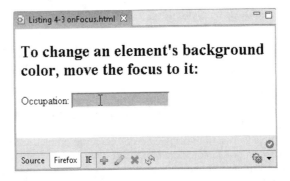

Listing 4-3   onfocus example

```html
<html>
    <head>
        <title>Listing 4-3</title>
        <script language="javascript" type= "text/javascript">
```

```
    //<![CDATA[
    function chgTextColor(i){
    document.getElementById(i).style.background="lightblue";
    }
    //]]>
  </script>
</head>
<body>
  <h2>To change an element's background color, move the focus
    to it:</h2>
  <form>
  Occupation: <input type="text" onfocus="chgTextColor(this.id);"
    id="occupation">
  </form>
</body>
</html>
```

onblur Event Handler

The onblur event handler, which works when the focus is removed from an element, comes in handy when you want to remind users of something they should have done to the element that had the focus, or want to question them about some aspect of that element. In Listing 4-4, we take the onfocus example you saw previously, add a second text box where the focus can be changed from the original text box (by clicking the text box or pressing TAB), and then create a message box that users have to attend to before they can continue, as shown in the following:

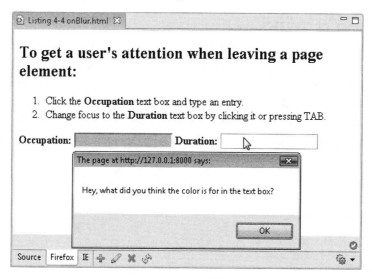

Listing 4-4   onblur example

```html
<html>
   <head>
      <title>Listing 4-4</title>
      <script language="javascript" type= "text/javascript">
         //<![CDATA[
         function chgTextColor(i){
         document.getElementById(i).style.background="lightblue";
         }
         //]]>
      </script>
   </head>
   <body>
      <h2>To get a user's attention when leaving a page element:</h2>
      <ol>
         <li>Click the <b>Occupation</b> text box and type an entry.</li>
         <li>Change focus to the <b>Duration</b> text box by clicking it
            or pressing TAB.</li>
      </ol>
      <form>
      <b>Occupation:</b> <input type="text" onfocus="chgTextColor(this.id);"
         id="occupation" onblur="window.alert('Hey, what did you think
the color is for in the text box?');">
         <b>Duration:</b> <input type="text" onfocus="chgTextColor(this.id);"
            id="duration">
      </form>
   </body>
</html>
```

Resizing a Window

The onresize event handler triggers and executes JavaScript code when a web page
window is resized. There are times (and those times can happen more often with certain
browsers than with others) that content on a web page doesn't resize when the web page
window itself is resized. To slap the browser into recognizing the change, you can force a
refresh, or reload, of the page using the onresize event handler. Listing 4-5 shows how
to do this. Figure 4-2 shows the status bar displaying a quick-refresh indication.

Listing 4-5   onresize example

```html
<html>
   <head>
      <title>Listing 4-5</title>
   </head>
   <body onresize="window.location.href=window.location.href;">
      <h2>To reload the web page, resize the window:</h2>
      <table border="1" width="100%">
         <tr>
            <td width="41%" height="21">I am really stretching this table out in
order to try and force a resize</td>
            <td width="59%" height="21">I am really stretching this table out in
               order to try and force a resize</td>
         </tr>
         <tr>
            <td width="41%" height="21">I am really stretching this table out in
               order to try and force a resize</td>
            <td width="59%" height="21">I am really stretching this table out in
               order to try and force a resize</td>
         </tr>
      </table>
   </body>
</html>
```

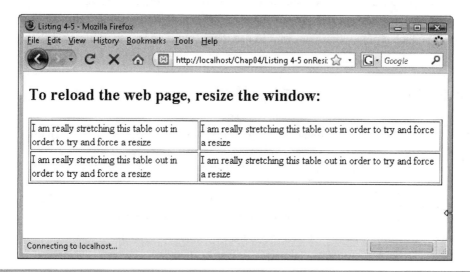

Figure 4-2   The green bar in the status bar indicates a quick refresh when the page is resized.

Using the Mouse and Keyboard Event Handlers

The most used of the event handlers is the group related to user mouse actions and keyboard inputs. Mouse events include actions by the user such as simply moving the mouse pointer, moving it on and off links, and pressing the mouse button to produce a click or double-click, as well as the pressing and releasing of the mouse button. Table 4-2 lists the related event handlers. (Keyboard events are discussed later in the chapter.)

In the next few sections, we have used a number of the mouse event handlers to show how these can be used in your code.

Working with onclick, ondblclick, and Arrays

While any number of elements on a web page can react to a user's click, none is more ubiquitous than the button. In this first example, along with the onclick event handler, we add a couple of other scripting elements to make things a little more interesting. First, an *array* is set up to more efficiently handle multiple variables. Next, a *function* is created to display messages when called. Finally, the onclick event handler is attached to screen elements to trigger the action.

Introducing Arrays

An *array* is a JavaScript object that allows you to store similar variables, indexed by number, so they can be used later in your script. By assigning values a number, not only do you reduce typing when you want to use them (write once, use many), but then you

Event Handler	Event Trigger
onclick	An element is clicked.
ondblclick	An element is double-clicked.
ondragdrop	An object is dragged-and-dropped into a window.
onmousedown	The user presses a mouse button.
onmousemove	The user moves the mouse pointer.
onmouseout	The user moves the mouse pointer from a link.
onmouseover	The user moves the mouse pointer to a link.
onmouseup	The user releases a mouse button.

Table 4-2 Click Event Handlers

also can employ other scripting features such as loops to further your efficiency. An array is created from a morphing of how we create variable and functions, in the form:

```
var arrayname=new Array()
```

where *arrayname* is a unique name you provide using the standard JavaScript syntax for naming variables and objects, and **var**, **new**, and **Array()** are scripting keywords that assign the soon-to-be-added variables to a new array.

You can assign variables (or parameters) to an array at the time you create the array (typically in the <head> section) or anywhere in your script thereafter. To assign variables after creating an array, you list them in the form:

```
var arrayname=new Array(3)
arrayname[0]="variablename0";
arrayname[1]=variablename1";
arrayname[2]=variablename2";
```

In this case, we know there will be three parameters in this array, so we set up the array as containing only three parameters, that is, **new Array(3)**. Later in our script we can add parameters in sequence either by continuing the original list, or simply by adding a line of code with the assignment. Alternatively, we could create the array with no parameters, that is, **new Array()**, and add variables as we need them. As objects, arrays have properties and methods that make them very useful tools in your scripting toolbox.

CAUTION

Arrays are efficient data-storage mechanisms that can easily lose their efficiency if used incorrectly. When you run a script with, say, a 100-parameter array, 100 bytes of data are placed in the memory stack. If you create a 100-parameter array, but inadvertently assign the last parameter an index of 500—for example, DogsInKennel[500]= "lassie";—you've just created a 500-parameter array, taking up 400 unused bytes in the stack. So check to be sure your index numbers are sequentially assigned.

Putting the Script Together

In the <head> section of Listing 4-6, the logic_list array is defined and populated with three variables. The callalert function is defined with a statement to display a message box when called. In the body, three buttons are created (shown next) that use the `onclick` event handler to call the `callalert` function with each of the three variables in the `logic_list` array.

Listing 4-6   onclick and array example

```html
<html>
    <head>
        <title>Listing 4-6</title>
        <script language="javascript" type= "text/javascript">
            //<![CDATA[
            var logic_list= new Array(2)
            logic_list[0]="Boy, do I need a European vacation";
            logic_list[1]="If only I had the money";
            logic_list[2]="Therefore, I need to keep working to earn
                enough money for my European vacation"
            function callalert(logic_list){
                window.alert(logic_list);
            }
            //]]>
        </script>
    </head>
    <body>
        <h2>Circular logic</h2>
```

```
     Click here for a solution... <input
        type="button"onclick=callalert(logic_list[0])>
        that has a small problem...  <input type="button"
        onclick=callalert(logic_list[1])>
        that seems to have a solution <input type="button"
        onclick=callalert(logic_list[2])>
  </body>
</html>
```

Adding the ondblclick Event Handler

As you might expect, the `ondblclick` event handler functions identically to the `onclick` event handler, except it requires a little extra effort on behalf of the user (a second click!). Listing 4-7 shows an example of using the `ondblclick` event handler that triggers a button displaying some text.

Listing 4-7   ondblclick example

```
<html>
   <head>
      <title>Listing 4-7</title>
   </head>
   <body>
      <h2>Click the button below to see if you won a prize! (If
         a single click doesn't work, try a double-click.)</h2>
      <input type="button" ondblclick="document.write('<h2>
         Congratulations, you won!!! An ex-prince from
         Nigeria will contact you with details on how to
         claim your prize!</h2>')">
   </body>
</html>
```

TIP

Two other event handlers react to mouse clicks, onmousedown and onmouseup. Depending on the action you are expecting the user to perform, these event handlers can often provide less error-prone results than onclick and ondblclick. Take, for example, the situation where a user clicks a link or button, but moves the mouse pointer off the target before releasing the mouse button. (Remember the definition of a click; that is, a click involves both the pressing and releasing of the mouse button.) If you use the onclick event handler, the trigger will not fire. If you use the onmousedown event handler, the trigger will fire on the initial press, irrespective of where the mouse pointer is when the button is released.

Moving the Mouse Pointer to Trigger Events

Like the click-type event handlers, a few handlers work when the mouse pointer is moved over an element, or off an element. The most common is the onmouseover and onmouseout pairing, which can be used for a variety purposes, but most notably in rollovers, where near-identical images are switched as the mouse pointer enters and leaves an image to give a sense of animation, as shown next. Listing 4-8 shows the code to include these two event handlers within the anchor tag (<a href) to create a link to an image. To create this script, you need two images that have the same dimension, as one is replaced by the other when the mouse pointer is moved on and off the image. The code includes the following details:

- `<a href="http://www.someLinkToPictures.com"` includes the opening tag, which creates a link to the image if the user clicks it instead of simply moving the mouse pointer on/off it.

- `onmouseover="document.swan.src='../Art/swan-onmouseover.jpg'"` displays the image in the src path when the image named "swan" is triggered by a mouse-over event.

- `onmouseout="document.swan.src='../Art/swan-onmouseout.jpg'">` displays the image in the src path when the image named "swan" is triggered by a mouse-out event (the mouse must move off the picture).

- `<img name="swan" border="0" width="307" height="230" alt="Dutch Swan" src="../Art/swan-onmouseout.jpg"></a>` defines the image that initially appears on the page.

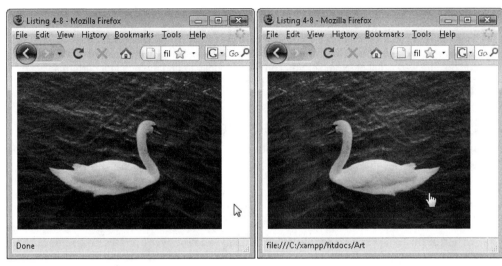

Before   After

NOTE

For the code examples in Listings 4-8 and 4-9 to be meaningful, we have used graphic files on my computer. If you want to replicate these examples, substitute a URL or path in the applicable `src` attribute to files of your choosing. In testing these listings, a stand-alone browser (Firefox or IE) works better than Aptana.

Listing 4-8   onmouseover and onmouseout example

```
<html>
    <head>
        <title>Listing 4-8</title>
    </head>
    <body>
        <a href="http://www.someLinkToPictures.com"
            onmouseover="document.swan.src='../Art/swan-onmouseover.jpg'"
            onmouseout="document.swan.src='../Art/swan-onmouseout.jpg'">
        <img name="swan" border="0" width="307" height="230" alt="Dutch Swan"
            src="../Art/swan-onmouseout.jpg"></a>
    </body>
</html>
```

NOTE

There are a number of variations on using the rollover to add interactivity to your scripts. The example shown in Listing 4-8 is really just the starting point for what you can do. The web is full of examples you can mimic legally to find the one that performs the actions you are specifically trying to achieve.

Using the Keyboard Event Handlers

In addition to receiving user input from the mouse, you can trigger events based on key actions from the keyboard, listed in Table 4-3. A majority of these events are related to online data entry forms, which are described in more detail in Chapter 5. In this chapter, the `onkeyup` event handler is used to demonstrate keyboard event handlers. In conjunction with a coding sample from Chapter 3, an event handler from earlier in this chapter, and two functions, a key release event is used to trigger a random message to the user.

The `<body>` section in Listing 4-9 performs three actions besides including some narrative X/HTML:

- `<body onload="setfocus()">` fires the `setfocus` function when the `onload` event handler is triggered.

- `<input input id="text1" type="text" onkeyup="presskey()">` creates a text box named `text1` and fires the `presskey` function when the user releases a pressed key.

The `<head>` section defines these two functions:

- **function** `setfocus()` encapsulates a statement that sets the focus to the text box (places the blinking insertion point at the left end of the box so it is ready to be entered) when the page is loaded.

Event Handler	Event Trigger
onkeydown	The user presses a defined key.
onkeypress	The user presses and holds down a defined key.
onkeyup	The user releases a pressed defined key.

Table 4-3 Keyboard Event Handlers

● **function** presskey() encapsulates the switch statement demonstrated in Chapter 3 to randomly display comments in alert message boxes.

Listing 4-9   onkeyup example

```
<html">
    <head>
        <title>Listing 4-9</title>
        <script language="javascript" type= "text/javascript">
            //<![CDATA[
            function setfocus(){
                document.all.text1.focus();
            }
            var randNum = Math.ceil(8*Math.random())
            function presskey(){
                switch (randNum) {
                    case 1:
                        window.alert("Hey dude, can you press a little
                        softer, please?");
                        break;
                    case 2:
                        window.alert("Ouch, take it easy, bub");
                        break;
                    case 3:
                        window.alert("C'mon, type like you mean it!");
                        break;
```

```
            case 4:
               window.alert("Is that all you got?");
               break;
            case 5:
               window.alert("Try pressing in the middle of
                  the key");
               break;
            default:
               window.alert("Where did you learn to spell?");
         }
      }
      //]]>
   </script>
</head>
<body onload="setfocus()">
   <h2>A little joke to play on your friends the next time they ask
      you to create a form:</h2>
   <ol>
      <li>Start typing a word in the text box below</li>
      <li>After closing the alert, refresh your screen by clicking
            Refresh Active Preview <img src="../art/refresh.gif">
at the bottom of the Aptana editor area. DO NOT
            PRESS F5. </li>
      <li>Continue until you've had enough.</li>
   </ol>
   <input input id="text1" type="text" onkeyup="presskey()">
</body>
</html>
```

NOTE

A few other event handlers focus on actions in a form. Chapter 5 is devoted to using JavaScript in forms, and many of these event handlers, listed in Table 4-4, are demonstrated in that chapter.

Event Handler	Event Trigger
onsubmit	A user submits a form.
onselect	A field in a form is selected.
onreset	A form is reset.
onchange	Contents of a form are changed.

Table 4-4 Form Event Handlers

Chapter 5
Working with and Validating Forms

Key Skills & Concepts

- Understanding Forms

- Creating Forms Using X/HTML

- Naming Forms on a Web Page

- Using Form Properties and Methods

- Working with Form Element Properties and Methods

- Understanding Validation

- Using Validation with Passwords

- Creating a Menu Bar

- Introducing Regular Expressions

Forms are the web mechanism by which information flows from the user to the web page. They collect information that is then used by the site. JavaScript adds automation to a form to respond to what the user enters.

Chapter 5 discusses how forms are created and used, their methods and properties, how to validate information in the form, and how to carry out navigation in a web site based on JavaScript navigation elements in a form.

Reviewing Forms

This section provides a short primer on forms and how to create them using X/HTML.

NOTE

For a more comprehensive look at creating and displaying forms with X/HTML and styling them with CSS, see *HTML, XHTML, and CSS QuickSteps, Second Edition,* by Guy Hart-Davis, published by McGraw-Hill/Professional, 2009.

Understanding Forms

A form, much like its paper incarnation, is an area on a page that contains subelements to allow a user to input information, an example of which is shown in Figure 5-1. The user

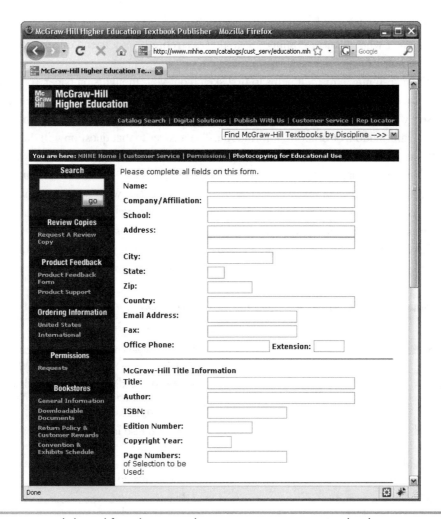

Figure 5-1   A web-based form has a similar appearance to its paper brethren.

is given boxes to fill in, options to select, and choices to make. Online forms have several advantages over paper forms:

- Online forms are easily and cheaply modified (no running to the copy store to run off another batch of 1000 order forms because a new item has been added).

- Input elements can be constructed to enforce user discipline, that is, data can be verified to exist (no blank fields), to be of a certain length (for example, credit card and Social Security numbers), or to otherwise fit certain criteria.

- Data is provided in digital form, immediately able to be entered into a database, without the time, cost, and inaccuracies inherent in data entry of written information.

There are three cardinal rules in creating a form: keep it simple, keep it short, and make it clear what the user is supposed to do (as a retired Navy friend once said, make it "sailor proof").

When designing a form, it helps to first sketch out your thoughts on paper. (Of course, if you are simply digitizing an existing paper form, that task is done for you.) First, ask yourself what type of information you want from the user, for example, contact information, account information, or ordering information. The answer to that question will dictate the questions you need to ask. For example, when soliciting contact information, ask for a name (and the format, such as *Full* or *Last, First*), title, address, e-mail address, and phone numbers. Make sure your text labels clearly convey to the user what you want from him or her, as shown in Figure 5-1. Also, check out forms on the Web that others are using for similar purposes, and see if there are any fields you need to consider adding.

Next, consider which form elements best serve the type of information you are gathering. Each form element, described in Table 5-1, caters to a specific purpose, and

Form Element	JavaScript Object Name	Usage
Button	button	Directs the user to another URL
Check box	checkbox	Obtains a yes/no-type response; can be used in a nonmutually exclusive grouping
Fieldset	NA	Allows you to display other form elements in a visible framed box, optionally with a legend (a nonscripting element)
Hidden field	hidden	Creates a field invisible to the user; commonly used to index submissions to the server
Password field	password	Creates a text box that displays asterisks (*) to mask entered characters
Radio (option) button	radio	Obtains a yes/no-type response within a mutually exclusive grouping
Reset button	reset	Returns a form to its default settings
Select box	select	Creates the infrastructure for a drop-down list box
Submit button	submit	Sends the data entered into a form to a destination such as a database or e-mail address
Text area	textarea	Allows large amounts of text to be entered, typically constrained only by the browser; useful for paragraphs, blogs, and essays
Text box	text	Allows for shorter, one-line text entries; typically 20 characters by default

Table 5-1 Form Elements

with the exception of `fieldset`, also has associated JavaScript objects, which allow you to validate and set values from a script. Most of these JavaScript objects are used later in this chapter.

Lastly, review the overall appearance and layout of the form. Cluster similar types of information together, and consider splitting a longer form into multiple forms if you need to provide intervening narrative or images, or if you feel your user will need a break. (As you'll see later in the chapter, it is quite easy to set up multiple forms on a single web page.)

Creating Forms Using X/HTML

Forms, as you may know already, are constructed using a two-part model. First, you use X/HTML to create and place the form and its elements on the web page. If you are familiar with creating static content on web pages, this should be familiar territory. The second, or active, phase involves using JavaScript to access your forms and to get them to do something using functions and other scripting.

A form is created by enclosing its elements within the `<form></form>` tags, effectively creating a form object. Optionally, you can divide a form into visible discrete sections using the `<fieldset></fieldset>` tag set. Listing 5-1 creates a basic form employing several form elements, as shown next. The following sections show you how you can use scripting in forms to activate them.

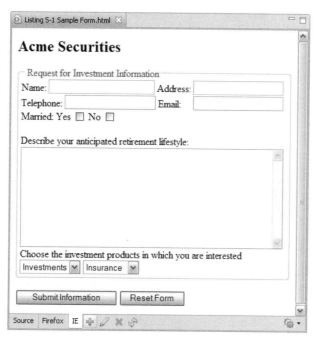

Listing 5-1   Form example

```html
<html>
   <head>
      <title>Listing 5-1 Sample Form</title>
   </head>
   <body>
      <h2>Acme Securities</h2>
      <form name="menu" action="mailto:teacher64@isp.com">
         <fieldset>
            <legend>Request for Investment Information</legend>
            Name: <input type="text" size="24">
            Address: <input type="text"><br>
            Telephone: <input type="text">
            Email:      <input type="text"><br>
            Married: Yes <input type="checkbox"> No <input
               type="checkbox"><p></p>
            Describe your anticipated retirement lifestyle:<br>
            <textarea name="report" rows="15" cols="50"></textarea>
            <br>Choose the investment products in which you are
            interested<br>
            <select name="investments" onchange="window.location=
               document.menu.investments.options
               [document.menu.investments.selectedIndex].value;">
            <option selected value="">Investments</option>
            <option value="stocks.html">Equities</option>
            <option value="bonds.html">Bonds</option>
            <option value="cds.html">CDs</option>
            </select>
            <select name="insurance" onchange="window.location=
               document.menu.insurance.options
               [document.menu.insurance.selectedIndex].value;">
            <option selected value="">Insurance</option>
            <option value="term.html">Term </option>
            <option value="whole.html">Whole Life</option>
            <option value="annuities.html">Annuities</option>
            </select>
         </fieldset>
      </form>
      <input type="submit" value="Submit Information">
      <input type="reset" value="Reset Form">
   </body>
</html>
```

Using JavaScript in Forms

As mentioned in the previous section, a form object is created from the `<form>` tag set. To apply JavaScript properties and methods to forms and their elements, a naming convention must be set up to identify which form and element scripting statements are being applied. In this section, you will first see how to identify forms and then be introduced to their properties, as well as to properties and methods associated with form elements.

Naming Forms on a Web Page

Forms are identified in one of two ways. The most straightforward of the two conventions, and the one described here, is to simply name the form (the other method, detailed in the following section, utilizes the `length` property of the form object). By naming the form, you create an instance of the form object.

NOTE

A downside of naming forms instead of using the `document.forms.length` property to identify forms is that you cannot use a form array to loop through each of the element in your forms. This limitation is normally outweighed by the convenience of quickly knowing which form is which without having to figure out the index number of a particular form. Of course, if you're working with only a couple of forms, either method is fine.

Naming forms allows you to access forms on a web page by a unique, meaningful name. To name a form, add the name attribute to the `<form>` tag as in the following syntax:

```
<form name="formname">
```

To call the form from a statement in your scripts, use this method:

```
document.formname
```

Listing 5-2 employs the `length` property of the form object to count the number of elements in a form (the `length` property is described later in the chapter and is used in other examples and listings). Note the naming of the form at the beginning of the `<body>` section and how it's called in the `alert` statement to provide information for the text in the message box. Several form elements are added using the X/HTML `<input>` tag set, shown next. These, and others like them, will be the basis on which we add scripting commands later in the chapter.

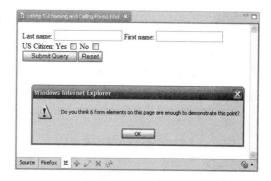

Listing 5-2	Naming and calling forms example

```html
<html>
   <head>
      <title>Listing 5-2 Naming and Calling Forms</title>
   </head>
   <body>
      <form name="count_elements">
         Last name: <input type="text">
         First name: <input type="text"><br>
         US Citizen: Yes <input type="checkbox">
            No <input type="checkbox"><br>
         <input type="submit"><input type="reset">
      </form>
      <script language="javascript" type= "text/javascript">
         //<![CDATA[
         window.alert("Do you think "+document.count_elements.length+"
            form elements on this page are enough to demonstrate this
            point?")
         //]]>
      </script>
   </body>
</html>
```

Form Properties and Methods

Table 5-2 lists and describes the properties and methods associated with the form object. While most of the form properties only contain values that relate to the attributes in the <form> tag (similar to the name attribute described in the previous section), a few provide more meaningful actions. These, and some of the form methods, are discussed in this section.

action Property

The action attribute of <form> directs the browser to send submitted form data to a destination, typically a URL where a server-side CGI or PHP processing script appends the data to a database. Alternatively, the form data could be directed to a JavaScript function that would handle the processing, or to an e-mail address. The action property allows you to recall these values, an example of which is shown here and coded in Listing 5-3. In the listing, the script has a write statement containing one argument with a concatenated literal text value and the dot syntax:

```
"+document.mailto.action);
```

JavaScript Element	Type	Description
`action`	Property	Specifies the destination of the CGI (Common Gateway Interface) or PHP script; value corresponds to the `<form>` action attribute
`elements[]`	Property	Specifies an array used to access elements in the form
`encoding`	Property	Specifies the type of encoding used in the form; value corresponds to the `<form>` type attribute
`length`	Property	Specifies the number of elements in the form; value corresponds to the length of the elements array associated with the form
`method`	Property	Specifies the type of method used when a form is submitted; value corresponds to the `<form>` method attribute
`name`	Property	Specifies the name of a form; value corresponds to the `<form>` name attribute
`target`	Property	Specifies the window where CGI or PHP output is directed; value corresponds to the `<form>` target attribute
`reset()`	Method	Displays a button in the form that when clicked by the user, resets the input in form elements to default values
`submit()`	Method	Displays a button in the form that when clicked by the user, sends the form values to a specific script

Table 5-2   Form Properties and Methods

where `document` denotes the document object, `mailto` is the form object name, and `action` is the form property that returns the value in the `<form>` action attribute.

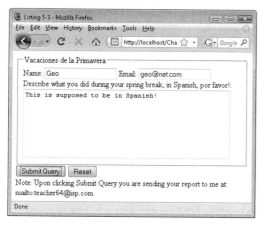

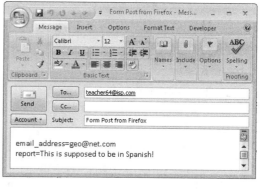

CAUTION
When using `mailto:` in the `action` attribute, the user's e-mail client opens a new message form, which is populated with the form data. The user must then click Send to send the mail data. The data isn't saved or processed for inclusion in a database or spreadsheet.

Listing 5-3   action property example

```html
<html>
    <head>
        <title>Listing 5-3 Action Property</title>
    </head>
    <body>
        <form name="mailto" method="post" enctype="text/plain"
            action="mailto:teacher64@isp.com">
            <fieldset>
                <legend>Vacaciones de la Primavera</legend>
                Name: <input type="text">
                Email: <input type="text" name="email_address"><br>
                Describe what you did during your spring break, in Spanish,
                    por favor!:<br>
                <textarea name="report" rows="15" cols="50"></textarea><br>
            </fieldset>
                <input type="submit">
                <input type="reset">
        </form>
        <script language="javascript" type= "text/javascript">
            //<![CDATA[
            document.write("Note: Upon clicking Submit Query you are
                sending your report to me at: "+document.mailto.action);
            //]]>
        </script>
    </body>
</html>
```

forms Array
Earlier in the chapter, we mentioned a way to identify and access forms other than by giving each name. Though not actually a form object property, it behaves much the same. Using the `forms` array, each form on a web page is sequentially numbered, starting at 0 (see Chapter 4 for a more detailed explanation about arrays). For example, to access the third form on a page, the syntax `document.forms[2]` would be used. Listing 5-4 illustrates this usage by including the `length` property of the form object.

As shown previously, the `length` property returns the value corresponding to the number of form elements in a form. This example has three forms, each with a different number of elements. The first form is named alpha (using the name form property), the second two are not named. In the script, the three `write` statements show how you can use the forms array notation to access forms in addition to naming them. Also, you can access a form by either its name or its forms array position, as shown in the first and third `write` statements.

Listing 5-4   forms array example

```html
<html>
   <head>
      <title>Listing 5-4 Forms Array</title>
   </head>
   <body>
      <form name="alpha">
         <fieldset>
            <legend>Hi, I'm the first form and I am called
               Alpha</legend>
            Name: <input type="text">
            Address: <input type="text"><br>
            Telephone: <input type="text">
            Email: <input type="text">
         </fieldset>
      </form>
```

```html
<p>
<form>
   <fieldset>
      <legend>Hi, I'm the second form and I don't have
         a name</legend>
      Product Name: <input type="text">
      Model: <input type="text"><br>
      Model Number: <input type="text">
      Serial Number: <input type="text"><br>
      <input type="submit">
      <input type="reset">
   </fieldset>
</form>
<p>
<form>
   <fieldset>
      <legend>Hi, I'm the third form and I don't rate a name,
         either</legend>
      Are you currently employed: Yes: <input type="checkbox">
      No: <input type="checkbox"><br>
      <input type="submit">
   </fieldset>
</form>
<p>
<script language="javascript" type= "text/javascript">
   //<![CDATA[
   document.write("In the form named Alpha, there are
      "+document.alpha.length+" elements.<br>");
   document.write("In the second form, there are
      "+document.forms[1].length+" elements.<br>");
   document.write("In the third form, there are "+document.forms[0].length+"
      elements. Oops, that's the results for the Alpha form. Actually, there
      are "+document.forms[2].length+" elements in the third form.");
   //]]>
</script>
</body>
</html>
```

elements [] Property

Within forms, each element can either be referred to by name (as forms are, described earlier) or by its position in the elements [] array (also like forms). The elements [] array is a property of the forms [] array. The two ways to identify and access form elements have the following form (numbering starts at zero):

- document.forms[0].elements[2], in which the third element in the first form on the page is referenced.

- document.third_form.second_element, in which the second element in the third form is referenced, both the form and the element being named.

To meaningfully work with a form element with JavaScript, you need to use its associated properties and methods. These are described in the following section.

reset() and submit() Methods

The `reset()` and `submit()` methods allow you to programmatically perform the actions of the Reset and Submit form element buttons, that is, to clear a form to its default values and to submit form values to a specified destination. Listing 5-5 and Figure 5-2 show how you can submit a form without a user manually performing that action, by using the `onblur` event handler to submit the form when focus is removed from a form element. (The `reset()` method works in a similar fashion.) Stealing a little thunder from the next section, this example uses the form property of the `textarea` element in conjunction with the **this** keyword to identify which form the element belongs to. This construction (`onblur="this.form.submit()"`) is an alternative to naming the form and then referring to it by name in the scripting attribute (`onblur="document.myformname.submit()"`).

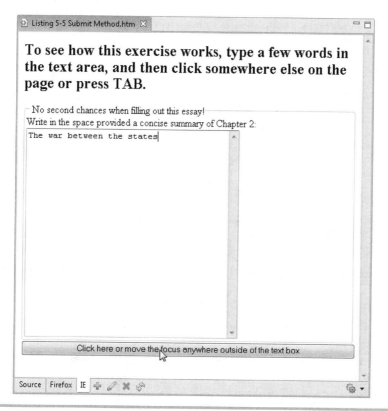

Figure 5-2 A form can be submitted by an event handler action such as a click.

NOTE

Using either the `reset()` method or the Reset form element button will reset a form to its default values. If you want to completely clear a form including default values, you need to add additional scripting that individually identifies each element and returns it to a cleared state.

Listing 5-5   submit() example

```
<html>
    <head>
        <title>Listing 5-5 Submit Method</title>
    </head>
    <body>
        <h2>To see how this exercise works, type a few words in the
            text area, and
            then click somewhere else on the page or press TAB.</h2>
        <form action="http://www.matthewstechnology.com/essay.php">
            <fieldset>
                <legend>No second chances when filling out this essay!</legend>
                Write in the space provided a concise summary of Chapter 2:
                    <textarea rows=20 cols=40 onblur="this.form.submit()"></textarea><br>
            </fieldset>
            <input type="submit" value="Click here or move the focus anywhere
                    outside of the text box">
        </form>
    </body>
</html>
```

Working with Form Element Properties and Methods

Earlier in the chapter, Table 5-1 listed the form elements that a form comprises. Here, Table 5-3 lists several properties and methods that are applicable to each. As you can see, many of these properties/methods are shared by several elements.

This next section provides examples of how some of these properties and methods can be used with form elements to achieve certain results. Many of the properties/methods that are not shown behave in a very similar manner to the ones being demonstrated.

defaultValue Property

In text boxes and text areas, you can display a default value for your users. If they change that value and then decide to return to the default value, they might be tempted to reset the entire form, which works but obliterates any other entries they may have made. A slicker way to handle this is to create a way that simply returns an element to its default value. Listing 5-6 shows the code for creating a function that returns the

Property/Method	Used by These Elements	Description
checked	Check box, radio button	Indicates if a check box is checked (true) or not (false)
defaultChecked	Check box, radio button	Indicates whether a check box is checked by default (true)
defaultValue	Text area, text box	Indicates the default value in a text area or text box
form	All	Returns the name of the parent form
name	All	Sets or returns the name of the element
options[]	Select box	Provides an array for options within an option list
selectedIndex	Select box	Indicates the index value of the selected option within the option list
type	All	Returns the type value of the element; for example, the type value for a check box is checkbox
value	All except select box	Sets the value of a specified element
blur()	All except hidden field	Removes the focus from an element
click()	All except hidden field, select box, text area, and text box	Acts as a click event on an element
focus()	All except hidden field	Places focus on an element
select()	Text area, text box	Selects the text area box or text box

Table 5-3 Form Element Properties and Methods

value of a text box to its default value when called by clicking the Return to Default Citizenship button. An onclick event handler does the calling in the <body> section. Try it for yourself, as shown in Figure 5-3.

Listing 5-6 defaultValue property example

```
<html>
  <head>
    <title>Listing 5-6 defaultValue Property</title>
    <script language="javascript" type= "text/javascript">
      //<![CDATA[
      function default_cit(){
      document.contact.citizen.value=document.contact.citizen
        .defaultValue;
      }
      //]]>
    </script>
  </head>
```

```
<body>
  <form name="contact">
    <fieldset>
      <legend>Personal Information</legend>
      Name: <input type="text" name="fullname">
      Email: <input type="text" name="email"><br>
      Citizenship: <input type="text" name="citizen"
      value="United States">
      <input type="button" value="Return to Default Citizenship"
        onclick="default_cit();">
    </fieldset>
    <input type="submit" value="Submit Personal Info">
    <input type="reset">
  </form>
</body>
</html>
```

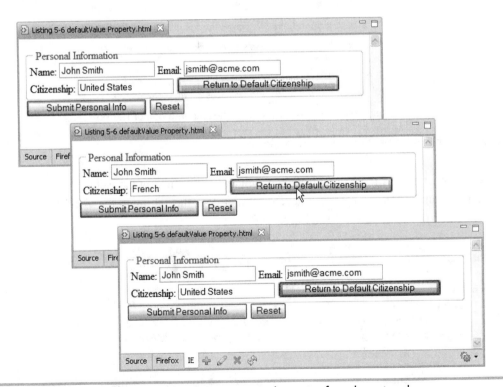

Figure 5-3 You can reset a field without resetting the entire form by using the
`defaultValue` property.

options[] and value Properties

As was noted in Table 5-3, the `options []` property is an array that provides an index for all the options in a drop-down select box, similar to the example shown next. Using the array indexing convention (remember, the numbering starts at 0 and continues sequentially as the options are listed), you can reference any of the options. In Listing 5-7, the `value` property is used to access the value referenced by two of the indexed array options, and then it is written to the page. The options list is shown next.

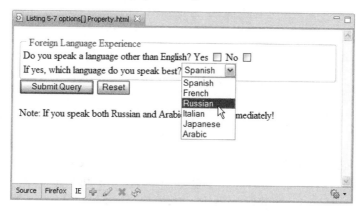

Listing 5-7   options[] property example

```html
<html>
   <head>
      <title>Listing 5-7 options[]Property</title>
   </head>
   <body>
      <form name="languageform">
         <fieldset>
            <legend>Foreign Language Experience</legend>
            Do you speak a language other than English?
            Yes <input type="checkbox" name="languageyes">
            No <input type="checkbox" name="languageno"><br>
            If yes, which language do you speak best?
            <select name="languages">
               <option selected value="Spanish">Spanish</option>
               <option value="French">French</option>
               <option value="Russian">Russian</option>
               <option value="Italian">Italian</option>
               <option value="Japanese">Japanese</option>
               <option value="Arabic">Arabic</option>
            </select>
         </fieldset>
```

```
      <input type="submit">
      <input type="reset">
   </form>
   <p>
   <script language="javascript" type= "text/javascript">
      //<![CDATA[
      document.write("Note: If you speak both "
         +document.languageform.languages.options[2].value+"
         and " +document.languageform.languages.options[5]
         .value+" contact us immediately!");
      //]]>
   </script>
  </body>
</html>
```

Focus and Blur Methods

The focus() and blur() methods perform the same actions as the event handlers of the same names described in Chapter 4; that is, focus() sets focus to a field through a user mouse click or tabbing action, and blur() removes the focus from an element. The main difference between the two is how each is activated in the script. You simply include methods, similarly to the properties described earlier in the chapter, in the hierarchical dot syntax in a scripting statement. The example shown in Listing 5-8 uses these two methods as attributes of the onclick event handler, producing the form shown next.

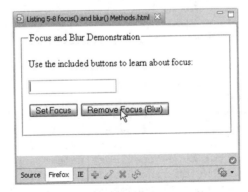

TIP

A handy way to use the focus() method in a form is to place the focus in a form element (that is, place the cursor in the element) after a validation script has returned the user to the element to correct his or her input. Validating JavaScript is described in more detail in the following section.

Listing 5-8 focus() and blur() methods

```html
<html>
   <head>
      <title>Listing 5-8 focus() and blur() Methods</title>
   </head>
   <body>
      <form name="focusandblur">
         <fieldset>
            <legend>Focus and Blur Demonstration</legend>
            <p>Use the included buttons to learn about focus:</p>
            <input type="text" name="demo" size="20"><p>
            <input type="button" name="focus" value="Set Focus"
               onclick="document.focusandblur.demo.focus();" />
            <input type="button" name="blur" value="Remove Focus
               (Blur)"
               onclick="document.focusandblur.demo.blur();" />
            <p>
         </fieldset>
      </form>
   </body>
</html>
```

Validating a Form

Earlier in the chapter the basic functioning and layout of a form was reviewed, and the sections that followed illustrated ways you could use JavaScript to get your forms to perform certain actions. The one aspect missing so far is one of the most common ways JavaScript is used in forms. This section discusses form validation and demonstrates ways you can use it in your forms.

Understanding Validation

Validation is a fancy way of checking for correctness of user input in a form. Since most input typically is included in a database for further processing or data mining, it's imperative that the data coming in is accurate and is in the correct format (it helps avoid the GIGO situation; that is, garbage in, garbage out). Whether to validate data, then, is not really the question (the answer is Yes), but rather, where to validate it. Submitted data is generally sent to a CGI or PHP script running on a server that certainly has the wherewithal to handle the validation tasks. However, that requires extra horsepower and a return trip to the browser, which can slow down the response to the user. A faster way to handle the validation is to perform it locally, on the user's computer in conjunction with the web browser.

CAUTION
JavaScript is not available in every browser ever constructed, so client-side validation may not wind up being performed. As time goes by and older browsers fall by the wayside, this problem becomes less relevant. However, Internet security folks recommend validating at both the client and the server to solve this problem and other security issues. Client-side validation is used to handle most common user input errors, while the server side has more robust validation to guard against dedicated hacker attacks.

For the most part, client-side validation can be as simple as verifying that a form element has not been left blank, checking for the presence of required characters, or accessing external databases for security confirmation. The sky's the limit as to what sort of data needs to be validated, so perhaps the best way to discover what is available and how to code it, is to take note of what others are doing on the Web in their own forms and scripts.

Using Validation with Passwords

One of the best demonstrations of client-side validation is ensuring basic information is provided correctly by the users. You can check that users enter characters they believe to be their password by having them enter it twice. (The actual verification to determine if the password is stored in a database is handled on the server side). Listing 5-9 at first glance appears to be an overly complex script, especially for the minimal output shown here, but taken in pieces related to the ways a validation script works and the different ways validation can be performed, it becomes quite tame.

Listing 5-9   validation example

```
<html>
   <head>
      <title>Listing 5-9 Validation</title>
      <script language="javascript" type= "text/javascript">
      //<![CDATA[
         var minlength=8;
         function validateform(){
            if (document.passwordform.fullname.value==""){
               window.alert("Please provide your full name");
```

```
                document.passwordform.fullname.focus();
                return false;
            }
            if (document.passwordform.pwd1.value==""){
                window.alert("Please enter a password");
                document.passwordform.pwd1.focus();
                return false;
            }
            if (document.passwordform.pwd1.value.length < minlength){
                window.alert("The password must be at least
"+minlength+" characters long");
                document.passwordform.pwd1.focus();
                return false;
            }
            if (document.passwordform.pwd1.value !=
                document.passwordform.pwd2.value){
                window.alert("Your two password entries are not the
                    same");
                document.passwordform.pwd1.focus();
                document.passwordform.pwd1.select();
                return false
            }
            else {
                window.alert("Thank you for submitting correct
                    data");
                return true;
            }
        }
        //]]>
    </script>
</head>
<body>
    <form name="passwordform" onsubmit="return validateform()"
        action="http://myserver.com/cgi-bin/formresults>.com">
        <fieldset>
            <legend>Validation Example</legend>
            Name: <input type="text" name="fullname" size="30"><br>
            Enter password:  <input type="password"
            name="pwd1"><br>
            Confirm password: <input type="password" name="pwd2"><br>
        </fieldset>
        <p>
        <input type="submit" value="Submit Validated Form">
        <input type="reset">
    </form>
</body>
</html>
```

Using the onsubmit Event Handler

The `<body>` section in Listing 5-9 appears much the same as you've seen in other examples in this chapter, producing the basic short form shown here. The one interesting aspect in this construction is the argument in the `onsubmit` attribute, that is, `onsubmit="return validateform()"`. This construction is a key element in how the validation process works.

When the user clicks the Submit Validated Form button, instead of sending the form values directly to the server specified in the `action` attribute, as has been the case in previous examples, the `onsubmit` event handler in the `<form>` tag set intercepts the request, calls the `validateform()` function (which is described in the next section), and using the **return** keyword, sees if the function returns a **true** or **false**. If **true**, the values are sent to the server; if **false**, no data is sent.

Dissecting the Function

The `validateform()` function comprises several **if** statements that perform the validation checks within the text box and two password boxes. If the condition of an **if** statement is true, the code continues running uninterrupted. If the condition is false, an alert message box appears to the user apprising of a problem.

The first two **if** statements in Listing 5-9 are nearly identical and simply check to make sure the Name text box and first password box are not blank. If either is blank, an alert is displayed (as shown next), a **false** is returned to the `onsubmit` event handler in the `<body>` section, and no form data is sent.

```
if (document.passwordform.fullname.value=="") {
    window.alert("Please provide your full name");
    document.passwordform.fullname.focus();
    return false;
}
```

NOTE

It is important to use fully qualified form field names—document.passwordform
.fullname and not just passwordform.fullname—if you want scripts to work in
Firefox. IE will work with the shortened name, but Firefox won't.

If an alert is displayed, note that the focus is brought back to the affected element
when the user closes the message box.

In the third **if** statement the length of the password entered by the user is compared
with the length specified in the minlength variable. If it's less than the value, an alert is
displayed, a **false** is returned to the onsubmit event handler in the <body> section,
and no form data is sent.

```
if (document.passwordform.pwd1.value.length < minlength) {
    window.alert("The password must be at least "+minlength+"
    characters long");
    document.passwordform.pwd1.focus();
    return false;
}
```

In the fourth and final **if** statement, the values of the two password boxes are compared
to ensure the entered password is identical to the password entered in the confirmation box.
As in the other **if** statements, a **false** generates an alert, and a **true** continues the script.

```
if (document.passwordform.pwd1.value !=
    document.passwordform.pwd2.value) {
    window.alert("Your two password entries are not the same");
    document.passwordform.pwd1.focus();
    document.passwordform.pwd1.select();
    return false
}
```

TIP

If you were to just compare the two passwords (passwordform.pwd1 !=
passwordform.pwd2) and not their values, it is possible that you would not get
equality when the two passwords are the same because the other attributes of the
variable, such as length, may differ.

The final actions in the function are handled by the **else** and final **return** statements. When all the **if** statements return **true**, the code processing reaches the **else** statement, which displays a confirmation alert to acknowledge to the user that all is well. When the alert is acknowledged, the function returns a **true**, which is received by the onsubmit event handler, which finally gives the green light for the form data to be sent to the URL specified in the action attribute.

```
else {
    window.alert("Thank you for submitting correct data");
    return true;
}
```

While this is a bit of a long example, it really is the tip of the iceberg in terms of what validation checks you can perform. For example, in addition to what was checked here, you could check to see that the password was a "strong" password by verifying that some capital letters, numbers, and special characters were included. Or, in the case of an e-mail text box, you could check to see if the user included both the @ character and a period (see Chapter 9 for an example of this). Using variations on the examples in Listing 5-9, you can construct your own validators to check the parameters important to your forms.

Using Form Extras

Forms can be used for a variety of purposes, and JavaScript is a key component to making them function. Besides validating data, scripting can be used, for example, to calculate payments and amortization on loan servicing web pages (investigate the Math object and its properties and methods for tools to introduce calculations in your forms). Also, many form elements can serve double duty as a way to create alternatives to buttons and link bars.

This section provides an example that shows how to build a drop-down list by using the select form element to create a menu that directs the user to other pages in your web site and introduces the use of regular expressions in forms.

Creating a Menu Bar

Button bars and link bars, as shown here, have traditionally been used to allow users to navigate around a web site. If you have categories of information that have several subcategories, you could organize your links within drop-down lists to consolidate all these choices. Listing 5-10 provides the start of a menu bar that employs several scripting elements and techniques previously discussed.

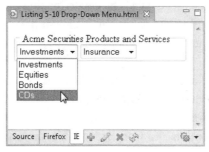

Listing 5-10 Drop-down menu example

```html
<html>
  <head>
    <title>Listing 5-10 Drop-Down Menu</title>
  </head>
  <body>
    <form name="menu">
      <fieldset>
        <legend>Acme Securities Products and Services</legend>
        <select name="investments" onchange="window.location=
          document.menu.investments.options[document.menu.
          investments.selectedIndex].value;">
```

```
                        <option selected value="">Investments</option>
                        <option value="stocks.html">Equities</option>
                        <option value="bonds.html">Bonds</option>
                        <option value="cds.html">CDs</option>
                        </select>
                        <select name="insurance" onchange="window.location=
                           document.menu.insurance.options[document.menu.
                           insurance.selectedIndex].value;">
                        <option selected value="">Insurance</option>
                        <option value="term.html">Term </option>
                        <option value="whole.html">Whole Life</option>
                        <option value="annuities.html">Annuities</option>
                    </fieldset>
                </form>
            </body>
        </html>
```

The structure of the menu bar is a form with two select form element boxes, whose composition was described earlier in the chapter (you can easily add more select boxes to increase the size of the menu bar). The key to making this work is capturing the user's selection of an option and passing the value of the option (the HTML page where you want the user directed) to an event handler's window.location property, which displays the page.

At first glance, it seems to make sense to use the onclick event handler, but we need another choice because we don't want any action to occur if the user clicks the selected value option, which in this case isn't an option, but which acts as the category heading for the list of options. To work around this, the onchange event handler is used, as shown here:

```
onchange="window.location=document.menu.investments.options
[document.menu.investments.selectedIndex].value;"
```

Within the window.location property attribute, the selectedIndex property of each select box options [] array holds the value of the index item selected by the user.

The last component of the attribute, value, is the value of the selected option, which in this case is the web page or URL you want displayed.

The only other interesting aspect of this code occurs in the selected value option:

```
<option selected value="">Insurance</option>
```

To ensure the selected value is a dead link acting as a category heading, we give it a null value.

Introducing Regular Expressions

As if JavaScript isn't full of enough terminology such as keywords, objects, properties, and methods, a whole other world of syntax awaits you in the form of regular expressions (often abbreviated as regex or RegExp). These are not the standard expressions shown in the last three chapters. Regular expressions are a shorthand convention that allows you to define a character pattern using a text string, letting you boil down lines of code into one. They are a powerful tool to detect, validate, and format text strings.

NOTE

A detailed journey into regular expressions is beyond the scope of someone just learning JavaScript. The purpose here is to make you aware of its existence and allow you to recognize it for what it is.

A regular expression is treated by the JavaScript interpreter as an object (with its own properties and methods) and takes the form:

```
re = /somepattern/;
```

where `re` is a variable name used to indicate the value denoted by the regular expression special characters contained within the forward slashes. A simple example of a regular expression used to match text strings consisting of a four-character serial number, starting with a letter followed by three numbers is

```
/^\b[a-d]\d\d\d\b$/
```

where

- **/ /** denotes a regular expression
- **^** denotes the beginning of the entire text string
- **\b** denotes a word boundary (not really needed in this example since we only have one word)
- **[a-d]** matches any character within the range of characters
- **\d** matches any digit 0–9 (same as using `[0-9]`)
- **$** denotes the end of the entire text string

So in a validated text box using the example expression, *A306* and *c598* would be accepted entries, but *1902, C3456,* and *D45c* would not match the criteria (*1902* doesn't start with a letter between *a* and *d, C3456* is five characters long, and *D45c* includes a trailing letter instead of a number).

Regular expressions will be a natural progression in your JavaScript education, requiring a bit more study, but providing a more streamlined way to create ever more complex scripts. Taking this concept a step farther, you can add more power and flexibility to your web pages by using the popular programming language PHP to code your pages. Chapter 6 introduces you to PHP and the server side of web programming.

Part III

Exercising the Server with PHP

n Part II of this book you saw how JavaScript activated dynamic web elements with scripts running in the client browser. In Part III you'll see how PHP, running in the server, provides another level of automation, including dynamically handling information and determining what a user views next.

NOTE

While JavaScript and PHP have many similarities, this section of the book has been written without reference to the JavaScript section, so you do not need to flip back and forth. At the same time you may find some duplication between the two sections.

Chapter 6 discusses the basic constructs used by PHP and how PHP is tied into an X/HTML script. Variables, operators, expressions, and functions are described, and examples are shown of their use. `if-else` and `switch` statements and the conditions that control them are demonstrated along with `for`, `while`, and `do` loops.

Chapter 7 reviews and demonstrates the file-handling capabilities of PHP, describing how to use PHP file-handling to set up a user login form, validate login information against a file, and establish session variables that can control access to restricted pages on a web site. Passing data among web pages is also discussed along with how the URL, session variables, and cookies are used to do that. Cookies are also discussed in terms of how they can be used to customize a page to a particular user.

In this Part III opener we'll provide some background on PHP and talk about what tools you should have running to work with PHP.

About PHP

PHP is a scripting language for developing dynamic web pages. PHP, which runs in a web server, is *interpreted,* meaning that the original human-readable script written by the developer is, each time it is used, converted to computer instructions. This contrasts with languages such as C and Java (not JavaScript), which are *compiled* instead of interpreted, meaning the original script is converted to computer instructions as a one-time process and stored in the converted form, so when it is used, it can immediately be executed and not have to wait for interpretation. While interpreted languages like PHP may be slightly slower, they can be changed immediately before they are used, giving them a lot of flexibility and making development much easier—something you'll appreciate as you go through the next four chapters.

PHP began life in 1994 when Rasmus Lerdorf developed it to help him add some dynamic elements to his *personal home page,* hence PHP. Since then it has spread like wildfire because it is powerful and easy to use, it integrates well with HTML, and it supports a number of databases, importantly, MySQL. Rasmus also put it in the public domain, which means that not only is it free to use, but anybody with the skill can enhance it. As a result a number of people have worked on it. Today it is in its fifth major revision (PHP 5) with a number of minor revisions along the way (as this is written, the latest stable version is PHP 5.2.8, with PHP 5.3 due out shortly and PHP 6 is in the works). PHP is now a fully mature professional scripting language, as you can see from its web site, http://www.php.net. It has a large number of user groups all over the world (valuable for getting help—see the PHP site for one in your area), sizable steering and documentation committees, and many developers working on it, for the most part on a volunteer basis. It also now has a more official sounding, if recursive, name—"PHP: Hypertext Preprocessor." While it is impossible to get an accurate count, many millions of web pages have been developed using it, and many professional web developers believe that PHP and MySQL are the best way to add a database to a web site of any size.

Tools Needed for PHP

To effectively work with PHP, you need to have a development environment that supports both the writing and the testing of PHP scripts. You'll need tools for

- **PHP script writing**, with code assistance and validation as you write the script
- **PHP script testing** on your development computer
- **Developmental support** in a browser, to help debuging

The Part I introduction describes and recommends packages that you can download for these tools, including

- **Aptana Studio**, an integrated development environment (IDE) that provides powerful authoring for HTML, CSS, and JavaScript by default, and with an add-on or plug-in, for PHP. The PHP plug-in will be discussed here.
- **XAMPP** is a combination of the Apache web server, the PHP and Perl servers, and the MySQL database server that all run on your computer and duplicate what you will see when you upload your web site to a commercial web host.
- **IE 6**, **IE 7**, and **Firefox** browsers are all needed to test and debug your scripts. Since large percentages of the web browsing population are using these browsers, it is important to try your web pages in all of them. IE 8, which is in final testing as this is written, is also a strong candidate for you to use for testing. It is available for both Windows XP and Windows Vista, as well as for Windows 7. In addition to simply trying out your pages on these browsers, we recommend a Web Developer's Toolbar available for Firefox.

If you do not already have Aptana Studio, XAMPP, IE 6, IE 7, Firefox, and the Firefox Web Developer's Toolbar, return to the Part I introduction and follow the instructions to download and install them. They are recommended for the discussion in the remaining chapters of this book.

Adding PHP to Aptana

Aptana Studio, as it is initially downloaded, does not include support for PHP. Fortunately the Aptana organization provides an excellent free plug-in for PHP that has a built-in PHP server for previewing your script within Aptana Studio, as well as full PHP code assist and formatting, and a PHP debugger. To download and install the Aptana PHP plug-in:

1. Start Aptana Studio as you normally would; if My Aptana is not open, click **Help | Aptana Help | My Aptana**.

2. In My Aptana, click **Plugins**. In the Platform tab, under Aptana PHP, click **Get It**.

3. Under Select The Features To Install, click the check box for **Site Providing Aptana PHP** and click **Next**.

4. Click **I Accept The Terms** and click **Next**. Finally click **Finish**. The downloading will take place. This can take several minutes.

5. When downloading is finished, click **Install All**. When the installation is complete, click **Yes** to restart Aptana Studio.

Setting Up PHP in Aptana

It is not obvious by looking at Aptana that PHP is installed, and if you click **File | New**, you will not see "Untitled PHP File" unless a PHP project has already been opened in your Aptana Studio. Do that next to get Aptana ready for the rest of this book.

1. In Aptana Studio running on your desktop, click **File | New | Project** to open the New Project dialog box.

2. In the New Project dialog box, open **Aptana Projects**, click **PHP Project**, and click **Next**. Both the project and a new file, index.php, will be created.

3. In the next New Projects dialog box, unselect **Use Default Location** if it is selected, click **Browse**, open **Computer** and your primary drive (probably **c:**), scroll down, and open **xampp** and **htdocs**. (c:\xampp\htdocs\ is the folder that the Apache server looks at for files.)

4. Enter a project name ("Examples" is used here), and click **Finish**. You should now have an index.php file with the single PHP statement with the PHP function phpinfo(), like this:

5. Click a browser tab and you'll see information about the PHP server that has been added to Aptana, as shown in Figure P3-1. Click **Source** to return there.

6. Click **Window | Preferences,** and then in the left column open **Aptana | Editors | PHP** and see all the settings for PHP. At this point you probably want to leave the default settings unchanged.

7. When you are ready, click **OK** to close the Preferences dialog box.

If you were able to do the preceding steps and get the results mentioned, you are assured that PHP has been installed.

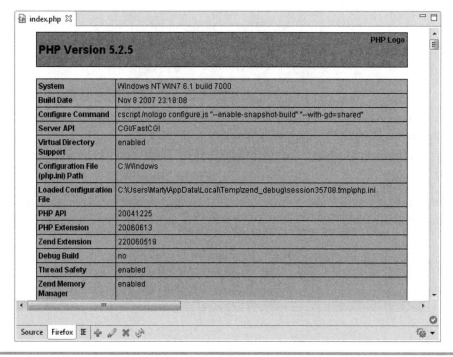

Figure P3-1 Seeing `phpinfo()` in Aptana proves that a PHP server has been installed there.

Chapter 6
Fundamentals of PHP

Key Skills & Concepts

- Using PHP with X/HTML

- Writing and Testing PHP

- Introducing PHP Basics

- Using Variables, Constants, and Operators

- Incorporating Statements and Expressions

- Creating Functions

- Applying Conditional Statements

PHP provides server-side programming, giving the web developer access to the web server that is hosting the web site, and to everything that is stored and/or runs there. Among these are other web pages, stored on that server or another server, web applications such as shopping carts and billing programs, and databases to both collect information and display information. PHP also has access to the server's file system so it can read and write information independent of the database. Most importantly, PHP can be used to build the web pages that are sent to the client so the pages can be customized to the person at the client, for example, to display a particular language or appropriate level of security for the user.

This chapter will introduce PHP, how it is integrated with X/HTML, and how it is written and tested on your computer outside of Aptana. The chapter will then review statements, variables, operators, and functions, and show examples of their use. Finally the chapter will conclude with an exploration of conditionals and the statements that use them, again with examples.

PHP Introduction

PHP is a way within a web page of telling the server that you want something done. It may be to open another web page, write in a file, or to extract information from a database. Whatever it is, in an X/HTML page, the developer has decided that he or she needs something from the server. This is the job of PHP. Note that it started from an

X/HTML page, so the first question is how to put PHP on an X/HTML page. The second question is what can be done with it once it is there.

Integrating PHP with X/HTML

The default PHP file created by Aptana in the Part III introduction has a .php extension and a single line of PHP script:

```
<?php phpinfo(); ?>
```

The .php extension tells the server that the file needs to go through the PHP interpreter. The `<?php ... ?>` tells the PHP interpreter that it needs to process whatever is in the middle, and to replace the PHP lines of script with X/HTML code sent to the browser so it can interact with the server. So the first two rules of PHP are

- PHP files must have a .php extension.
- PHP script must be surrounded by `<?php ... ?>`.

NOTE

In some situations, you can use `<? ... ?>` without the php, but unless you are developing for a very controlled environment like an intranet, we strongly suggest that you include the php, to make sure your script works in all environments, and to simply alert or remind whoever is looking at the script that they are looking at PHP.

Given those two rules, you can put PHP script anywhere in an X/HTML file. For example, Listing 6-1 shows the preceding PHP line in the body of an X/HTML page that is saved with a .php extension. The result is shown in Figure 6-1.

NOTE

Figure 6-1 shows how Firefox displays the X/HTML and PHP page using XAMPP, which contains the latest PHP server. This differs somewhat from the way that Aptana displays PHP, as you saw in the Part III opener.

Listing 6-1   PHP example

```
<!DOCTYPE html PUBLIC "-//W3C//DTD XHTML 1.0 Strict//EN"
"http://www.w3.org/TR/xhtml1/DTD/xhtml1-strict.dtd">
<html xmlns="http://www.w3.org/1999/xhtml" lang="en" xml:lang="en">
   <head>
   <meta http-equiv="Content-Type" content="text/html; charset=iso-8859-1">
      <title>Listing 6-1</title>
   </head>
```

```
<body>
    <h1>This is an Example of PHP Embedded in X/HTML</h1>
    <p>The PHP code displays information about the PHP server.</p>
    <?php
        phpinfo();
    ?>
</body>
</html>
```

NOTE
The remaining listings in this chapter will not include the `<!DOCTYPE>` and `<meta>` statements, as well as the `<html>` attributes, to make the listings more compact.

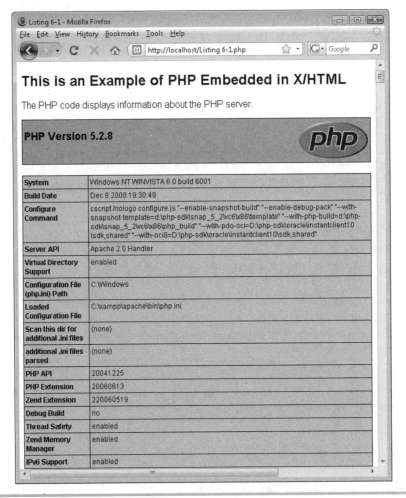

Figure 6-1 PHP operates from any part of an X/HTML page.

Writing and Testing PHP

As you write and test PHP script with the tools discussed in this book, you will want to do the writing and some testing with Aptana, and to do additional testing using the Apache and PHP servers in XAMPP with several browsers. To do that, you need to open an Aptana PHP project where XAMPP can see it, and create and store your PHP files in the project. This is what was done in the "Setting Up PHP in Aptana" section in the Part III introduction. Here's how to go to the next step and put the PHP statement in an X/HTML page:

1. In Aptana click **File | New | HTML File**. In the New HTML dialog box the Container should show the project you created in the Part III introduction; "Examples" was suggested. If it doesn't show, click **Browse**, select your project, and click **Finish**.

2. Between the <body> tags enter the statements shown in Listing 6-1.

3. Click **File | Save As**, enter a name with a .php extension, like "Listing 6-1.php," and click **OK**.

4. Click one of the browsers in Aptana, and you should see both your X/HTML title and paragraph, as well as the PHP server information generated by the phpinfo() function.

5. Click the **XMAPP icon** on your desktop to open the XAMPP Control Panel. Click **Start** for both Apache and MySQL. When both modules say "Running" and the Start buttons have changed to Stop buttons, as shown next, click **Close**.

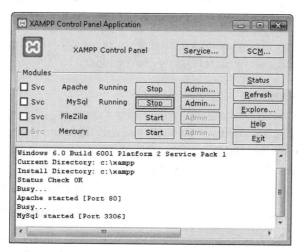

6. Open a browser, IE or Firefox; in the address bar, type localhost/Listing 6-1.php; and press ENTER. You should see the image shown in Figure 6-1.

If you do not see the correct results in steps 4 and 6, then either the installation of the Aptana PHP plug-in or XAMPP did not go correctly, or the setup of the project and file is not correct.

If it works in Aptana and not in your browser, then make sure XMAPP is running as described in step 5. If so, look at what is in the address bar. If it is "http://localhost/ Listing 6-1.php," then use the Windows Explorer to see if the file is in c:\xampp\htdocs\ Listing 6-1.php (note, the Apache server is case sensitive). If may be in another folder within htdocs. If so, add that to the address bar in your browser.

If you see the display in your browser and not in Aptana, then either the plug-in is not working or, more likely, you have not set up the project correctly. The best way to cure this is to completely redo it. Go back to the Part III introduction, and redo the instructions under "Setting Up PHP in Aptana." If you think that the Aptana PHP plug-in is not working, go back and try to reinstall it. Aptana will tell you if it is already installed.

It is very important, before you go further in this chapter, that you make sure that Aptana Studio, the Aptana PHP plug-in, and XAMPP, along with two or three IE browsers and Firefox, are all running. You need to be able to test your work as you go along.

TIP

Aptana, Apache Friends, and PHP all have forums and user groups that you can contact with questions on how to resolve problems.

PHP Basics

PHP has several basic facilities that both give it power and make it easier to use. These include the ability to display information at any point in your script, adding comments in several ways, and a set of useful coding conventions.

Display Information

In debugging script it is often helpful to display a comment or a variable while the script is being used. PHP gives you two way to do this with the echo() and print() functions, which are very similar, and for many purposes they are the same. Listing 6-2 shows both functions, which produce this image.

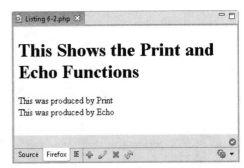

Listing 6-2   print/echo example

```
<html>
   <head>
      <title>Listing 6-2</title>
   </head>
   <body>
      <h1>This Shows the Print and Echo Functions</h1>
      <?php
         print "This was produced by Print <br />";
         echo "This was produced by Echo";
      ?>
   </body>
</html>
```

Both `print` and `echo`, while called "functions" and included in function lists, are unlike most functions in that that their arguments are not required to be in parentheses, although you can use parentheses if you want. The quote marks are required unless the argument is a number, although you can use either single or double quote marks.

Since the information within the quotes is sent to the browser for processing, you can include X/HTML tags and have them treated as if they are in a line of X/HTML. The `<br />` in Listing 6-2 shows this. This also means that you can place text on multiple lines within a single set of quotes.

There are only two significant differences between `print` and `echo`. `print` returns a value (1) when it is processed, so you can test to see if that happened (explained later in the chapter). `echo` does not do that, but `echo` can take multiple arguments, separated by commas, while `print` can take only one.

Examples of the various ways that `print` and `echo` can be used are shown in Listing 6-3, with the results shown here.

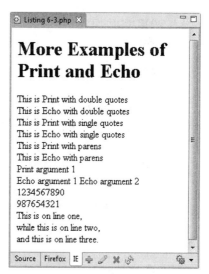

Listing 6-3.php

More Examples of Print and Echo

This is Print with double quotes
This is Echo with double quotes
This is Print with single quotes
This is Echo with single quotes
This is Print with parens
This is Echo with parens
Print argument 1
Echo argument 1 Echo argument 2
1234567890
987654321
This is on line one,
while this is on line two,
and this is on line three.

Source   Firefox   IE

Listing 6-3 More print and echo examples

```
<body>    <h1>More Examples of Print and Echo</h1>
   <?php
      print "This is Print with double quotes <br />";
      echo "This is Echo with double quotes <br />";
      print 'This is Print with single quotes <br />';
      echo 'This is Echo with single quotes <br />';
      print ("This is Print with parens <br />");
      echo ("This is Echo with parens <br />");
      print "Print argument 1<br />"; #Second causes error
      echo "Echo argument 1  ", "Echo argument 2<br />";
      print 1234567890 ;  //Without quotes
      echo "<br />" , 987654321 , "<br />";
      print "This is on line one,<br />
         while this is on line two, <br />
         and this is on line three.";
      /* echo and print are essentially
         the same with one argument. */
   ?>
</body>
```

NOTE
In Listing 6-3 the echo of a number without quotes cannot start with a zero because
PHP interprets that as an octal (base 8) number, which cannot contain a "9," so the
whole number is evaluated as "0."

Commenting Script
PHP allows you to add comments to your script in three ways, as was shown in Listing 6-3:

● On a single line starting with #

```
#This is a comment
```

● On a single line starting with //

```
//This is also a comment
```

● On multiple lines enclosed with /*   */

```
/* This is a comment that can
be on several lines. */
```

TIP
It is strongly recommended that you comment your script profusely to make it easier to
work with in the future.

Coding Conventions

PHP is fairly easygoing as far as conventions are concerned. In the first three listings, though, you have probably noticed several conventions that should be added to your PHP rules:

- Each PHP statement should end with a semicolon (;). The only exception is the last statement before the closing ?>, which can have a semicolon, but it is not required.

- Text, any combination letters and numbers, also called a *string,* in an argument needs to be enclosed in quotation marks, either single (' ') or double (" "). (Some differences are explained in a Note later in this section.) Quotation marks must be in like pairs.

- Legitimate numbers, which can have a decimal point, do not have to be in quotation marks.

- Multiple arguments are separated by commas (,).

- Most functions require that their arguments be enclosed in parentheses.

TIP

When you are debugging script and you get the message "Syntax Error," check to see if a semicolon is missing at the end of the previous line. Often that is the problem.

You may have wondered since quotation marks are used to identify a string, how you display a quotation mark that is part of the string to be printed or echoed. For this purpose PHP uses the backslash (\) in what is called an *escape sequence,* like this:

```
print "My name is \"Marty\"";
```

Most of the characters that PHP assigns a special use for can be used as a literal character by preceding it with a backslash. In addition PHP has defined several escape sequences. Here are some of the more common escape sequences:

- \" produces a double quotation mark.
- \' produces a single quotation mark.
- \\ produces a backslash.
- \$ produces a dollar sign.
- \r produces a carriage return.
- \n produces a linefeed.
- \t produces a tab.

NOTE

While either single or double quotation marks can be used to enclose a string, in some circumstances one or the other is preferable. With single quotation marks enclosing the string, you can use literal double quotation marks without the backslash in the string, as shown next. With single quotation marks, though, escape sequences other than \ ' or \ \ will display the backslash and not perform their function. With double quotation marks, all escape sequences work.

```
print 'My name is "Marty"';
```

Parts of PHP

PHP, while a relatively simple language compared with C or Java, is still very complex, as you would expect of any comprehensive language such as PHP. In this section we'll take PHP apart and explore PHP information types, statements, variables, operators, and functions. In the following part we explore control structures, classes, and objects.

NOTE

As with any language, a large number of elements are in each part of the language, far more than can be covered here. To look at the complete list, go to http://www.php .net/manual/en/langref.php.

Types of Information

PHP is not as sensitive as other languages to the type of information you are working with, and you normally do not have to specify a data type, such as integer or string. PHP will determine it for itself by the context in which you are using it. It is still a good idea for you to keep in mind the type you are working with. The possible data types are shown in Table 6-1. There is substantial further discussion of these later in this chapter, including how the type is set, unset, and used with variables and arrays.

All of the examples in Table 6-1, except for NULL, are also arrays. Other notes on data types include

- The Boolean FALSE is equivalent to the integer 0, the floating point number 0.0, an empty string or a string of "0", an array of zero elements, or NULL. Everything else is TRUE.

- Integers are by default decimal (base 10) numbers. To make a number octal (base 8), precede it with 0 (zero), for example, 02 or 06. To make a number hexadecimal (base 16), precede it with 0x, for example, 0x4 or 0x8.

- Very large integers (larger than 2,147,483,647) are considered floating point numbers.

Data Type	Name	Description	Examples
Arrays	`arr`	A set of two or more pieces of data that can be any of the first six data types in a comma-separated list	98101, 'WA', 'Seattle', '123 E 3rd'
Booleans	`bool`	Either "TRUE" or "FALSE"; not case sensitive, but commonly uppercase	TRUE, FALSE
Floating point numbers	`float`	A fractional number with a decimal; may be negative, and may use scientific notation	7.34, −21.89, 2.31e3
Integers	`int`	A whole number without a decimal; may be negative	43, 928, −4
Null	`null`	The absence of any value	NULL
Strings	`string`	A series of characters (one of 256 letters, numbers, and special characters) enclosed in either single or double quotation marks	"Mike", 'Seattle', "1495 W. 18th St"
Objects	`object`	Script that is repeatedly called	
Resources	`resource`	A reference to an external element; commonly used with MySQL	

Table 6-1   PHP Data Types

- If you divide two integers, you get a floating point number unless the numbers are evenly divisible.

- Floating point numbers are not accurate to the last digit because of the infinite progression of fractions like one-third. Therefore, you should not compare two floating point numbers for equality.

- A string containing a number (either integer or floating point) immediately following the left quote, can be used as a number. For example, `"18.2"` and `"4 cars"` can both be used as numbers, while `"his 4 cars"` cannot.

- A specific value in an array is identified with a *key*, which can be an integer, a string that evaluates as an integer, the truncated integer portion of a floating point number, the Boolean TRUE, which evaluates to the integer 1, or FALSE, which evaluates to the integer 0.

NOTE

In this book, as in the PHP Manual, two additional pseudo-types are used for discussion purposes only: "mixed" is used for a combination of any of the first six types, and the "numbers" type is used for a combination of integers and floating point.

Variables and Constants

As you write PHP script, you need to name items that you are working with so you can repeatedly refer to them. There are two common types of items you can name:

- **Variables**, which are items that can contain different values at different times during script execution, start with a dollar sign ($) followed by a name that you give it.

- **Constants**, which will contain the same value throughout the execution of your script, are by convention all uppercase names that you give them. For example, NULL is a constant.

The name that you give to either variables or constants (or any other label in PHP) is case sensitive, can begin with either the letters *a–z* or *A–Z*, or an underscore (_), can be of any length, and can contain letters, numbers, underscores, and the characters in western European alphabets. While you may find that some special characters will be allowed, the best practice is to not use them.

PHP keywords with specific meaning that you should not use with variables, constants, or other labels in PHP are listed in Table 6-2.

A large number of predefined constants in PHP are used for a variety of purposes, like true constants (M_PI = 3.1415926535898 and M_E = 2.718281828459), constants used with particular functions (SORT_NUMERIC and SORT_STRING used with sort functions), constants used to define something (CAL_GREGORIAN and CAL_JULIAN used with calendars), and constants used for formatting (DATE_ATOM and DATE_RFC822 used with the date functions). You can find a list of predefined constants within each major section of predefined functions in the PHP Manual Function Reference at http://www.php.net/manual/en/funcref.php.

abstract	and	array	as	bool	break
case	catch	class	clone	const	continue
declare	default	do	echo	else	elseif
enddeclare	endfor	endforeach	endif	endswitch	endwhile
extends	false	final	float	for	foreach
function	global	goto	if	implements	int
interface	instanceof	namespace	new	null	object
or	print	private	protected	public	static
string	switch	throw	try	true	use
var	while	xor			

Table 6-2 PHP Keywords

A good practice is to make variable and constant names more self-descriptive and in the process, to stay away from any possibility of conflict with a predefined name. For example, if you are collecting a buyer's name and address, you might be tempted to use $name, $street, and $city. While nothing is wrong with those names, it is a better practice to get in the habit of using compound names both that are more descriptive and that stay away from common names, for example, $buyer_name, $buyer_street, and $buyer_city. It may take a couple of seconds more to type these names, but they are not going to be confused with similar names. Also, most programmers get really good at cutting and pasting to reduce typing.

TIP

If you are having trouble finding a bug in a program, look at the names you have assigned variables and constants, and try changing any that could possibly have a conflict with other names, such as changing $name to $buyer_name.

Operators

Having created a variable or a constant, you are going to want to assign it a value. PHP has defined a number of operators of various types, as shown in Table 6-3, to do this.

NOTE

Another set of comparison operators, called "ternary operators," will be discussed under "Control Structures" later in this chapter.

If you combine several operators in a single expression, the order of precedence is as follows, beginning with the highest or first executed: ++, --, !, ~, @, *, /, %, +, -, ., <<, >>, <, <=, >, >=, <>, ==, !=, ===, !==, &, ^, |, &&, ||, =, +=, -=, .=, and, xor, or. You can use parentheses to get around the order of precedence. Other notes about the PHP operators are as follows:

- The modulus (%) does not give the percent the first number is of the second; rather it gives the remainder, that part that is left after whole division.

- The equal sign (=) does not mean "equal," it means "assign" or "replace." For comparisons, such as "is a equal to b," use the double equal sign (==).

- If $a = 2 and $b = 2.0, they are not identical, because one is an integer and the other is a floating point number.

Type of Operator	Name	Example	Explanation
Arithmetic			Performs arithmetic
+	Add	`$a + $b`	Sum
-	Subtract	`$a - $b`	Difference
*	Multiply	`$a * $b`	Product
/	Divide	`$a / $b`	Quotient
%	Modulus	`$a % $b`	Remainder
Assignment			Replaces a value with another
=	Assign	`$a = 7;`	Sets $a to 7

+=	Increment	`$a = 7;`
		`$a += 2;`
		`returns 9`
			Increments $a by 2

.=	Concatenate	`$a = "Joe ";`
		`$a .= "Blow";`
		`returns "Joe Blow"`
			Adds a string to an existing string

[]=	Append	`$array []= $something`	Appends $something to the end of the array
Bitwise			Turns specific bits in an integer on or off
&	And	`$a & $b`	Sets bits in both $a and $b
|	Or	`$a | $b`	Sets bits in either $a or $b
^	Xor	`$a ^ $b`	Sets bits in $a or $b, but not both
~	Not	`~$a`	Does not sets bits in $a
<<	Shift left	`$a << $b`	Shifts bits $a by $b steps to the left (each step is multiplying by 2)
>>	Shift right	`$a >> $b`	Shifts bits in $a by $b steps to the right (each step is dividing by 2)
Comparison			Compares two values
==	Equal	`$a == $b`	Returns TRUE if $a equals $b
===	Identical	`$a === $b`	Returns TRUE if $a is identical to $b
!= or <>	Not equal	`$a != $b` or `$a <> $b`	Returns TRUE if $a is not equal to $b
!==	Not Identical	`$a !== $b`	Returns TRUE if $a is not identical to $b
<	Less than	`$a < $b`	Returns TRUE if $a is less than $b
>	Greater than	`$a > $b`	Returns TRUE if $a greater than $b

Table 6-3 PHP Operators

Type of Operator	Name	Example	Explanation
<=	Less than or equal to	`$a <= $b`	Returns TRUE if $a is less than or equal to $b
>=	Greater than or equal to	`$a >= $b`	Returns TRUE if $a is greater than or equal to $b
Incremental			Changes the value by one
++	Increment	`++$a` `$a++`	Adds one to $a and returns $a Returns $a, then adds one to it
--	Decrement	`--$a` `$a--`	Subtracts one from $a and returns $a Returns $a, then subtracts one from it
Logical			Logical consequence
and &&	And	`$a and $b`	Returns TRUE if both $a and $b are TRUE
or ||	Or	`$a or $b`	Returns TRUE if either $a or $b is TRUE
xor	Xor	`$a xor $b`	Returns TRUE if either $a or $b is TRUE, but not both
!	Not	`!$a`	Returns TRUE if $a is not TRUE
Other			
@	Error off	`@my_function()`	Disables display of errors in expression
` `	Execute	`` ` date ` ``	Executes what is within the back ticks (these are not single quotes), like DOS commands

Table 6-3 PHP Operators *(continued)*

Listing 6-4 shows examples of the use of PHP variables and operators. The results this script returns are shown in the illustration on the following page.

NOTE

The variable names in the following script, for example $a or $b, will be replaced with the value contained in the variable when they are displayed with `echo` or `print`, unless you *escape* them (treat them as literal characters) by putting a backslash (\) in front of the variable. This is true *both* inside double quotes as well as outside of any quotation marks and is called *interpolation*. If you use single quotes to enclose a variable name, the name, not the contents, will be displayed.

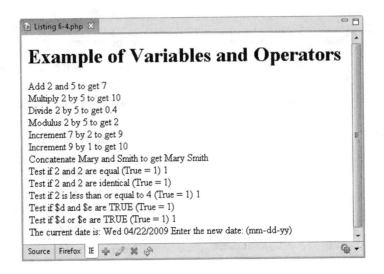

Listing 6-4 Examples of variables and operators

```html
<html>
   <head>
      <title>Listing 6-4</title>
   </head>
   <body>
      <h1>Example of Variables and Operators</h1>
      <?php
         //Math
         $a = 2; $b = 5;
         echo "Add $a and $b to get  ", $a + $b, "<br />";
         echo "Multiply $a by $b to get  ", $a * $b, "<br />";
         echo "Divide  $a by $b to get  ", $a / $b, "<br />";
         echo "Modulus  $a by $b to get  ", $a % $b, "<br />";
         //Increment and Concatenate
         $a = 7;
         echo "Increment $a by 2 to get ", $a += 2, "<br />";
         echo "Increment $a by 1 to get ", ++$a, "<br />";
            $first_name = "Mary "; $last_name = "Smith";
         echo "Concatenate $first_name and $last_name to get  ",
            $first_name . $last_name, "<br />";
         //Comparison
         $a = "2"; $b = 2.0; $c = 4; $d = $a == $b; $e = $a === $b;
         echo "Test if $a and $b are equal (True = 1)  ", $a == $b,
            "<br />";
         echo "Test if $a and $b are identical (True = 1)  ",
            $a === $b, "<br />";
```

```
    echo "Test if $a is less than or equal to $c (True = 1)   ",
        $a <= $c, "<br />";
    //Logical
    echo "Test if \$d and \$e are TRUE (True = 1)   ", $d and $e,
        "<br />";
    echo "Test if \$d or \$e are TRUE (True = 1)   ", $d or $e,
        "<br />";
    //Execute
    echo ` date ` ;
    ?>
  </body>
</html>
```

Statements and Expressions

PHP scripts contain either comments or statements. A statement is anything that is in between semicolons or the opening and closing PHP tags. Often a statement is a single line of code ending in a semicolon, but you can have several statements on a single line, and you can have statements that take several lines. Most statements contain one or more expressions, but a few are only a single keyword, such as **break** or **else**.

Expressions are anything that has a value or evaluates to a value. Values are anything that can be assigned to a variable, so values can be any of the data types: integer, floating point, string, boolean, array, or object. While the NULL data type is the absence of a value, it is still considered a value for this discussion.

Expressions can contain expressions, or said another way, expressions are building blocks that can be used to build other expressions. For example, $a = 2 is three expressions, 2, $a, and $a = 2.

Functions

A function is a piece of script that does something and can be repeatedly called within a larger script. Some internal functions already exist, and some user-defined functions you write. Some functions require *arguments,* which are values that you pass to the function, which uses them to compute a return value. Other functions simply return a value when they are called.

Internal Functions

You can use a great many internal or predefined PHP functions to do many different tasks. To explore the full set of PHP functions, see the online PHP Manual Function Reference at http://www.php.net/manual/en/funcref.php.

The following sections describe a *few* of the more heavily used internal functions as examples in the given category. Again, these are only a small sample of the available functions.

Array Functions Array functions provide the means to work with arrays in a number of ways. Several of these are shown in Table 6-4 and are demonstrated in Listing 6-5.

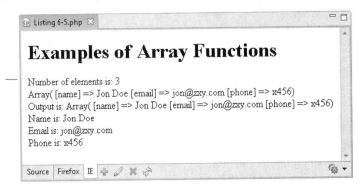

Listing 6-5 Examples of array functions

```html
<html>
   <head>
      <title>Listing 6-5</title>
   </head>
   <body>
      <h1>Examples of Array Functions</h1>
      <?php
         $nameEntry = array(
            "name" => "Jon Doe", "email" => "jon@zxy.com",
            "phone" => "x456", );
         echo "Number of elements is: ", count($nameEntry), "<br />";
         print_r($nameEntry);
         $output = print_r($nameEntry, true);
         echo "<br /> Output is: ", $output, "<br />";
         echo "Name is: ", $nameEntry [name], "<br />";
         echo "Email is: ", $nameEntry [email], "<br />";
         echo "Phone is: ", $nameEntry [phone], "<br />";
      ?>
   </body>
</html>
```

Function	Description	Explanation
array()	Builds an array of arguments	Arguments are a series of *key => value* statements separated by commas. Keys can be integers or strings. Values can be any type.
count()	Counts elements in an array	Argument is an array name; the elements are the number of key/value pairs.
print_r()	Prints a variable including an array in readable form	Argument is a variable (or array) name. With an optional second argument = TRUE, the contents of the variable or array are returned for use by another variable instead of being printed.

Table 6-4   Several Array Functions

Date/Time Functions   The date and time functions provide access to and work with the current date and time at the server running the script. A few of these are shown in Table 6-5, demonstrated in Listing 6-6, shown next:

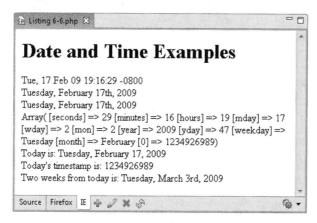

Function	Description	Explanation
date()	Formatted date and time as a string	Requires a format string and optionally a timestamp if the local time is not desired
Getdate()	An array of the date and time components	Takes an optional timestamp if the local time is not desired
time()	Current "Unix" timestamp	Returns the number of seconds since 1-1-1970, 00:00:00 GMT to the current moment at your server

Table 6-5   A Couple of Date and Time Functions

Listing 6-6   Examples of date and time functions

```html
<html>
   <head>
   <title>Listing 6-6</title>
   </head>
   <body>
      <h1>Date and Time Examples</h1>
      <?php
         echo date(DATE_RFC822), "<br />";
         $date_format = "l, F jS, Y";
         echo date($date_format), "<br />";
         echo date("l, F jS, Y"), "<br />";
         print_r(getdate());
         $date_array = getdate();
         echo "<br />Today is: ", $date_array[weekday],
            ", ", $date_array[month], " ", $date_array[mday],
            ", ", $date_array[year], "<br />";
         echo "Today's timestamp is: ", time(), "<br />";
            //Seconds since 1-1-1970
         $twoweeks = (14 * 24 * 60 * 60);
            //seconds in 2 weeks
         $twoweeksFrNow = Time() + $twoweeks;
         echo "Two weeks from today is: ",
            date("l, F jS, Y", $twoweeksFrNow), "<br />";
      ?>
   </body>
</html>
```

TIP
All the formatting codes for the date() function, such as the ones used in Listing 6-6, are shown at http://www.php.net/manual/en/function.date.php.

Math Functions   Math functions allow you to perform mathematical routines. Some of these are shown in Table 6-6 and are demonstrated in Listing 6-7.

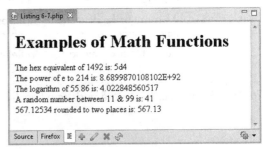

Function	Description	Explanation
`dechex()`	Converts a decimal integer to a hexadecimal number	Returns a string representing the hexadecimal number.
`exp()`	Calculates powers of e	Returns a floating point number of e to the power of the floating point argument.
`log()`	Calculates the natural logarithm	Returns a floating point number of the logarithm of the floating point argument. An optional argument can specify a different base other than the default of e.
`rand()`	Generates a random number	Without an argument this generates an integer between 0 and 32,768. Optionally, minimum and maximum integers may be specified, separated by a comma.
`round()`	Rounds a number to number of decimal digits	Returns a floating point number after arithmetically rounding a floating point number. Optionally, the precision or number of decimal digits may be specified.

Table 6-6   A Few Math Functions

Listing 6-7   Examples of math functions

```
<html>
   <head>
      <title>Listing 6-7</title>
   </head>
   <body>
      <h1>Examples of Math Functions</h1>
      <?php
         echo "The hex equivalent of 1492 is: ", dechex(1492), "<br />";
         echo "The power of e to 214 is: ", exp(214), "<br />";
         echo "The logarithm of 55.86 is: ", log(55.86), "<br />";
         echo "A random number between 11 & 99 is: ", rand(11,99),
            "<br />";
         echo "567.12534 rounded to two places is: ", round(567.12534, 2),
            "<br />";
      ?>
   </body>
</html>
```

String Functions   String functions allow you to work with strings. You have already seen two string functions, echo () and print (). Several others of these are shown in Table 6-7, demonstrated in Listing 6-8, and shown in the illustration on the following page.

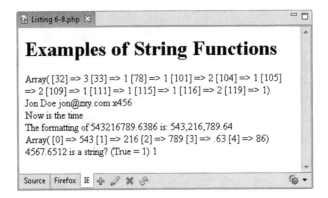

NOTE

The count_char() function has five modes (0 through 4). Modes 0 through 2 are arrays that return the count of, for mode 0, all 255 characters; for mode 1, all characters present; and for mode 2, all characters not present. Modes 3 and 4 are strings that list, for mode 3, all unique characters present; and for mode 4, all characters not present.

Function	Description	Explanation
count_chars()	Counts occurrence of characters in a string	Arguments are the string and optionally a mode, which determines if the return is an array or a string, and what is to be counted. See Note above.
implode() or join()	Joins array elements to form a string	Arguments are the array and optionally the character, which defaults to a space, to be placed between elements.
is_string()	Determines if a value is a string	Argument is a variable, which is evaluated and returns TRUE if is a string.
ltrim()	String formed by removing white space and specified characters on left	Arguments are the string and optionally a list of characters to remove. Without a list, spaces, tabs, carriage returns, new-lines, and vertical tabs are removed.
number_format()	String formed by formatting a number with a decimal point and thousands separator	A floating point number is formatted with an optional integer number of decimal digits (1, 2, or 4, not 3). Optionally, the decimal point and thousands separator characters can be specified.
str_split()	Splits a string into array elements	Arguments are the string and optionally the number of characters in each element, with a default of 1.
Strval()	Converts a numeric variable to a string	Argument must be an integer or floating point number.

Table 6-7   Examples of String Functions

Listing 6-8   Examples of string functions

```php
<html>
   <head>
      <title>Listing 6-8</title>
   </head>
   <body>
      <h1>Examples of String Functions</h1>
      <?php
         $textString = "Now is the time!";
         $textArray = count_chars($textString, 1);
         print_r($textArray);
         $nameEntry = array(
            "name" => "Jon Doe", "email" => "jon@zxy.com",
            "phone" => "x456",
            );
         echo "<br />", implode("  ",$nameEntry), "<br />";
         $aLongString = "            Now is the time";
         echo ltrim($aLongString), "<br />";
         echo "The formatting of 543216789.6386 is: ",
            number_format(543216789.6386, 2), "<r />";
         print_r(str_split(543216789.6386, 3)) ;
         echo "<br />", $newString, "  is a string? (True = 1) ",
            is_string($newString) , "<br />";
      ?>
   </body>
</html>
```

NOTE
In "Control Structures," later in this chapter, you'll see a much better display
of count_chars().

User-Defined Functions

As you write PHP scripts, you'll often find that you want to repeatedly use the same
code. You could simply copy the code to all the places you want to use it, but if you
want to change that code, you would have to change it everywhere it was copied. The
solution for this is to create a function containing the code you want to repeat, and simply
call that function everywhere you want to use it. Functions also let you segment or
compartmentalize your code, making it easier to debug and maintain.

There is even a bigger reason for using functions. Up to now, all the PHP code in this chapter is meant to run, or execute, as the page is loaded, *but after* the page is displayed, in contrast to some JavaScript that executes *before* the page is displayed. If you don't want the PHP script executed as the page is loaded, you can create a function, place it above the X/HTML header, and it won't be run until it is called.

Like predefined or internal functions, user-defined (just "user" from here on) functions may optionally have arguments that are passed to them, and may return a value after they are executed. Once a user function has been defined, it is *called* or used just like an internal function. The function itself can do anything you can do with PHP, using all of the features of PHP including calling other functions, or even calling itself to create a recursive function. (You need to limit recursive functions to make sure they can't endlessly act recursively, or an error will result. A good rule of thumb us to limit recursion to no more than 100 times.)

User functions are defined with the **function** and **return** keywords by using this form:

```
function name($argument1, $argument2,...)
{
    [any PHP statements];
    return $returnValue;
}
```

The name that you give to a function uses the same naming rules as variables, constants, and other labels. It is case sensitive, can begin with either the letters *a–z* or *A–Z,* or an underscore (_), can be of any length, and can contain letters, numbers, underscores, and the characters in western European alphabets.

Listing 6-9 shows an example of a user function with the result shown next. Many other examples are shown in this and following chapters.

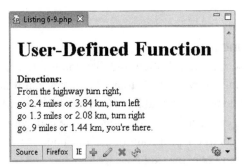

Listing 6-9   User-defined function

```
<html>
    <head>
        <title>Listing 6-9</title>
    </head>
    <body>
        <h1>User-Defined Function</h1>
        <?php
            function tokm($miles)
            {
                $km = $miles * 1.6;
                return $km ;
            }

            echo "<b>Directions:</b>", "<br />", "From the highway
            turn right,"
            , "<br />",
            "go 2.4 miles or ", tokm(2.4), " km, turn left", "<br />",
            "go 1.3 miles or ", tokm(1.3), " km, turn right", "<br />",
            "go .9 miles or ", tokm(.9), " km, you're there.", "<br />";
        ?>
    </body>
</html>
```

Control Structures

The scripts so far in this chapter have been executed from the first statement to the last statement without interruption or change of direction, with the exception of the repeated function calls in Listing 6-9. Often you will want to ask if the script should go one way or another, or go back and reexecute a particular piece of code. That is the purpose of control structures, which include if/else statements; while, do-while, and for statements; and switch statements, among others.

if/else Statements

The if/else statements are the primary decision-making construct in PHP. It allows you to specify that if some expression is TRUE, then a group of statements will be executed, else a different group of statements will be executed. It takes this form:

```
if (conditional expression) {
    statements executed if TRUE;
    }
```

```
else   {
   statements executed if FALSE;
   }
```

The else group of statements are optional and are needed only if you want do something other than continue with the script if the conditional expression is FALSE. Also you can nest if/else statements using elseif, like this:

```
if (conditional expression) {
   statements executed if TRUE;
   }
elseif (second conditional expression)   {
   statements executed if second conditional is TRUE;
   }
else {
   statements executed if second conditional is FALSE;
   }
```

In all cases the conditional expression must result in a Boolean TRUE or FALSE (1 or 0). If a variable simply exists, that is, it has been defined as containing something other than NULL, FALSE, or 0, then it is TRUE.

TIP

If you define a variable as containing a constant like NULL, TRUE, or FALSE, you must remember *not* to put it in quotation marks.

Many conditional expressions are comparisons that test if two elements are equal, greater than, or less than. Remember that when you test for equality in PHP, you must use a double equal sign (==), not a single one, which means assignment.

Listing 6-10 shows several examples of if/else statements, the results of which are shown next. A number of examples will be shown in the following chapters.

Listing 6-10   if/else statements

```php
<html>
    <head>
        <title>Listing 6-10</title>
    </head>
    <body>
        <h1>If/Else Examples</h1>
        <?php
            if ($a) {
                echo "True", "<br />";
            }
            else {
                echo "False", "<br />";
            }
            $a = "Something";
            if ($a) {
                echo "True", "<br />";
            }
            else {
                echo "False", "<br />";
            }
            $state = "CA";
            if ($state == "WA" ) {
                echo "Pacific Northwest", "<br />";
            }
            elseif ($state == "OR") {
                echo "Pacific Northwest", "<br />";
            }
            else {
                echo "Somewhere Else", "<br />";
            }
        ?>
    </body>
</html>
```

Ternary Operator

A shorthand method of doing if/else decision making in PHP scripts uses the ternary operator (? :), where ? replaces the if test and follows the conditional expression, and the : replaces else. The following statement produces the same results as the if statement that follows it.

```php
echo ($a) ? "True" : "False", "<br />";
if ($a) {
    echo "True", "<br />";
```

```
        }
    else {
        echo "False", "<br />";
        }
```

Joining several `if` statements, as you would with `elseif`, is not recommended with the ternary operator since PHP's behavior is not defined.

TIP

Use a parenthesis if you want to use multiple ternary operators.

while and do-while Statements

The `while` and `do-while` statements are looping constructs that allow you to repeatedly execute a piece of code until a conditional expression is no longer TRUE. The `while` statement is the foundation of this set of statements and takes one of the following forms:

```
while (conditional expression) {
    statements executed while TRUE;
    }
```

```
while (conditional expression) :
    statements executed while TRUE;
    endwhile;
```

The `do-while` statement is similar to the `while` statement, except that the conditional expression is at the end of the statement instead of the beginning. The `do-while` statement takes this form:

```
do {
    statements executed while TRUE;
    }
while (conditional expression);
```

The most common conditional expression is to compare a counter with some end value. In other words, to initialize a counter, and then to loop though some statements, incrementing the counter with each loop, until the counter exceeds the end value. Listing 6-11 shows examples of this for both `while` and `do-while`, with the results shown next. You can see that in this case there is no difference between `while` and `do-while`.

NOTE

Code in `do-while` is guaranteed to execute at least once, since the condition isn't checked until after the first execution. A `while` statement may not ever execute if the condition immediately evaluates to false.

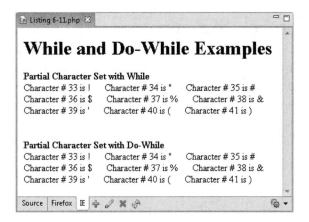

Listing 6-11   while and do-while examples

```html
<html>
   <head>
      <title>Listing 6-11</title>
   </head>
   <body>
      <h1>While and Do-While Examples</h1>
      <?php
         echo "<b>Partial Character Set with While</b><br />";
         $i = 33;
         while ($i <= 41) {
            echo "Character # ", $i , " is ", chr($i);
            echo "      Character # ", $i + 1 ,
               " is ", chr($i + 1);
            echo "      Character # ", $i + 2 ,
               " is ", chr($i + 2), "<br />";
            $i = $i + 3;
         }
         echo "<br /> <br /> <b>Partial Character Set with
            Do-While</b><br />";
         $i = 33;
         do {
            echo "Character # ", $i , " is ", chr($i);
            echo "      Character # ", $i + 1 ,
               " is ", chr($i + 1);
            echo "      Character # ", $i + 2 ,
               " is ", chr($i + 2), "<br />";
            $i = $i + 3;
         }
         while ($i <= 41);
      ?>
   </body>
</html>
```

for and foreach Statements

The `for` and `foreach` statements are additional looping constructs. The `for` statement, which is similar to its counterpart in other languages, places the initialization of the counter, its conditional limit, and its incrementing all in a series of expressions immediately following the `for`. The `for` statement can take one for the following forms:

```
for (initializing expression; conditional expression; incrementing expression)
    {
    statements executed while TRUE;
    }


for (initializing expression; conditional expression; incrementing expression):
    statements executed while TRUE;
endfor;
```

In its basic form, the `for` expression might be `for ($i = 1; $i <= 5; $i++)`, where `$i++` increments `$i` after it is used. If any of these expressions are handled elsewhere in the script, they can be left blank in the `for` expression, which at its minimum is `for ( ; ; )`.

The `foreach` statement is used to iterate through arrays and cannot be used on any other type of variable. It can display the value of each element in an array or alternatively it can display the key and the value of each element in an array. It therefore has one of the two following forms:

```
foreach ($array as $value) {
    statements executed for each element;
    }


foreach ($array as $key => $value) {
    statements executed for each element;
    }
```

When you first begin to execute a `foreach` statement, the array pointer is automatically reset to the first element. When you end the execution of a `foreach` statement, the array pointer remains at the last element, whose value remains contained by `$value`. You can use `unset ($value)` to remove it, and use `reset ($array)` to reset the array pointer.

Listing 6-12 shows examples of both `for` and `foreach` statements, with the results shown next. The `for` statement can be used in a manner very similar to `while`. The `foreach` statement makes the display of the `count_char` array much easier to read (compare with Listing 6-8).

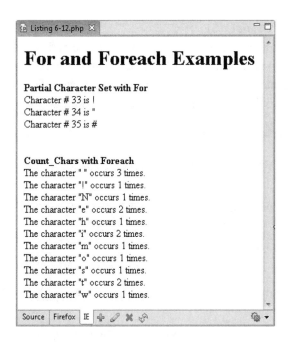

For and Foreach Examples

Partial Character Set with For
Character # 33 is !
Character # 34 is "
Character # 35 is #

Count_Chars with Foreach
The character " " occurs 3 times.
The character "!" occurs 1 times.
The character "N" occurs 1 times.
The character "e" occurs 2 times.
The character "h" occurs 1 times.
The character "i" occurs 2 times.
The character "m" occurs 1 times.
The character "o" occurs 1 times.
The character "s" occurs 1 times.
The character "t" occurs 2 times.
The character "w" occurs 1 times.

Listing 6-12   for and foreach examples

```html
<html>
    <head>
        <title>Listing 6-12</title>
    </head>
    <body>
        <h1>For and Foreach Examples</h1>
        <?php
            echo "<b>Partial Character Set with For</b><br />";
            for ($i = 33; $i <= 35; $i++) {
                echo "Character # ", $i , " is ", chr($i), "<br />";
            }
            echo "<br /> <br /> <b>Count_Chars with Foreach</b><br />";
            $textString = "Now is the time!";
            $textArray = count_chars($textString, 1);
            foreach ($textArray as $key => $val) {
                echo "The character \"", chr($key) , "\" occurs ",
                    $val, " times. <br />";
            }
        ?>
    </body>
</html>
```

switch Statements

The switch statement is similar to a series of if/elseif statements. The switch statement is used where you want to compare a single variable to a number of different values and do something different depending on the value. Three additional keywords are used with switch: case, break, and default, taking this form:

```
Switch ($avariable) {
    case 1:
        statements executed while TRUE;
        break;
    case 2:
        statements executed while TRUE;
        break;
    case 3:
        statements executed while TRUE;
        break;
    default:
        statements executed while all are FALSE;
}
```

Each case expression in the switch statement compares the switch variable with the case value, which can be string; if it is equal, the statements following the case expression are executed, and then the break expression sends the script's flow to the first statement after the switch's closing curly-brace. If none of the case expressions is successful, the statements following the default expression are executed, and the script's flow exits the switch statement. Listing 6-13 demonstrates how this works, which provides these results:

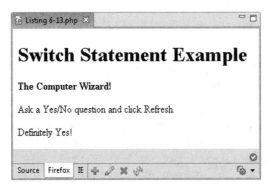

Listing 6-13   switch statement example

```
<html>
   <head>
      <title>Listing 6-13</title>
   </head>
   <body>
      <h1>Switch Statement Example</h1>
      <p><b>The Computer Wizard!</b></p>
      <p>Ask a Yes/No question and click Refresh.</p>
      <?php
         $randNum = rand(1,5);
         switch ($randNum) {
         case 1:
            echo "Definitely Yes!";
            break;
         case 2:
            echo "Probably Yes!";
            break;
         case 3:
            echo "Definitely Maybe!";
            break;
         case 4:
            echo "Probably No!";
            break;
         case 5:
            echo "Definitely No!";
            break;
         default:
            echo $randNum, "<br />"; //Display the number
            echo "Computer Malfunction, Try Again";
         }
      ?>
   </body>
</html>
```

In the following chapters, you'll see how to take the many pieces of PHP and weave them into a script that actually does something useful like passing data between web pages or between sessions, or reading and writing files on the server to create a guest book, or authenticating a user.

In addition to the online PHP Manual there are also two excellent books on PHP: *PHP: The Complete Reference,* by Steven Holzner, published by McGraw-Hill/ Professional, 2008; and *How to Do Everything with PHP & MySQL,* by Vikram Vaswani, published by McGraw-Hill/Professional, 2005.

Chapter 7
Using PHP by Itself

Key Skills & Concepts

- Understanding Basic File Functions

- Considering Additional File Functions

- Using Session Variables

- Adding Cookies

- Establishing Server Variables

- Completing the Index Script

- Building the Registration Scripts

- Creating the Sign-In Scripts

- Establishing a Site Page

P HP is often thought of as simply the mechanism for working with a MySQL database. It is, though, a full-featured programming language with not only all the features you saw in Chapter 6, but it also includes powerful file-handling tools, browser information features, and techniques for creating and using cookies and session variables. This chapter explores these powerful capabilities of PHP and in the process describes how to use PHP file management to set up a user login form, validate login information, determine the type of browser, and establish session variables that can protect access to a web site. Passing data among web pages using session variables and cookies is also discussed.

TIP

It is useful to have the PHP Manual and the PHP Function Reference bookmarked or set up as favorites in your browser so you can quickly refer to them. The manual is at http://www.php.net/manual/en/, and the function reference is at http://www.php .net/manual/en/funcref.php.

PHP File and Directory Management

One of the major benefits of server-side programming is that you can read and write information on the server's storage devices. PHP has an extensive set of functions that let you not only read and write files, but also change file attributes; copy, move, and delete files; work with directories; and much more. In this section we'll discuss and briefly demonstrate some of the more important file functions. In the final major section of this chapter, we'll show how to create a user authentication system by using the file commands.

Basic File Functions

The basic PHP file process has the following elements:

- Establish a file connection, or *file pointer* (also called a "handle"), between PHP and a file using the `fopen()` function.

- Write a data string to an opened file by using the `fwrite()` function.

- Read a certain number of bytes into a string from an opened file by using the `fread()` function.

- Terminate a file pointer with the `fclose()` function.

Table 7-1 provides more information about these basic file functions, and Listing 7-1 provides a brief demonstration of how these functions are used.

TIP

If you name the file pointer variable `$fp`, it will match what Aptana suggests for file functions that require the file pointer argument.

Function	Description	Explanation and Arguments
`fclose()`	Terminates a file pointer	The only argument is the file pointer created with `fopen()`. Returns TRUE for a successful close and FALSE otherwise.
`fopen()`	Connects to a file and creates a file pointer	The required arguments are a string with the path and filename, and a string with the mode (see Table 7-2 for the list of modes). Returns a file pointer that can be used with other file functions or FALSE.
`fread()`	Reads a certain number of bytes into a string	The required arguments are the file pointer created with `fopen()`, and the number of bytes to be read. Returns a string with data read or FALSE.
`fwrite()`	Writes a string to a file	The required arguments are the file pointer created with `fopen()`, and the string to be written. Optionally, the number of bytes to be written can be added. Returns the number of bytes written or FALSE.
`rewind()`	Resets the file pointer to the beginning of the file	The only argument is the file pointer created with `fopen()`. Returns TRUE if successful, and FALSE otherwise.

Table 7-1 Basic File Functions

Mode	Explanation
a	Write only, starting at the end of the file or creating a new file, appending new information to what previously existed in the file.
a+	Write and read, starting at the end of the file or creating a new file, appending new information to what previously existed in the file.
r	Read only, from the beginning of the file.
r+	Read and write, from the beginning of the file.
w	Write only, after deleting any file contents or creating a new file.
w+	Write and read, after deleting any file contents or creating a new file.
x	Create a new file and write only, from the beginning of the file. Returns FALSE if the file exists.
x+	Create a new file and write and read, from the beginning of the file. Returns FALSE if the file exists.

Table 7-2 `fopen()` Modes

Figure 7-1 proves that the script in Listing 7-1 does work, providing this response online:

NOTE
You see the multiple lines in the file shown in the preceding illustration only if you run the script multiple times. The `a+` parameter of `fopen` allows this to happen.

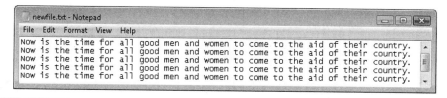

Figure 7-1   Placing \r\n (carriage return, linefeed) at the end of each line causes the file to display as separate lines instead of one continuous string of text. It also can be used to read a line at a time.

Listing 7-1   Basic file functions

```
<html>
  <head>
     <title>Listing 7-1</title>
  </head>
  <body>
     <h1>Basic File Functions</h1>
     <?php
        echo "<br />", "Create or Open the file.", "<br />";
           $fp = fopen("newfile.txt", "a+");
           if ($fp){
              echo "newfile.txt created.", "<br />";
           }
           else {
              echo "newfile.txt cannot be opened.", "<br />";
           }
        echo "<br />", "Write the file.", "<br />";
           $bytes = fwrite ($fp, "Now is the time for all good men and women
              to come to the aid of their country. \r\n");
           if ($bytes){
              echo $bytes, " byte written.", "<br />";
           }
           else {
              echo "File not written.", "<br />";
           }
        echo "<br />", "Rewind and read the file.", "<br />";
           rewind($fp);
           $data = fread ($fp, $bytes);
           if ($data){
              echo $data, "<br />";
           }
           else {
              echo "File not read.", "<br />";
           }
        echo "<br />", "Close the file.", "<br />";
           if (fclose ($fp)) {
              echo "newfile.txt closed", "<br />";
           }
```

```
        else {
            echo "newfile.txt not closed.", "<br />";
        }
    ?>
    </body>
</html>
```

TIP

As your scripts get longer, it becomes very tempting to close up your code, such as putting if statements on one line and not indenting. The problem with that is the code becomes harder to visually check and therefore is prone to problems.

Additional File Functions

While fread() and fwrite() are very functional, as you've seen, PHP provides a number of other ways to read and write data on a server's storage devices. Both fread() and fwrite() are aimed at reading or writing parts of a file to or from strings. PHP can also read to an array, read a character at a time, read a line at a time, and move around within a file using the functions described in Table 7-3, which are demonstrated in Listing 7-2, the results of which are shown in Figure 7-2.

CAUTION

fseek() can move the file pointer beyond the end of a file, so you may want to test for that and use a negative number of bytes with the SEEK_END constant.

Function	Description	Explanation and Arguments
feof()	Determines if the pointer is at end of file (EOF)	The only argument is the file pointer created with fopen(). Returns TRUE if the EOF is reached and FALSE otherwise.
fgetc()	Reads a single character from an open file	The only argument is the file pointer created with fopen(). Returns a string with the character read or FALSE if the EOF is reached.
fgets()	Reads a line designated by \n from an open file	The required argument is the file pointer created with fopen(), and optionally, the number of bytes to be read. Returns a string with data read or FALSE.
file()	Reads an entire file into an array, where each element is a line designated by \n	The required argument is a string with the path and filename. The default is to read as binary data, but you can change that with the FILE_TEXT constant as the second argument.
filesize()	Determines the size of a file	The only argument is a string with the path and filename. Returns the file size in bytes or FALSE.

Table 7-3 Additional File Functions

Function	Description	Explanation and Arguments
fseek()	Moves the file pointer of an open file	The required arguments are the file pointer created with fopen(), and the number of bytes to move the pointer. The default is to move from the beginning of the file, but adding the SEEK_CUR constant as the third argument adds the number of bytes to the current position, while using the SEEK_END constant as the third argument *adds* the bytes to the EOF. Returns a 0 for success, otherwise −1.
ftell()	Provides the current position of the file pointer of an open file	The only argument is the file pointer created with fopen(). Returns the number of bytes from the beginning of the file as an integer, or FALSE.

Table 7-3   Additional File Functions *(continued)*

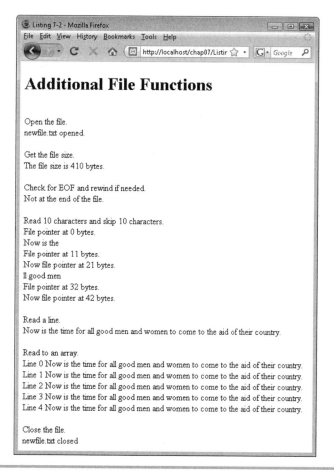

Figure 7-2   PHP gives you a number of ways to read and roam about a file.

NOTE

Listing 7-2 uses the newfile.txt file created with Listing 7-1, after that script has been run five times, creating five lines, each 82 characters or bytes long, for a total of 410 bytes.

Listing 7-2   Additional file functions

```
<html>
   <head>
      <title>Listing 7-2</title>
   </head>
   <body>
      <h1>Additional File Functions</h1>
      <?php
         $file = "newfile.txt";              echo "<br />", "Open the file.", "<br />";
            $fp = fopen($file, "r");
            if ($fp){
                echo "newfile.txt opened.", "<br />";
            }
            else {
                echo "newfile.txt cannot be opened.", "<br />";
            }
         echo "<br />", "Get the file size.", "<br />";
            $bytes = filesize ($file);
            if ($bytes){
                echo "The file size is ", $bytes, " bytes.", "<br />";
            }
            else {
                echo "File size not available.", "<br />";
            }
         echo "<br />", "Check for EOF and rewind if needed.", "<br />";
            if (feof($fp)){
                rewind($fp);
                echo "Returned to the beginning of the file.", "<br />";
            }
            else {
                echo "Not at the end of the file.", "<br />";
            }
         echo "<br />", "Read 10 characters and skip 10 characters.", "<br />";
            echo "File pointer at  ", ftell($fp), " bytes.", "<br />";
            while (ftell($fp) < 42) {
               while ($i < 11) {
                   $char = fgetc ($fp);
                   echo $char ;
                   $i++ ;
               }
               $i = 0;
               echo "<br />";
               echo  "File pointer at  ", ftell($fp), " bytes.", "<br />";
               fseek($fp, 10, SEEK_CUR);
               echo "Now file pointer at ", ftell($fp), " bytes.", "<br />";
            }
```

```
        echo "<br />", "Read a line.", "<br />";
            rewind($fp);
            $data = fgets ($fp);
            if ($data){
                echo $data, "<br />";
            }
            else {
                echo "File not read.", "<br />";
            }
        echo "<br />", "Read to an array.", "<br />";
            $textArray = file($file);
            foreach ($textArray as $line => $text) {
                echo "Line ", $line, " ", $text, "<br />";
            }
        echo "<br />", "Close the file.", "<br />";
            if (fclose ($fp)) {
                echo "newfile.txt closed", "<br />";
            }
            else {
                echo "newfile.txt not closed.", "<br />";
            }
    ?>
    </body>
</html>
```

TIP

As Listing 7-2 shows, while you are debugging a script, it is very helpful to put in a number of echoes to display what is happening, and to comment-out specific sections until you isolate a problem. In the final version of the script, the echoes can become comments.

PHP file functions, which number many more than mentioned in this and the previous section, provide a comprehensive ability to work with files. To see the full set of file functions, see http://www.php.net/manual/en/ref.filesystem.php.

Cookies and Session and Server Variables

Web pages use variables to temporarily store information while that page is being used. It is likely, though, that you will want to collect and store information from the user, from the script being run, and from the server, and to use that information on other pages during the current session, or across multiple sessions. In this section, we'll discuss creating and using session variables, cookies, and server variables to perform that function of collecting and storing. Start by comparing the three objects in Table 7-4.

Object	Created with	Accessed with	Stored on	Duration
Session variable	`$_SESSION`	`$_SESSION`	Server	Session or less
Cookie	`setcookie()`	`$_COOKIE`	Client	Until expires
Server variable	Automatically	`$_SERVER`	Server	Unlimited

Table 7-4 Comparison of External Variables

Session variables, cookies, and server variables are all PHP predefined, or built-in, variables called *superglobals* because they are available throughout a web site on as many pages as are contained in the domain. The superglobals used here are `$_SESSION`, `$_COOKIE`, and `$_SERVER`. Their use will be explained in the following sections. All the superglobals discussed in this book have the `$_` leading characters and here, as well as in many other reference sources, are displayed in all capital letters, although that is not a requirement. You'll see other superglobals later in this book.

Superglobals are *associative arrays,* arrays whose key, or array index, is a string instead of an integer. Generally the *key* is an element name, while the *value* is the element value. For example: `$_SESSION["name"]` = `$name;` where `["name"]` is the *key* for the array element and the contents of $name is its *value.* Some superglobal arrays, such as `$_SESSION` and `$_COOKIE`, allow you to define the keys, while others, such as `$_SERVER`, have predefined keys. You will see examples of these in the sections that follow.

TIP

When you are entering the string for an associative array's key, you can do it without the quotes. This is, however, a bad practice, because PHP considers the string with quotes as a different entity than the string without quotes, so it is very easy to confuse the two, creating an error in the script that is hard to find.

Session Variables

Session variables allow you to collect and use information across multiple pages in a web site during a single *session* or encounter between a user and a web site. To define a session, you must start it with the `session_start()` function, which must precede all other code sent to the client including `<html>` and `<head>`. You can then store information in the `$_SESSION` array. If you go to another page and again start it with the `session_start()` function, you can retrieve the information in the `$_SESSION` array. Listing 7-3a and Listing 7-3b demonstrate this with the results shown next.

TIP

Testing session variables as described in "Session Variables," using `http://localhost/` with the Apache server may not work. Instead use `http://127.0.0.1/`, and it should be fine.

Listing 7-3a   Creating a session variable

```php
<?php
    session_start()
?>
<!DOCTYPE html PUBLIC "-//W3C//DTD XHTML 1.0 Strict//EN">
<html>
    <head>
        <title>Listing 7-3a</title>
    </head>
    <body>
        <h1>Session Variables, Page 1</h1>
        <?php
            $name = "Joe";
            $amount = "$14.92";
            echo "Store session variables:", "<br />";
                $_SESSION["name"]   = $name;
                $_SESSION["amount"] = $amount;
                $_SESSION["time"]   = time();
            echo "Name is: ", $_SESSION["name"], "<br />";
            echo "Amount is: ", $_SESSION["amount"], "<br />";
            echo "Time is: ", date('Y m d H:i:s', $_SESSION["time"]), "<br />";
        ?>
    </body>
</html>
```

> **Listing 7-3b** Using a session variable

```php
<?php
    session_start()
?>
<!DOCTYPE html PUBLIC "-//W3C//DTD XHTML 1.0 Strict//EN">
<html>
    <head>
        <title>Listing 7-3b</title>
    </head>
    <body>
        <h1>Session Variables, Page 2</h1>
        <?php
            echo "Read session variables:", "<br />";
            echo "Name is: ", $_SESSION["name"], "<br />";
            echo "Amount is: ", $_SESSION["amount"], "<br />";
            echo "Time is: ", date('Y m d H:i:s', $_SESSION["time"]), "<br />";
        ?>
    </body>
</html>
```

NOTE
Session variables have a limited life, which is set by the `session.cache_expire` value in the pnp.ini file on the server. Depending on the use, this can be set from a few minutes to a number of hours in increments of a minute. The default is 180 minutes or three hours.

Cookies

Cookies store information on client computers. Once a cookie has been stored, or *set,* the same site (really *domain*) that created it will automatically receive that information the next time it is connected to the client. This allows the site to recognize a returning client. Cookies are created with the `setcookie()` function and accessed with the `$_COOKIE` superglobal array.

NOTE
Many people do not allow cookies to be stored on their computer due to security concerns.

Using setcookie()

You create and store a cookie using the `setcookie()` function, which must be placed before any other output in your script, including the `<html>` and `<head>` tags. It has the following form:

```
setcookie(name [,value [,expire [,path [,domain [,secure
    [,httponly]]]]]])
```

The `name` argument is the only one required. The rest are optional and may be left blank if none to the right are present. If you wish to skip an argument and enter one to the right, fill in with the empty string (""), except for $expire, which requires (0). The meaning of the arguments is

- **name** is the name of the cookie and can be any label using upper- and lowercase letters, numbers, and the underscore.

- **value** is the information you want stored with the cookie, as a string.

- **expire** is the time in seconds since 1/1/1970 that you want the cookie to expire. You can create this with the `time()` function, which will give you the number of seconds since 1/1/1970 to the current moment, and then add the number of seconds you want the cookie active. For example, `time()+(60*60*24*10)` would let the cookie be active for ten days from the current time. The default is 0, which means that the cookie will expire at the end of the session.

- **path** is the path on the server where the cookie will be available. If the path is set to "/", the entire domain will have access to the cookie.

- **domain** is the domain where the cookie will be available. If you want the cookie available to all subdomains, precede the domain with a period. For example, `.somedomain.com`.

- **secure**, if set to TRUE, says that the cookie should be sent only over a secure connection such as HTTPS. The default is FALSE.

- **httponly**, if set to TRUE, says the cookie should only be accessible with the HTTP protocol. The default is FALSE.

The `value` argument can be anything that you can put in a string, such as a name or an amount. If you want to store several separate pieces of information in a cookie, you need to use several cookies to do that. From the standpoint of PHP and the server, though, you can think of a set of cookies sent from one site to one client as an array. On the client they are stored as separate pieces of information, but in PHP you can address them as elements of a single array. Listing 7-4, later in this chapter, will provide an example of this.

CAUTION

Cookies are viewable by spyware applications, so do not use cookies to store sensitive information like usernames, passwords, and account numbers.

Using $_COOKIE

After a cookie has been set, the next time the domain that set it reconnects with the client, the client will automatically return the cookie information to the server, and it will be stored in the $_COOKIE superglobal array. You must close the connection with the client in which you set the cookie and reopen the connection before $_COOKIE will contain the information.

Listing 7-4a demonstrates a web site named "MatTech" storing a customer's first name, the date of her or his last order, and the type of merchandise purchased using cookies that don't expire for 90 days and are available throughout the domain that set the cookies. Listing 7-4b demonstrates receiving and displaying the information, like this:

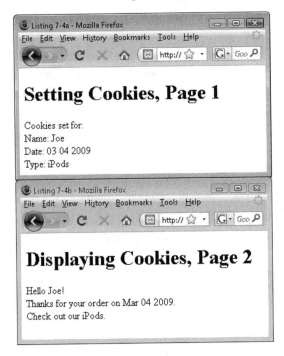

Listing 7-4a Setting a cookie

```php
<?php
    //Set cookies for name, date, and type of purchase
    $name = "Joe" ;
    $date = time() ;
    $type = "iPods" ;
    $expire = time()+(60*60*24*90);
```

```php
    setcookie("MatTech[name]", $name, $expire, "/");
    setcookie("MatTech[date]", $date, $expire, "/");
    setcookie("MatTech[type]", $type, $expire, "/");
?>
<!DOCTYPE html PUBLIC "-//W3C//DTD XHTML 1.0 Strict//EN">
<html>
    <head>
        <title>Listing 7-4a</title>
    </head>
    <body>
        <h1>Setting Cookies, Page 1</h1>
        <?php
            echo "Cookies set for:", "<br />";
            echo "Name: ", $name, "<br />";
            echo "Date: ", date('m d Y', $date), "<br />";
            echo "Type: ", $type, "<br />";
        ?>
    </body>
</html>
```

Listing 7-4b   Displaying a cookie

```php
<html>
    <head>
        <title>Listing 7-4b</title>
    </head>
    <body>
        <h1>Displaying Cookies, Page 2</h1>
        <?php
            if (isset ($_COOKIE["MatTech"])) {   //Check if there
                echo "Hello ", $_COOKIE["MatTech"][name], "! <br />";
                echo "Thanks for your order on ", date('M d Y',
                    $_COOKIE["MatTech"][date]), ". <br />";
                echo "Check out our ", $_COOKIE["MatTech"][type], ". <br />";
            }
        ?>
    </body>
</html>
```

TIP

To delete or unset a cookie, set a new one with the same name, a value of " ", and a date prior to the current date, such as `time()-3600`. If you set an array of cookies, you must delete them all. Listing 7-4c shows what is needed to delete the cookies set in Listing 7-4.

Listing 7-4c Deleting a cookie

```php
<?php
    //Delete cookies for name, date, and type of purchase
    $expire = time()-(60*60);
    setcookie("MatTech[name]", "", $expire, "/");
    setcookie("MatTech[date]", "", $expire, "/");
    setcookie("MatTech[type]", "", $expire, "/");
?>
```

Server Variables

Server variables provide information about the server, the software that is running on it, the current script that produced the request, and about the client and its software. The server in communication with the client produces this information and stores it in the superglobal array $_SERVER. Each web server produces a slightly different set of elements in the array, which are defined by their associative keys. Listing 7-5 is a short script for displaying the $_SERVER array elements on your server. Figure 7-3 shows the server variables generated with the Apache server from XAMPP on my computer, while Figure 7-4 shows some of the variables generated with Aptana's built-in server, which is only used for debugging purposes and so has a number of variables more.

Listing 7-5 Server variables generator

```php
<html>
    <head>
        <title>Listing 7-5</title>
    </head>
    <body>
        <h1>Exploring Server Variables</h1>
        <?php
         foreach ($_SERVER as $key => $value) {
            echo "<b> $key   :   </b> $value ", "<br />";
         };
        ?>
    </body>
</html>
```

Figure 7-3 Server variables generated by the XAMPP Apache web server

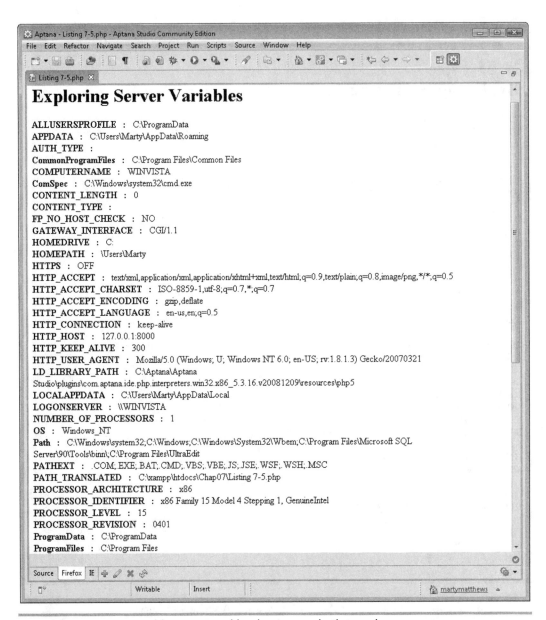

Figure 7-4 Server variables generated by the Aptana built-in web server

To look at and use server variables, use the particular key with $_SERVER. Since the value of most keys is a long and differing string, you don't want to check for equality, but rather check if the string contains a particular word. Listing 7-6 shows how to check if the browser being used is Firefox, with the following results using respectively Internet Explorer, Firefox, and Google Chrome:

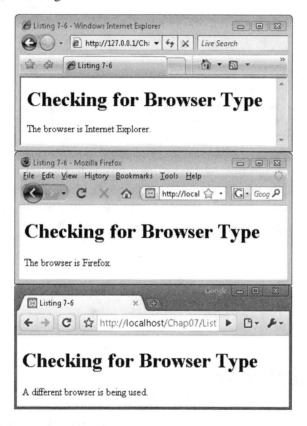

Listing 7-6   Checking for browser type

```html
<html>
   <head>
      <title>Listing 7-6</title>
   </head>
   <body>
      <h1>Checking for Browser Type</h1>
      <?php
       if(strpos($_SERVER[HTTP_USER_AGENT], "MSIE")) {
          echo "The browser is Internet Explorer. <br />";
       }
```

```
        elseif(strpos($_SERVER[HTTP_USER_AGENT], "Firefox")) {
            echo "The browser is Firefox. <br />";
        }
        else {
            echo "A different browser is being used. <br />";
        }
    ?>
  </body>
</html>
```

NOTE

Listing 7-6 does not identify Firefox in the Aptana built-in Firefox browser because the string does not include that word. Also, the word "Mozilla" is in both the IE and Firefox strings.

The `strpos()` function used in Listing 7-6 is both powerful and interesting. Its stated purpose is to find the position of the first occurrence of one string in another string. It is most frequently used, though, to simply find if one string exists in another, as is done in Listing 7-6 and again in Listing 7-11. The PHP manual talks of this as finding a "needle in the haystack."

TIP

To find the complete set of server variables and their meaning, go to http://www.php.net/manual/en/reserved.variables.server.php.

User Authentication

User authentication allows you to limit who has access to a web site. It requires that all users register for the site, providing a name, a unique ID (usually an e-mail address), and a password. This information is stored in a disk file with the ID and password encrypted so they cannot be misused. The fact that a person has registered (not their ID and password) is placed in a cookie on the user's computer, so he or she will not be asked to register again. A user wishing to enter a site is asked to enter his or her ID and password, which is encrypted and compared against the encrypted value in the file of registered users. If the ID and password correctly match a file entry, the user is admitted to the site. The fact that a user has been admitted to the site (not his or her ID and password) is stored in a session variable so the user can freely move from one site page to another without having to reenter the information.

Figure 7-5 shows a flowchart of a system to perform the user authentication function. It includes six scripts in four areas:

- **The initial site** index.php script, which checks if the user has a cookie.

- **The registration area** with two scripts, one for the user to enter his or her information, and the other to encrypt the user information, write it to disk, and to create and set a cookie.

- **The sign-in area** with two scripts, one for the user to enter their information, and the other to encrypt the user information, compare it with the disk information, and create and set a session variable.

- **A regular site page**, which checks for the presence of the session variable.

Each of these will be discussed in the following separate sections.

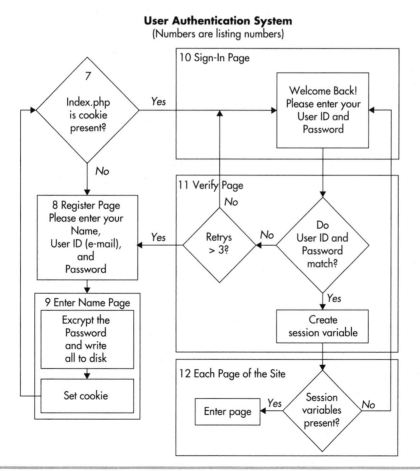

Figure 7-5 User Authentication System flowchart

CAUTION

This User Authentication System is meant for demonstration purposes *only* and is *not* intended as a fully secure procedure to protect access to a site. It also is not meant for very many users, since the entire disk file of users is read into memory each time it is used. Use it only as an example of PHP code and possibly as a starting point for your own system. *Any use of this system is at your own risk.*

In the next several chapters, you'll see how using a database for the files would greatly help a user authentication system and support a large number of users.

The Index Script

When a site is loaded, the script that automatically opens without being specifically requested is the index script, in this case index.php. For that reason the user authentication system will use that script to start the authentication. If any other script in the site is opened, the script will check to see if the user has signed in, and if not, will direct the user to sign in. The user will not be able to enter any script on the site if the script has the protection code on it.

The index.php script (see Listing 7-7) has a very simple series of PHP statements that asks if the user has a cookie for the site. (The example scripts use a site name of Matthews Technology, and the abbreviation "MatTech." To actually use this code, you would want to change that name.) If the user has a cookie from a previous visit to the site and registered there in the last 180 days, a session variable is created with their name, current date, and a retry variable used in signing in. The user is then directed to the signin.php script. If the user does not have a cookie, he or she is sent to the register.php script.

The index.php script has several unique elements:

- The script is pure PHP code, has no X/HTML code, and nothing is displayed to the user from that script. You'll see we do that several times in this system.

- The script uses the isset() function to determine if the cookie exists. Remember that if a domain has set a cookie on a user's computer, it will be automatically returned to the domain's server the next time the user connects to the server.

- The header("Location:... ") function is used to transfer execution to another web script by using the HTML header to inform the server to send another script. This function *must* be executed before any other output is sent to the user, such as an echo statement or the <html> or <head> elements.

TIP

Start out with a lot of `echo` statements to assist in the debugging, and use XHTML `<a href=...>` (anchor) elements in place of the PHP header statements, since `header` cannot be used after any output, for example the `echo` statements.

Listing 7-7	index.php

```php
<?php
    session_start();
    //Check if user has a cookie.
    if (isset ($_COOKIE["MatTech"])) {
        //If so, set session and go to sign in.
        $_SESSION["name"] = $_COOKIE["MatTech"][name];
        $_SESSION["retry"] = 0;
        $_SESSION["time"] = time();
        header( "Location: signin.php");
    }
    else {
        //If not, go to registration.
        header( "Location: register.php");
    }
?>
```

The Registration Scripts

As mentioned, there are two registration scripts: register.php, which handles the user input and enterName.php, which does the processing. It is possible to do all this on one script, as you will see done in some of the PHP/MySQL examples, but the two-script solution provides a clean introduction to this process.

Input Form

The register.php script, which you can see in Listing 7-8, is a table containing a form with three fields, Name, User ID, and Password, as shown in Figure 7-6. When the user completes filling out the form, whose contents are placed in the $_POST superglobal array, and clicks **Register**, the form `action` transfers execution to the enterName.php script.

TIP

JavaScript can be used with `Body (onload)` event to automatically go to the first form field.

Listing 7-8   register.php

```html
<!--User enters name, ID, and password.-->
<html>
    <head>
        <title>Listing 7-8 Registration Page</title>
    </head>
    <body>
        <div>
            <img src="MatTech.gif" alt="Matthews Technology" />
        </div>
        <div id="form">
            <!-- Go to enterName.php after clicking Register -->
            <form action="enterName.php" method="post" id="registerForm">
            <table width="150" border="1" cellspacing="3" cellpadding="5" >
                <tr height= 50>
                    <th colspan= "2" valign="middle" >
                        <p id="head">Welcome to Matthews Technology!</p>
                        <p id="body">Please enter your Name,<br />User ID, and
                            Password</p>
                    </th>
                </tr>
                <tr>
                    <td width="40">
                        <p class="label">Name:</p>
                    </td>
                    <td width="100">
                        <input type="text" name="name" value="" size="60" />
                    </td>
                </tr>
                <tr>
                    <td>
                        <p class="label">User ID:</p>
                    </td>
                    <td>
                        <input type="text" name="userid" value="" size="60" />
                    </td>
                </tr>
                <tr>
                    <td>
                        <p class="label">Password:</p>
                    </td>
                    <td>
                        <input type="password" name="passwd" value="" size="20" />
                    </td>
                </tr>
            </table>
                <input type="submit" name="submit" value="Register" />
            </form>
        </div>
    </body>
</html>
```

Figure 7-6   The registration form could use a CSS to spruce it up a bit.

Encryption and Save to Disk

The enterName.php script, shown in Listing 7-9, is the second pure PHP script. It picks up the name entered at registration and passed to this script through the $_POST superglobal. This is combined with the current time and the expiration time to create and set a cookie on the user's computer. The user ID and password, entered at registration, are combined and then encrypted with SHA1 (Secure Hash Algorithm 1), for 160-bit encryption. Next the current time, the user's name, and the encrypted ID and password are placed into an array, and the array is written to disk with the file_put_contents() function (because it allows an array to be appended to an existing disk file). System execution is then transferred back to index.php.

Listing 7-9   enterName.php

```php
<?php
/* Cookie is written. Then the user id
 *  and password are encrypted and that and
 *  the name are written to disk. */
```

```php
//Information for cookie, expires in 6 months.
$name = $_POST['name'] ;
$date = time() ;
$expire = time()+(60*60*24*180);

//Set cookie.
setcookie("MatTech[name]", $name, $expire, "/");
setcookie("MatTech[date]", $date, $expire, "/");

//Combine userid and password and encrypt it.
$userPasswd = $_POST['userid'] .= $_POST['passwd'];
$encryptid_pw = sha1($userPasswd);

//Build an array of data and write it to disk.
$entry = array( 'index' => time(),
                'name' => $name,
                'encrypt' => $encryptid_pw,
              );
if (!$byteswrite = file_put_contents('namelist.txt',
    $entry, FILE_APPEND)) {
      echo "<br />File not written.<br />";
    }

//Return to Index.php.
header( "Location: index.php");
?>
```

The Sign-In Scripts

Once again the two sign-in scripts, signin.php and verify.php, could be in one script, but are split for the clarity of this exercise.

Signing In

Once the user has a cookie on her or his computer, the user goes immediately to signin.php. This is again a form within a table, shown in Figure 7-7 and Listing 7-10, that uses the $_POST superglobal to pass the user ID and password to verify.php by using the form action when the user clicks **Sign In**.

NOTE

You should not get to signin.php without being registered, but the "Not registered? Click here!" is added so you can get back to register.php without having to delete the cookie.

Figure 7-7   The fact that the user ID and password are transmitted over the Internet unencrypted is a major security flaw. Using HTTPS to do this would help.

Listing 7-10   signin.php

```
<!-- User enters id and password. -->
<html>
   <head>
      <title>Listing 7-10 Sign-In</title>
   </head>
   <body>
      <div>
         <img src="MatTech.gif" alt="Matthews Technology" />
      </div>
      <div id="form">
         <!-- Display the sign-in form. After filling in, go to verify script. -->
         <form action="verify.php" method="post" id="signinForm">
         <table width="100" border="1" cellspacing="3" cellpadding="5" >
            <tr height= 50>
               <th colspan= "2" valign="middle" >
                  <p id="head">Welcome Back!</p>
                  <p id="body">Please enter your<br />User ID and Password</p>
                  <p id="body">Not registered? <a href="register.php">Click
                     here!</a></p>
               </th>
            </tr>
```

```
            <tr>
               <td width="50">
                  <p class="label">User ID:</p>
               </td>
               <td width="120">
                  <input type="text" name="userid" value="" size="60" />
               </td>
            </tr>
            <tr>
               <td>
                  <p class="label">Password:</p>
               </td>
               <td>
                  <input type="password" name="passwd" value="" size="20" />
               </td>
            </tr>
         </table>
            <input type="submit" name="submit" value="Sign In" />
         </form>
      </div>
   </body>
</html>
```

Verifying the Input

The verify.php script, which you can see in Listing 7-11, reads the entire namelist.txt file into the $namelist string using the file_get_contents() function. It then combines the user ID and password that were entered at sign-in and encrypts that combination. The strpos() function is then used to see if the encrypted combination is contained in $namelist. If the encryption is there, the session variable is updated, and execution is transferred to the site scripts. If the encryption is not found on the disk file, the $retry variable is incremented and checked to see if it is greater than 3. If so, execution is transferred to register.php, otherwise the $retry variable is stored in the $_SESSION variable, and execution is transferred to signin.php.

Listing 7-11 verify.php

```php
<?php
   session_start();

// Verify user's id and password, and create session.

      //Read the name list file.
      if(!$namelist = file_get_contents('namelist.txt')) {
         echo "<br />File not read.<br />";
      }
```

```php
//Combine the user ID and password and encrypt it.
$userPasswd = $_POST['userid'] .= $_POST['passwd'];
$testentry = sha1($userPasswd);

//Determine if the encrypted user ID and password are in file.
if(strpos($namelist, $testentry)){

    //If there, reset the session and enter site.
    $_SESSION["retry"] = "admit";
    $_SESSION["time"] = time();
    header( "Location: enterSite.php");
}
else {
    //If not, add to Session Retry and test > 3
    $retry = $_SESSION["retry"];
    $retry++;
    if ($retry > 3) {
        //If greater than 3 go to register.
        header( "Location: register.php");
    }
    else {
        //If less than 3, reset Session Retry and go to Sign in
        $_SESSION["retry"] = $retry;
        header( "Location: signin.php");
    }
}
?>
```

A Site Page

The code snippet that goes on each regular site page (see Listing 7-12) checks to see if
`$_SESSION["retry"]` is present and equal to "admit." If so, the user is greeted, and
execution flows into the regular page. Otherwise, execution is returned to index.php,
where the user has to prove she has a cookie, or she will have to register, and in either
case she will have to sign in.

TIP

Instead of including the snippet of PHP code in Listing 7-12 on each regular site page,
save just the PHP snippet as its own file; then as the first line of every site page insert
`<?php require_once(enterSite.php); ?>`. One feature of the `require` and
`require_once` functions is that the balance of the script on the page will not execute
until the code referenced by the function successfully executes. It halts execution with a
fatal error. This contrasts with the `include` and `include_once` functions, which do
not halt execution of the remaining script. The `_once` prevents the snippet from being
loaded more than once.

Listing 7-12 enterSite.php

```php
<?php
   session_start();
//Having successfully signed in...
   //Check to see if session variable present and is "admit"
   if (isset($_SESSION["retry"]) && $_SESSION["retry"] == "admit") {
      //If so, continue.
      echo "Hello ", $_SESSION["name"], "!<br />";
   }
   else {
      //If not, return to the site Index page.
      header( "Location: index.php");
   }
?>
```

Many things can be done to enhance this system. The first is probably to make the pieces that collect the user ID and password use HTTPS and thus secure that transfer. The second is to use a CSS to make the data collection forms look better. Two other areas that we'll address in Chapter 9 are better handling of error messages, such as those returned from disk read and write errors, and handling the user trying to enter unusual characters and other content (like pasting an image) into the form.

Part IV

Powering Databases with MySQL and PHP

In Chapter 7 you saw how with PHP you can read and write a disk file for user authentication. While that worked, it was limited in that you had to read the entire file into memory, and search it there to do what was needed. In Part IV you'll see how MySQL, a full-fledge relational database management system (RDBMS), greatly enhances the process of reading, writing, maintaining, changing, searching, and rearranging information stored in computer files. It is the third major tool used to make web sites dynamic, and while a web site requires HTML and PHP in addition to MySQL, MySQL does the heavy lifting when it come to the handling of data.

Chapter 8 discusses the fundamentals of MySQL and how it is used with PHP. It begins with a look at relational databases, SQL (Structured Query Language), and the basics of working with databases. It then describes how phpMyAdmin is used over the Internet or an intranet to create, change, and manage MySQL databases. Finally, the PHP functions that are used to manipulate a MySQL database are discussed, with examples of how they are used.

Chapter 9 reviews and demonstrates both the database-handling capabilities of PHP and MySQL through examples of data entry, validation, storage, and retrieval, and also demonstrates searching or querying a database, updating and deleting records, and formatting and displaying database information on a web page.

In this Part IV opener, we'll provide some background on MySQL, and talk about what tools you should have running in order to work with PHP and MySQL.

About MySQL

MySQL is a relational database management system that uses the Structured Query Language to store, work with, and retrieve information over the Internet. MySQL is called "the world's most popular open source database," with many millions of web sites using it. MySQL is a web resource that runs on a web server as does PHP. MySQL is built to handle large-volume, multiuser database access. Wikipedia claims that MySQL is used by several high-traffic web sites including Flickr, Facebook, Wikipedia, Google, Nokia, and YouTube. MySQL, because of its ease of use, speed, and reliability, is also very usable for smaller sites, and that explains its widespread use.

NOTE
The GNU General Public License discussed here is a model license for free software that was developed for the Swedish GNU operating system. "GNU" is not an acronym, but the name of an antelope like animal.

MySQL was developed and first released in 1995 by MySQL AB, a Swedish company that is now a subsidiary of Sun Microsystems. MySQL AB makes the program available under a GNU General Public License (GPL) in addition to proprietary licenses. GPL stipulates that any system that uses MySQL must be distributed under a similar license. It is this arrangement that makes MySQL available with XAMPP. As this is written (Spring 2009), XAMPP includes MySQL 5.1.30. MySQL AB/Sun Microsystems offers the MySQL Community Server, which can be freely downloaded, but which requires significant expertise to set up, integrate, and manage. It also offers MySQL Enterprise, which comes with many tools and technical support to make the job much easier, for a price. XAMPP makes using MySQL relatively easy and is a good way to start a project. Version 5.1.32 is currently available from MySQL AB, as well as version 6.1 in alpha state for development and testing. In all cases MySQL is a mature, full-featured, professional RDBMS, as you can see from its web site, http://www.mysql.com. Many professional web developers believe that PHP and MySQL are the best way to add a database to a web site of any size.

Tools Needed for MySQL

To effectively work with MySQL, you need to have the same tools that have been described in earlier section introductions of this book. The Part I introduction describes and recommends packages that you can download to accomplish this work, including

- **Aptana Studio**, an integrated development environment that provides powerful authoring for HTML, CSS, and JavaScript by default, and with an add-on or plug-in, for PHP.

- **XAMPP** is a combination of the Apache web server, the MySQL database server, and the Perl and PHP servers that all run on your computer and duplicate what you will see when you upload your web site to a commercial web host with those servers.

- **IE 6**, **IE 7**, and **Firefox** browsers are all needed to test and debug your scripts. Since the majority of the web-browsing population uses these browsers, it is important to try your web pages in all of them. IE 8, which is in final testing as this is written, is also a strong candidate for you to use for testing. It is available for both Windows XP and Windows Vista, as well as for Windows 7.

If you do not already have Aptana Studio, XAMPP, IE 6, IE 7, and Firefox, return to the Part I introduction, and follow the instructions to download and install them. They are needed for the discussion in the remaining chapters of this book.

TIP

This and the next chapter will require XAMPP to be running and at least one browser to be opened to http://localhost/xampp. If you have an XAMPP icon on the desktop, double-click it. Otherwise click **Start | All Programs | Apache Friends | XAMPP | XAMPP Control Panel**. In the XAMPP Control Panel, click **Start** opposite Apache, and click **Start** opposite MySQL, as shown in the following illustration.

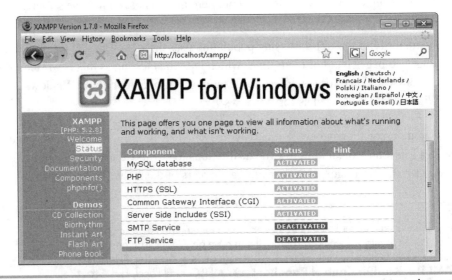

Load a browser and, in the address bar, type http://localhost/xampp, and then click **Status** on the left. The first five services should be activated, as you can see in Figure P4-1.

TIP
If you have problems seeing your web site on http://localhost/, try http://127.0.0.1/.

This section of the book also depends heavily on foundational knowledge of PHP, as presented in Part III of the book. If you don't have that knowledge, it is strongly recommended that you return to that part and familiarize yourself with PHP before tackling Part IV.

Figure P4-1 "Localhost" is the Apache web server running on your computer and provides access to MySQL.

Chapter **8**
Fundamentals
of MySQL

Key Skills & Concepts

- Understanding an RDBMS

- Understanding SQL

- Using MySQL

- Opening and Exploring phpMyAdmin

- Creating and Using a Database in phpMyAdmin

- Manipulating a Database

- Obtaining Database Information

- Administering a Database

- Combining PHP MySQL Functions

MySQL gives a web site the ability to store, retrieve, and manipulate large amounts of information quickly and efficiently. This allows a web site to present a large catalog of items for sale, to provide access to and searchability of a large archive of information, or to register and service a large group of individuals, such as members of an organization.

This chapter will look at relational databases, SQL (Structured Query Language), and the basics of working with MySQL directly. It then describes how phpMyAdmin is used over the Internet or an intranet to create, change, and manage MySQL databases. Finally, the PHP functions that are used to exercise a MySQL database are discussed with examples of how they are used.

Relational Databases and SQL

As an RDBMS, MySQL is in the top tier of database engines, and by implementing SQL, it is a member of the most sophisticated of those products. Other products in this group include Oracle, IBM's DB2, and Microsoft's SQL Server. To fully understand MySQL and its power, it is important to understand RDBMS and SQL.

Columns or fields

BkID	Book Title	Author	Publisher	Price	Category
1	Nightfall	Asimov	Bantam	5.99	Sci. Fic.
2	Patriot Games	Clancy	Berkley	4.95	Thriller
3	2010	Clarke	Ballantine	3.95	Sci. Fic.
4	Lie Down with Lions	Follett	Signet	4.95	Mystery
5	A Thief of Time	Hillerman	Harper	4.95	Mystery
6	The Fly on the Wall	Hillerman	Harper	4.95	Mystery
7	Hornet Flight	Follett	Signet	7.99	WW II
8	The Innocent Man	Grisham	Dell	7.99	Non Fiction
9	Mission of Honor	Clancy	Berkley	7.99	Thriller

Table →

Rows or records →

An individual field

Figure 8-1 A database is a table with records and fields.

Understanding an RDBMS

A database in its simplest form is a *table* of information, as shown in the Excel list of books in Figure 8-1. Each book entry is a row in the table and is called *record*. Each piece of information in a book entry, such as the title or author, is a column in the table, and is called a *field*.

The table in Figure 8-1 is called a *flatfile,* where all the information in the database is in a single table. Notice that there are several books that have the same author, the same publisher, or the same category. If these fields were made into their own tables that contain additional information, it would simplify the Books table, provide more information, and save storage space. (Savings are very small in this database, but if you have a large database, they would be significant.) The resultant four tables, which are shown in Figure 8-2, form a *relational database.*

In a relational database, repeated pieces of information are stored in separate tables and related to one another through their *key,* or index, a unique value assigned to each record in the table. In the table that it indexes, the key is called the *primary key.* When that key is used in another table, it is called a *foreign key.* For example, in the Authors table the Aid (author ID) is the primary key, but in the Books table the Aid is a foreign key relating the Authors table to the Books table. The full set of relationships in the Books database is shown here.

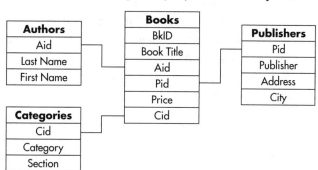

BkID	Book Title	Aid	Pid	Price	Cid		
3	2010	3	3	3.95	1		
5	A Thief of Time	5	5	4.95	3		
7	Hornet Flight	4	4	7.99	2		
4	Lie Down with Lions	4	4	4.95	3		
9	Mission of Honor	2	2	7.99	2		
1	Nightfall	1	1	5.99	1		
2	Patriot Games	2	2	4.95	2		
6	The Fly on the Wall	5	5	4.95	3		
8	The Innocent Man	6	6	7.99	2		

Aid	Last Name	First Name		Pid	Publisher	Address	City
1	Asimov	Isaac		1	Bantam	666 5th Ave	New York
2	Clancy	Tom		2	Berkley	200 Madison	New York
3	Clarke	Arthur		3	Ballantine	201 E 50th	New York
4	Follett	Ken		4	Signet	375 Hudson	New York
5	Hillerman	Tony		5	Harper	10 E 53rd	New York
6	Grisham	John		6	Dell	666 5th Ave	New York

Cid	Category	Section
1	Sci. Fic.	F-14
2	Thriller	G-10
3	Mystery	E-9

Figure 8-2 A relational database places repetitive information into separate tables.

The process of taking a field with repeated values and placing the field in its own table, is called *normalization*. It not only reduces the space taken up by a database, but it also significantly enhances the maintainability of a database. Without normalization, if you wanted to change a value in a field, you would have to change all occurrences of the value everywhere in the database. With normalization, you only have to change a single occurrence.

Understanding SQL

SQL, or the Structured Query Language, is an efficient means of working with a database using statements similar to spoken English. SQL was originally developed at IBM and has since become an international standard that is used by a number of RDBMSs. SQL was designed as a structured, declarative query language for relational databases. SQL statements generally begin with a declarative keyword, such as **CREATE, DELETE, INSERT, OPEN, SELECT**, and **UPDATE**. This is then followed by one or more clauses beginning with one or more of these keywords: **FROM, GROUP BY, HAVING, JOIN, ORDER BY**, and **WHERE**. For example, using the Books database and table defined earlier:

```
SELECT * FROM books WHERE price > 5.00 ORDER BY books.title;
```

will select all records (the asterisk) from the Books table where the Price is greater than $5.00, and order the resulting list by Book Title. Listing 8-1 shows additional examples of SQL statements that build the Books table with five fields, three of which are variable character strings of either 255 or 60 maximum characters. The BkID field is an integer that must have a value (NOT NULL) and is the primary key for the table. The data for six books is then inserted into the table. In the first five of them every field has a value, so the fields are not specified. For the sixth book, two of the fields are missing, so the ones that are present must be specified. Then the table is updated to change the price for book 3 and to change the title for book 5 to correct a misspelling. Finally book 6 is removed from the table.

Listing 8-1   Examples of SQL Statements

```
CREATE TABLE books (
     bkid int NOT NULL PRIMARY KEY,
     title varchar(255),
     author varchar(60),
     publisher varchar(60),
     price decimal(10,2));
INSERT INTO books VALUES
     (1, 'Nightfall', 'Asimov', 'Bantam', 5.99);
INSERT INTO books VALUES
     (2, 'Patriot Games', 'Clancy', 'Berkley', 4.95);
INSERT INTO books VALUES
     (3, '2010', 'Clarke', 'Ballantine', 3.95);
INSERT INTO books VALUES
     (4, 'Lie Down with Lions', 'Follett', 'Signet', 4.95);
INSERT INTO books VALUES
     (5, 'A Theif of Time', 'Hillerman', 'Harper', 4.95);
INSERT INTO books (bkid,title,price) VALUES
     (6, 'The Innocent Man',7.99);
UPDATE books SET price=5.99 WHERE bkid = 3;
UPDATE books SET title='A Thief of Time' WHERE bkid = 5;
DELETE FROM books WHERE bkid = 6;
```

There are, of course, many other SQL keywords and clauses, as well as a variety of data types and functions. The purpose of the book, though, is to explore how to use MySQL with PHP. While MySQL is closely tied to SQL, there are some differences, so we'll leave SQL with this brief introduction.

Using MySQL

The MySQL server can be used in a variety of ways. Here we'll look at three of them: directly through the MySQL command-line client; online through the phpMyAdmin user interface; and programmatically through PHP. In this section we will briefly look at the command-line client; in the next major section we'll explore phpMyAdmin; and in the major section after that we'll go into depth on using PHP to exercise MySQL.

The MySQL command-line client is mainly for determining if MySQL is installed and running on a computer, and for doing some quick maintenance on a database. Major setup and maintenance of a database is done with phpMyAdmin, while recurring use of a database is done programmatically, which in this book means PHP.

Starting the MySQL Command-Line Client

The MySQL command-line client is placed on your computer when XAMPP is installed and is in the c:/xampp/mysql/bin folder. If it is not already running, start XAMPP and then load and try MySQL with these instructions:

1. If you have an XAMPP icon on the desktop, double-click it. Otherwise click **Start | All Programs | Apache Friends | XAMPP | XAMPP Control Panel**.

2. In the XAMPP Control Panel, click **Start** opposite Apache, and click **Start** opposite MySQL, as shown in the introduction to Part IV.

3. Open the Windows Explorer by clicking **Start | Computer** ("My Computer" in Windows XP).

4. Change to the c:/xampp/mysql/bin folder by double-clicking the **c:** drive, scrolling down to, and opening **xampp | mysql | bin**.

5. Open the MySQL command-line client window by double-clicking **mysql.exe**, as shown in Figure 8-3.

6. At the mysql> prompt type

   ```
   select version(), current_date;
   ```

   and press **ENTER**. Your command window should look like this:

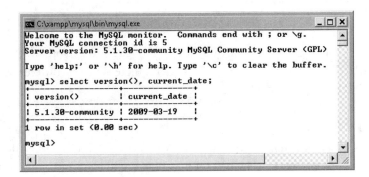

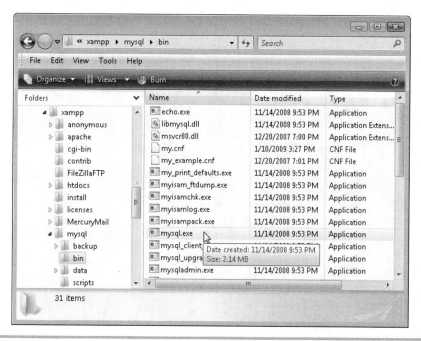

Figure 8-3 XAMPP provides a full suite of web development software, including a full version of MySQL.

7. If you have been able to do these instructions and get the results shown, then MySQL is properly installed and running. If not, you need to go back over your installation and possibly these instructions to see where the error is.

8. If you are immediately going on to the next section, do so directly. Otherwise type <u>exit</u>, and press ENTER.

NOTE

Some earlier installations of XAMPP were installed in the Program Files folder, so the path to mysql.exe would be c:/program files/xampp/mysql/bin.

Build a Table on the Command Line

Build a bit of the Books table, do a query on it, and then delete it with these instructions (see Figure 8-4 for the results):

1. If you exited the command-line window, use as much of the immediately preceding instructions as needed to reopen it.

Figure 8-4 The MySQL command-line client is a bit tedious and probably not your first choice for working with MySQL.

2. To attach the Books table to an existing database, see what databases are available by typing at the mysql> prompt:

```
SHOW DATABASES;
```

and pressing ENTER.

3. To use the Test database, at the mysql> prompt, type

```
USE test;
```

and press ENTER.

4. To begin creating the new table, at the mysql> prompt, type

```
CREATE TABLE books (
      bkid int NOT NULL PRIMARY KEY,
      title varchar(255),
      author varchar(60));
```

and press ENTER. This code can be entered all on a single line, or, by using SHIFT-ENTER (new-line), it can be on several lines as shown here.

5. Add books to the database at the `mysql>` prompt by typing

```
INSERT INTO books VALUES
      (1, 'Nightfall', 'Asimov');
```

and press **ENTER**. Again, this can be on one or two lines.

6. Continue adding books, and at the `mysql>` prompt, type

```
INSERT INTO books VALUES
      (2, 'Patriot Games', 'Clancy');
```

and press **ENTER**.

7. At the `mysql>` prompt, type

```
INSERT INTO books VALUES
      (3, '2010', 'Clarke');
```

and press **ENTER**.

8. List the books in the database, sorted by title. At the `mysql>` prompt, type

```
SELECT * FROM books ORDER BY title;
```

and press **ENTER**.

9. Delete the table. At the `mysql>` prompt, type

```
DROP TABLE books;
```

and press **ENTER**.

10. Close the MySQL command-line client. At the `mysql>` prompt, type

```
exit;
```

and press **ENTER**.

TIP

The MySQL command-line client is a good tool for small, quick fixes to a database; for small, one-time queries; and for testing how a MySQL command will respond.

Using phpMyAdmin

phpMyAdmin is an online graphical user interface for working with a MySQL database and was written in PHP. It is one of the programs that comes with XAMPP. The principal use of phpMyAdmin is to initially create databases and their tables that will be exercised programmatically with PHP, and to do occasional maintenance on a database. It is not meant for the day-to-day use of the database, which is accomplished with PHP or other programs.

In this section we'll explore phpMyAdmin, review its security and how to change it, create a database with a table, and look at the details of a database specification, including the various data types.

Opening and Exploring phpMyAdmin

Open and explore phpMyAdmin with these steps:

1. If it is not already running, open the XAMPP Control Panel and start both Apache and MySQL as described earlier in this chapter.

2. Open a browser and in the address bar, type http://localhost/xampp/, and press ENTER.

3. In the left column, click **phpMyAdmin**, which should open as shown in Figure 8-5.

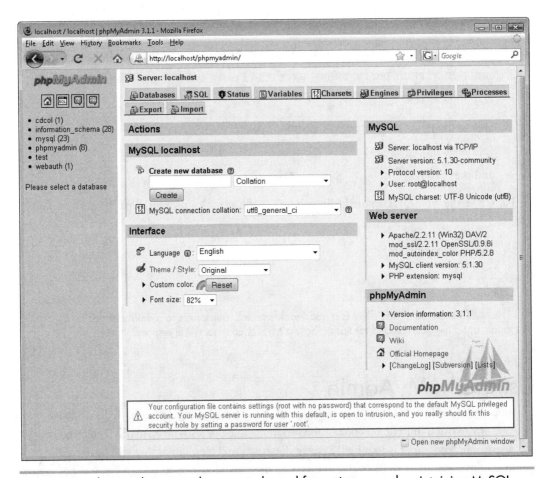

Figure 8-5 phpMyAdmin provides a control panel for setting up and maintaining MySQL.

The phpMyAdmin window shown in Figure 8-5 provides a list of built-in databases on the left side with the number of tables in parentheses. On the right are various settings, the current versions of MySQL, Apache, PHP, and phpMyAdmin, as well as documentation for phpMyAdmin. In the middle you can create a new database and change the interface. Across the top are ten tabs that provide a lot of additional information about the resident MySQL databases and the ability to change settings and, in the SQL tab, to do everything you can do in the MySQL command-line client.

At the bottom of the window, you'll see a warning that phpMyAdmin's default settings do not include a password for the default username "root." This means that anybody who knows the username "root," and many people do, can access your database and do what they wish with it. While you are working on your own computer using localhost (or 127.0.0.1), your risk is not great, but when you upload your site to a commercial host, it becomes critical that you set the username to something other than "root" and use a strong password. The next section shows you how to do that.

Setting Privileges

You can set and change a password, and add and delete users through the Privileges tab of phpMyAdmin—providing you have the privileges to do that, which the root user does (another reason to set a password for root, even on your own computer). Do that next:

1. From the phpMyAdmin Home page (shown in Figure 8-5; if you're not there, click **Server:localhost** above the tabs), click the **Privileges** tab. The User Overview opens, as shown in Figure 8-6.

   You can see that root user is set up (at least in my case) for both localhost and 127.0.0.1, has no password set in either case, and has all privileges, including the ability to grant privileges to others.

2. Click the **Edit Privileges** icon on the right end of the first root user listed. The top of the detail privileges page opens. Here you can see the full list of privileges that can be set.

3. Scroll down until you see Change Password, and click in the text box opposite Password.

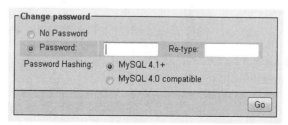

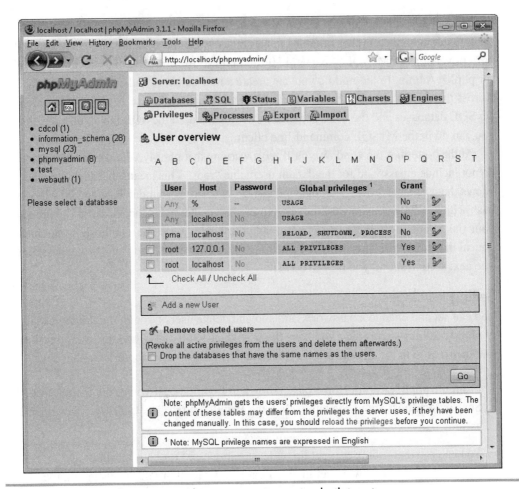

Figure 8-6 MySQL has a comprehensive security system built into it.

4. Type the password you want to use (for greatest strength, make it six to eight characters long and a combination of upper- and lowercase letters, numbers, and at least one special character).

5. Press TAB, retype the same password, and click **Go**. Click the **Privileges** tab again.

6. If you have a second root user, click the **Edit Privileges** icon opposite it, and follow the preceding instructions to set a password for it.

7. If you don't have a second root user, or after you have set the second root user's password, you will get an error message when you try to do anything in phpMyAdmin, such as go back to the Home page, because you have not entered your new password.

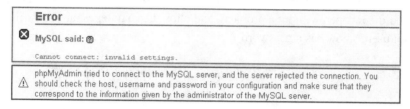

8. You need to tell phpMyAdmin's configuration to use your new password for the root user. Open Aptana. In the File panel or File menu, open c:\xampp\phpmyadmin\config .inc.php.

9. In Aptana's edit pane, scroll down until you see

```
$cfg['servers'][i]['password'] = ' ';
```

as shown in Figure 8-7.

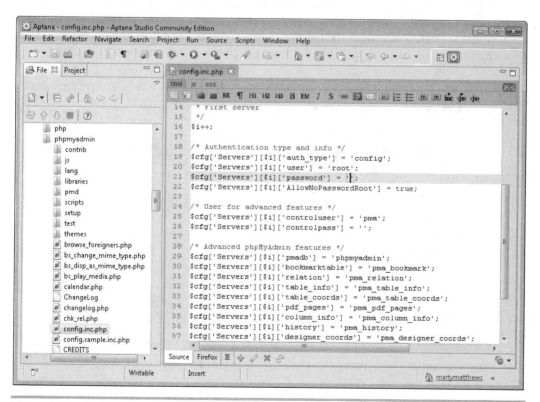

Figure 8-7 The phpMyAdmin configuration file must be told about the root password.

10. Between the final pair of single quotes, type your password, leaving no spaces within the quotes.

11. Save the config.inc.php file, close Aptana, try once more to open phpMyAdmin, which should now open without a problem, and click the **Privileges** tab. You will see that the root user(s) now has a password.

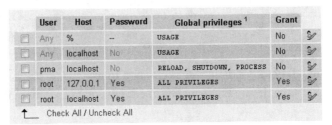

	User	Host	Password	Global privileges [1]	Grant	
☐	Any	%	--	USAGE	No	✎
☐	Any	localhost	No	USAGE	No	✎
☐	pma	localhost	No	RELOAD, SHUTDOWN, PROCESS	No	✎
☐	root	127.0.0.1	Yes	ALL PRIVILEGES	Yes	✎
☐	root	localhost	Yes	ALL PRIVILEGES	Yes	✎

↑ Check All / Uncheck All

Create and Use a Database in phpMyAdmin

To fully exercise phpMyAdmin, you need to create a database, add a table to it, and add some data to the table. You can then do queries and manipulate the data.

Create a Database and Its Table

Use the following steps to build the full Books database shown earlier in Figure 8-2.

1. In the phpMyAdmin Home page in the Create New Database text box, type <u>Books</u> and click **Create**. A message appears telling you the database has been created.

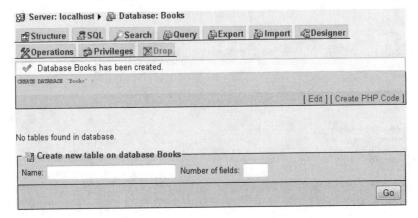

2. Under Create New Table, in the Name text box, type <u>Books</u>, press **TAB**, and type <u>6</u> for the Number Of Fields in the Books table. Click **Go**. The field entry window opens, as shown in Figure 8-8.

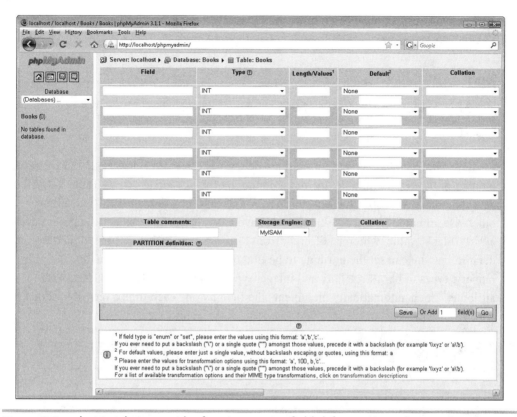

Figure 8-8 phpMyAdmin provides for an extensive field definition (not often used).

3. In the first field, type <u>Bkid</u>, leave INT (integer) for the Type, tab over to Index, select **Primary**, and click **A_I** for Auto Increment. Leave the remaining fields blank.

4. Fill in the remaining fields as shown next. For the Type, press **v** to get VARCHAR.

Server: localhost ▸ Database: Books ▸ Table: Books

Field	Type	Length/Values[1]	Default[2]
Bkid	INT		None
Title	VARCHAR	255	None
Author	VARCHAR	60	None
Publisher	VARCHAR	60	None
Price	DECIMAL	10,2	None
Category	VARCHAR	20	None

5. When you have completed entering the fields, click **Save**. You will get a message that table Books has been created, as shown in Figure 8-9.

NOTE

Unless you specify otherwise, a NULL or blank field is not allowed. Since we did not specify (check) NULL as we were building the table, all fields have Null-No, shown in Figure 8-9.

In the Books table, we have used three data types (INT, VARCHAR, DECIMAL), but a number of types are available, the more common of which are shown in Table 8-1. All data types have a NULL value (the absence of any value) by default if NULL is allowed; otherwise all numeric and date/time types have a 0 value, while text and set types have a " " (blank) value, which is different from NULL. All numeric types are signed by default, but you can set the attribute to be UNSIGNED. You can also set an attribute for numeric types to be ZEROFILL, and integer types can have the AUTO_INCREMENT attribute, which automatically increments the field by one each time a record is added.

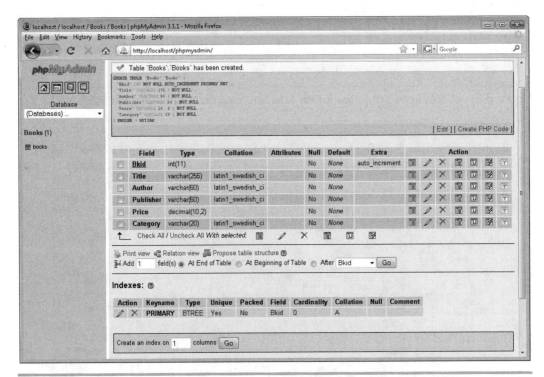

Figure 8-9   At the top of the phpMyAdmin new table page is the MySQL code for building the table.

Text fields store characters based on the specified or default character set and collation sequence (see the following Note on collation sequence). Binary data types are used to store nontext information such as still images and audio and video segments.

Type	Name	Length	Contents
Numeric	TINYINT	1 byte	−128 to +127, or 0–255 unsigned.
Numeric	SMALLINT	2 bytes	−32,768 to +32,767 or 0 to 65,535 unsigned.
Numeric	MEDIUMINT	3 bytes	−8,388,608 to +8,388,607 or 0 to 16,777,215 unsigned.
Numeric	INT	4 bytes	−2,147,483,648 to +2,147,483,647 or 0 to 4,294,967,295 unsigned.
Numeric	BIGINT	8 bytes	−9,223,372,036,854,775,808 to +9,223,372,03 6,854,775,807 or 0 to 18,446,744,073,709,55 1,615 unsigned.
Numeric	FLOAT(t,d)	4 bytes	Single-precision floating-point number of t total digits, of which d are to the right of the decimal place. Good for smaller numbers with up to 7 decimal places.
Numeric	DOUBLE(t,d)	8 bytes	Double-precision floating-point number of t total digits, of which d are to the right of the decimal place. Good for larger numbers with up to 15 decimal places.
Numeric	DECIMAL(t,d)	Varies	Decimal number of t total digits, of which d are to the right of the decimal place, stored in binary format, packing 9 decimal digits into 4 bytes. Will expand for large numbers.
Text	CHAR(t)	0 to 255	Fixed maximum number of characters (t) padded with blanks on the right, but removed when retrieved. Length is the number of t characters in bytes.
Text	VARCHAR(t)	0 to 65,535	Variable number of characters up to a maximum of (t), not padded. Length is the actual number of characters in bytes plus 1 byte up to 255 characters or plus 2 bytes above 255.
Text	TINYTEXT	0 to 255	Variable number of characters up to a maximum of 255, not padded. Length is the actual number of characters in bytes plus 1 byte.
Text	TEXT	0 to 65,535	Variable number of characters up to a maximum of 65,535, not padded. Length is the actual number of characters in bytes plus 2 bytes.

Table 8-1 MySQL Data Types *(continued)*

Type	Name	Length	Contents
Text	MEDIUMTEXT	0 to 16,777,215	Variable number of characters up to a maximum of 16,777,215, not padded. Length is the actual number of characters in bytes plus 3 bytes.
Text	LONGTEXT	0 to 4,294,967,295	Variable number of characters up to a maximum of 4,294,967,295, not padded. Length is the actual number of characters in bytes plus 4 bytes.
Binary	TINYBLOB	0 to 255	Variable number of bytes up to a maximum of 255, not padded. Length is the actual number of bytes plus 1 byte.
Binary	BLOB	0 to 65,535	Variable number of bytes up to a maximum of 65,535, not padded. Length is the actual number of bytes plus 2 bytes.
Binary	MEDIUMBLOB	0 to 16,777,215	Variable number of bytes up to a maximum of 16,777,215, not padded. Length is the actual number of bytes plus 3 bytes.
Binary	LONGBLOB	0 to 4,294,967,295	Variable number of bytes up to a maximum of 4,294,967,295, not padded. Length is the actual number of bytes plus 4 bytes.
Date/Time	DATE	3 bytes	Stored as YYYY-MM-DD and can range from 1000-01-01 to 9999-12-31.
Date/Time	TIME	3 bytes	Stored as HHH:MM:SS, can range from −838:59:59 to 838:59:59, and can be displayed as D HH:MM:SS, where D is the number of days up to a maximum of 34.
Date/Time	DATETIME	8 bytes	Stored as YYYY-MM-DD HH:MM:SS and can range from 1000-01-01 00:00:00 to 9999-12-31 23:59:59.
Date/Time	TIMESTAMP	4 bytes	Stored as the number of seconds from 1970-01-01 00:00:01 and can go to 2038-01-09 03:13:07. Normally displayed as YYYY-MM-DD HH:MM:SS.
Date/Time	YEAR(t)	1 byte	A two-digit or four-digit (YEAR(2) or YEAR(4)) year from 1901 to 2155. Two-digit years 00 to 69 are assumed to be 2000 to 2069, and years 70 to 99 are assumed to be 1970 to 1999.
Set	ENUM(v1,v2,v3)	1 or 2 bytes	Stores exactly one of up to 65,535 specified string values in a list. Length is dependent on the number of values.
Set	SET(v1,v2,v3)	1 to 8 bytes	Stores zero or more of up to 64 specified string values in a list. Length is dependent on the number of values chosen.

Table 8-1 MySQL Data Types *(continued)*

NOTE

As you create a table in phpMyAdmin, you'll notice that the default collation sequence is `latin1_swedish_ci`. This results from its ancestry and is not really a problem, but if you would like to better reflect U.S. English, use `latin1_general_ci`. (This handles most western European languages. You can select either `ci`, meaning case insensitive, or `cs`, meaning case sensitive.) You can set this on a field-by-field basis or for an entire table by clicking the **Operations** tab while viewing a table, and, under Table Options, selecting `latin1_general_ci` for the collation, as shown next, and clicking **Go**. You can also set it at the database level through the **Operations** tab.

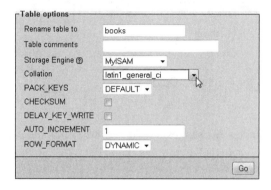

TIP

If a field's data type is `TIMESTAMP`, that field will automatically be filled with the current date and time when the record is created. You want to forbid a manual entry to be made in this field. If you want a field to both have an automatic date and time, and allow a manual entry, make its data type `DATETIME` and enter `NOW()` as the default, which provides the current date and time.

Add Records to Your Table

Now that you have a table in phpMyAdmin, add some records to it, and then you can query it:

1. If you left phpMyAdmin at the end of the last set of steps, restart XAMPP and phpMyAdmin, and reopen the Books database and the Books table, so the center body of your window looks like Figure 8-9.

2. Click **Insert**. Enter the information in Table 8-2. In all cases leave the Bkid field blank. It will be filled in automatically. Uncheck **Ignore** at the top of the second record. In the remaining five fields, enter under Value the following nine records, clicking **Go**, **Insert**, and unchecking **Ignore** again after every-other record:

3. After clicking **Go** the last time, you should be returned to the Structure tab of the Books table. Click the **Browse** tab to see the records you entered. They should look like Figure 8-10.

Title	Author	Publisher	Price	Category
Nightfall	Asimov	Bantam	5.99	Sci. Fic.
Patriot Games	Clancy	Berkley	4.95	Thriller
2010	Clarke	Ballantine	3.95	Sci. Fic.
Lie Down With Lions	Follett	Signet	4.95	Mystery
A Thief of Time	Hillerman	Harper	4.95	Mystery
The Fly on the Wall	Hillerman	Harper	4.95	Mystery
Hornet Flight	Follett	Signet	7.99	Thriller
The Innocent Man	Grisham	Dell	7.99	Thriller
Mission of Honor	Clancy	Berkley	7.99	Thriller

Table 8-2 Information for the Books Database

4. If you want to make any changes in your records, click the pencil icon on the left of the record. Make the needed changes, and then click **Go**. 🖉

CAUTION

❌ The red *X* icon deletes a record. Although you are given a warning, it is easy to click the *X* instead of the pencil icon, go whipping through the warning, and not realize what you have done until it is too late (there is no undelete). (Can you tell I've done that a couple of times?)

Query Your Table

Queries in phpMyAdmin are very similar to what you did in the command-line client, except that phpMyAdmin helps you write the script. Try that next.

1. From the Browse page (Figure 8-10) in phpMyAdmin, click the **SQL** tab. The Run SQL Query window will open with the query started, like this:

Run SQL query/queries on database books: ⑦

```
SELECT * FROM `books` WHERE 1
```

Fields
Bkid
Title
Author
Publisher
Price

Bookmark this SQL query:

☐ Let every user access this bookmark ☐ Replace existing bookmark of same name

[Delimiter ;] ☑ Show this query here again   Go

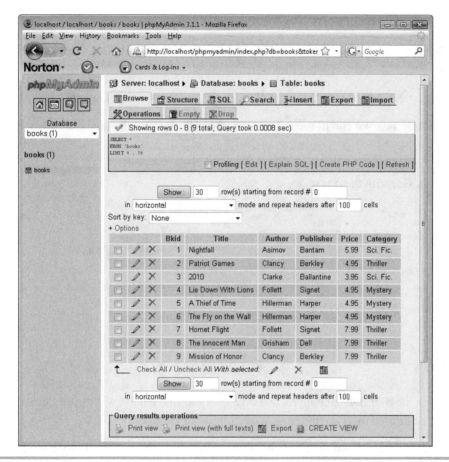

Figure 8-10   Browsing a table in phpMyAdmin lets you sort and review the records that have been entered.

2. Drag over the "1" on the right end of the query, and double-click **Price** in the Fields list.

3. Click at the right end of the query, type >5.00; and click **Go**. The results are shown next:

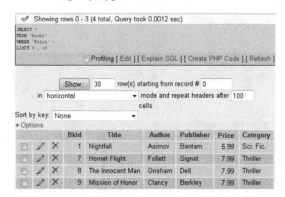

4. Click the **SQL** tab and do a query of only the Title and Author fields.

5. Drag over the asterisk, double-click **Title** in the Fields list, type a **,** (comma), and double-click **Author** in the Fields list.

6. Drag over the "1" on the right end of the query, and double-click **Category** in the Fields list.

7. Click at the right end of the query, type ="Thriller"; (note the double quotes), like this:

```
SELECT `Title`, `Author` FROM `books` WHERE
`Category` = "Thriller";
```

8. Click **Go**, with these results:

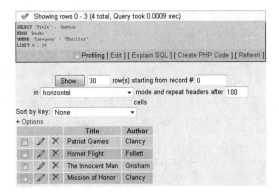

9. Click the **SQL** tab once more, and do a query to find a book where you know only part of the title. In this case the book with "Lions" in the title.

10. Drag over the "1" on the right end of the query, and double-click **Title** in the Fields list.

11. Click at the right end of the query, type LIKE "%Lions"; like this:

```
SELECT * FROM `books` WHERE `Title` LIKE "%Lions";
```

12. Click **Go** to get this book:

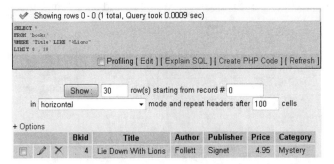

13. phpMyAdmin and your browser can be closed at this point.

Exploring PHP MySQL Functions

While phpMyAdmin is a good tool for setting up databases and tables, and for testing queries, to use MySQL in an Internet application, you need a programming language. One of the best, if not the best, for that purpose is PHP. Almost all web-hosting sites provide both PHP and MySQL, and you have XAMPP to test the pair on your computer without cost. Many millions of sites, both large and small, use PHP and MySQL. Using MySQL with PHP is straightforward and not difficult. It is an extension of what you have already learned about SQL and MySQL.

To use MySQL, PHP uses a set of functions that perform the SQL commands and much more through accessing the MySQL application programming interface (API). These functions can be split into three categories: database manipulation, database information, and database administration.

NOTE

Throughout this and the next chapter's discussion of the PHP MySQL functions, we will precede each function with `mysql`. There is also `mysqli`, which is the improved (i) version of `mysql` that came into being with PHP 5.0 and is for use with MySQL 4.1.3 and later. While many similarities exist between `mysql` and `mysqli`, and in many cases you can simply replace `mysql` with `mysqli`, `mysqli` is aimed at object-oriented programming, and some subtle differences between the two are beyond the scope of this book.

Database Manipulation

PHP's database manipulation functions for MySQL are the heavy lifters of the group, opening, closing, querying, and retrieving database contents, as shown in Table 8-3.

NOTE

As with the rest of the book, there are many more PHP MySQL functions than can be discussed here. For the full list, see http://www.php.net/mysql.

The process of using an existing MySQL database with PHP follows these steps:

- Connect to MySQL.
- Select a database.
- Perform a query.
- Process results.
- Release the results memory.
- Disconnect from MySQL.

Function	Description	Arguments and Comments
mysql_close	Disconnects from MySQL	Optionally the connection ID. mysql_close usually isn't needed.
mysql_connect	Connects to MySQL	Host server name, username, password. Returns the connection ID.
mysql_create_db	Creates a MySQL database	Name of db to be created. Optionally the connection ID.
mysql_drop_db	Deletes a MySQL database	Name of db to be deleted. Optionally the connection ID.
mysql_fetch_array	Gets a row as any type of array	Result of a query, type of array: MYSQL_ASSOC, MYSQL_NUM, or MYSQL_BOTH (the default).
mysql_fetch_assoc	Gets a row as an associative array	Result of a query. Field names are the indexes.
mysql_fetch_object	Gets one or more fields in a row	Result of a query. Optionally the class name and an array of parameters.
mysql_fetch_row	Gets a row as an enumerated array	Result of a query. Field numbers are the indexes, beginning with 0.
mysql_query	Queries a MySQL database	SQL query statement. Optionally the connection ID.
mysql_result	Gets contents of one field in one row	Result of a query, row number starting at 0, field name or offset.
mysql_select_db	Selects a MySQL database	Name of the database to be selected. Optionally the connection ID.

Table 8-3 Database Manipulation Functions

The last two steps are optional, but they are a good practice and become mandatory if you are working with multiple databases.

Connect to MySQL

Connecting to MySQL is really "logging into" a particular MySQL database server with a username and password. Like this:

```
$connection = mysql_connect("localhost", "root", "password");
```

This assumes you are using the default username root, which can be replaced by any username you have set up, and you replace *password* with the password you created earlier in this chapter under "Setting Privileges."

If mysql_connect is able to connect, the variable $connection contains the connection identifier that is automatically used by the other PHP MySQL functions. This connection remains open for as long as the script is running. When the script ends, the connection is deleted. If you open several connections, you need to specify the connection identifier in other PHP MySQL functions. If a connection is not made, then `$connection` contains `FALSE`. You can use this in three ways:

- `if` statement:

```
if ($connection = mysql_connect("localhost", "root", "password")){
   echo "Connected.";
   }
else {
   echo "Cannot Connect.";
   }
```

- Ternary operator

```
$connection = mysql_connect("localhost", "root", "password");
   echo $connection ? "Connected." : "Cannot Connect.";
```

- `or die` clause:

```
$connection = mysql_connect("localhost", "root", "password")
   or die ("Cannot Connect.");
   echo "Connected.";
```

Notice that the `or die` is a clause of `mysql_connect`, and there isn't a `;` (semicolon) until the end of the clause. Also, the `die()` function is very similar to `echo`.

TIP
When you move your database and web site from your computer (localhost) to some web host, you probably will have to change the `mysql_connect` host name, username, and password to fit that host.

Select a Database
Once you are connected to the MySQL server, you need to identify the database you want to use, which is a simple statement:

```
mysql_select_db("books");
```

If you have several connections, you can specify the one you want to use. If you use the connection you established immediately preceding, the statement would be

```
mysql_select_db("books", $connection);
```

If you want to return a message if the database is not available, use (you don't have to assign it a variable, but that may be useful)

```
$database = mysql_select_db("books", $connection)
   or die("Database Books not available.");
```

Perform a Query

The query is a MySQL select statement assigned to a PHP variable:

```
$query = "SELECT * FROM books WHERE price>5.00";
```

To perform the query, it needs to be in a query statement:

```
$result = mysql_query($query)
    or die("Couldn't do query.");
```

If needed, the server connection can be added as shown with mysql_select_db.

Process Results

Once you have done the query, you will want to do something with the data. The variable $result contains a resource that allows other PHP MySQL functions to get individual rows and fields in the database. These can be displayed or otherwise processed. There are several functions that can be used to get the information, depending on what you want to do with it. The two most commonly used functions are mysql_fetch_assoc($result), which gets an associative array with the field names as the indexes, and mysql_fetch_row($result), which gets an enumerated array with field numbers (beginning at zero) as the indexes.

```
while($row = mysql_fetch_assoc($result)) {
    echo $row['bkid']. "\t". $row['title']. "\t". $row['author'].
        "\t". $row['price']. "\n";
}

while($row = mysql_fetch_row($result)) {
    echo $row[0]. "\t". $row[1]. "\t". $row[2].
        "\t". $row[4]. "\n";
}
```

Notice that in the preceding two examples, only some of the fields are displayed (publisher and category have been left out) to simplify the example.

Complete the Query

To complete the query, you simply need to free the memory that is taken up with the result of the query, and then close the connection. Neither of these is mandatory; both tasks are also done when the script closes, but they are simple steps that are a good habit to get into so they won't be forgotten when they are needed. The two functions look like this:

```
mysql_free_result($result);

mysql_close($connection);
```

Put It Together

The composite of all of these functions to perform a MySQL database query is shown in Listing 8-2, the result of which looks like this:

Listing 8-2   Query of Books database

```
<!DOCTYPE html PUBLIC "-//W3C//DTD XHTML 1.0 Strict//EN">
<html>
   <head>
      <title>Listing 8-2</title>
   </head>
   <body>
      <h1>Query the Books Database</h1>
      <h3>List books priced above $5.00</h3>
      <?php
       //Connect to the database Books
      $connection = mysql_connect("localhost", "root", "password")
         or die("Cannot connect.");
      mysql_select_db("books")
         or die("Database Books not available.");
      //Select books > $5.00
      $query = "SELECT * FROM books WHERE price>5.00;";
      $result = mysql_query($query)
         or die("Couldn't do query.");
      //Display the books selected
      while($row = mysql_fetch_row($result)) {
         echo $row[0]. " - ". $row[1]. " - ". $row[2]. " - $".
            $row[4]. "<br />";
      }
      //Free memory and close the database
      mysql_free_result($result);
      mysql_close($connection);
      ?>
   </body>
</html>
```

Database Information

As you use a MySQL database with PHP, you will need or want information about the database and its tables, rows, and fields. PHP has a number of functions for this purpose, many of which are shown in Table 8-4.

TIP

Database information functions are particularly useful to debug a script; find out what is happening in your database; find what table, row, and field you are accessing; or to find what error messages you are receiving.

Function	Description	Arguments and Comments
`mysql_affected_rows`	Gets number of rows affected by previous operation	Optionally the connection ID
`mysql_client_encoding`	Gets name of character set	Optionally the connection ID
`mysql_db_name`	Gets name of the database	Pointer from `mysql_list_dbs`, row number, and optionally the field name
`mysql_error`	Returns the error message from the previous operation	Optionally the connection ID
`mysql_fetch_lengths`	Returns an array of field lengths in the last row retrieved.	Result pointer from a query

`mysql_field_len`
`mysql_field_name`
`mysql_field_table`
`mysql_field_type`
	Returns the length, name, table name, or type of a specified field	Result pointer from the last query and the field number (beginning at 0)

`mysql_get_client_info`
`mysql_get_host_info`
`mysql_get_server_info`
	Returns the client version, the type of host connection, or the MySQL server version	Optionally the connection ID

`mysql_info`	Returns detailed information about the last query	Optionally the connection ID
`mysql_insert_id`	Gets the ID or key generated by `AUTO_INCREMENT`	Optionally the connection ID
`mysql_list_dbs`	Returns a resource get a list of databases	Optionally the connection ID
`mysql_num_fields` `mysql_num_rows`	Gets the number of fields or rows in the last query	Result pointer from the last query
`mysql_stat`	Gets the current server status	Optionally the connection ID

Table 8-4 Database Information Functions

How you use the database information functions depends on what you want to do. Here are some examples:

- `mysql_affected_rows`, which gets the number of rows affected by the last `INSERT`, `UPDATE`, `REPLACE`, or `DELETE` SQL query, provides this information to use with control functions to iterate through a set of rows. It is for types of queries other than `SELECT` or `SHOW`, which get the same information from `mysql_num_rows`.

- `mysql_error`, which returns the textual error message from the most recent MySQL operation, can be displayed with an `or die()` function or an `echo` statement.

- `mysql_field_type`, which returns the type of field such as `int`, `real`, and `string` can be use in formatting and in the determination of further processing.

- `mysql_insert_id`, which returns the ID or key that was automatically created through `AUTO_INCREMENT` by the last `INSERT` query, is used to reference the record that was just created.

- `mysql_num_rows`, which gets the number of rows affected by the last `SELECT` or `SHOW` SQL query, provides this information to use with control functions to iterate through a set of rows. It is for types of queries other than `INSERT`, `UPDATE`, `REPLACE`, or `DELETE`, which get the same information from `mysql_affected_rows`.

Database Administration

The database administration functions perform several maintenance duties on a database. Several of these functions are shown in Table 8-5.

Function	Description	Arguments and Comments
mysql_data_seek	Moves the row pointer to specified row	Result pointer from the last query and the new row number (beginning at 0).
mysql_field_seek	Sets the result pointer to specified field number	Result pointer from the last query and the new field number (beginning at 0).
mysql_free_result	Frees the memory used by the last query	Result pointer from the last query.
mysql_ping	Checks if a MySQL server connection exists, and if not, reconnects	Optionally the connection ID.
mysql_real_escape_string	Prepares special characters in a string for use in SQL	String to be escaped. Optionally the connection ID.
mysql_set_charset	Sets the character set	Character set name. Optionally the connection ID.

Table 8-5 Database Administration Functions

Examples of how several of the database administration functions might be used are

- `mysql_data_seek`, which moves the MySQL row pointer to a specific row, can be used with `mysql_fetch_row` to get a specific row.

- `mysql_ping`, which checks to see if a script is still connected to a MySQL server, and reconnects it if it isn't, can be used after a lengthy idle period to possibly reestablish a connection.

- `mysql_real_escape_string`, which prepares ("escapes") the special characters in a string so they will not cause an error when included in a SQL statement, should be used with any string that is sent to MySQL that could possibly contain special characters.

NOTE
`mysql_real_escape_string` replaces `mysql_escape_string`, which is deprecated and will provided a warning notice if it is used. `mysql_real_escape_string` takes into account the particular character set being used and can be specific to a particular connection.

Combining PHP MySQL Functions

Listing 8-3 combines a number of the PHP MySQL functions by retuning to the Books database used earlier, having the user enter part of a title, and searching for and displaying the full book information. Among the other features are

- Use a form that returns to the PHP in the same script.
- Pause on the form until Submit is clicked.
- Strip the title that is entered of any white space, and make sure it is not blank.
- Escape special characters with `mysql_real_escape_string`.
- Display the error text on a query error with `mysql_error`.
- Display the book that is found using an associative array.

The output of this script is displayed in Figure 8-11.

Listing 8-3   Combining PHP MySQL functions

```
<!DOCTYPE html PUBLIC "-//W3C//DTD XHTML 1.0 Strict//EN">
<html>
   <head>
     <title>Listing 8-3</title>
   </head>
```

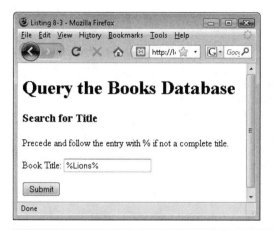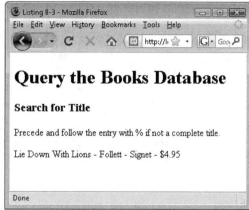

Figure 8-11 The query form disappears when the results are displayed.

```
<body>
    <h1>Query the Books Database</h1>
    <h3>Search for Title</h3>
    <p>Precede and follow the entry with % if not a complete title.</p>
    <?php

    //Wait for submit
    if (!$_POST['submit']) {

    //Enter search information
    ?>
        <form action="<?=$_SERVER['PHP_SELF']?>" method="post">
            <p>Book Title: <input type="text" name="title" /></p>
            <p><input type="submit" name="submit" value="Submit" /></p>
        </form>
    <?php
    }
    else {

    //Remove white space, check for blanks, and escape special characters
        $title =  (trim($_POST['title']) == '') ?
            die ("Please enter a title.")
            : mysql_real_escape_string($_POST['title']);

    //Connect to the Book database
        $connection = mysql_connect("localhost", "root", "password")
            or die("Cannot connect.");
        mysql_select_db("books")
            or die("Database Books not available.");
```

```
    //Select book with partial title
        $query = "SELECT * FROM books WHERE Title LIKE '$title'";
        $result = mysql_query($query)
            or die("Error in query: ". mysql_error());

    //Display book with associative array
        while($row = mysql_fetch_assoc($result)) {
            echo $row['Title']. " - ". $row['Author']. " - ".
                $row['Publisher']. " - $". $row['Price']. "<br />";
        }
        mysql_free_result($result);
        mysql_close($connection);
    }
    ?>
</body>
</html>
```

In the following chapter, you'll see a number of additional ways of combining PHP and MySQL with HTML, CSS, and JavaScript to create a comprehensive class registration and payment system.

In addition to the PHP and MySQL online manuals, an excellent book on MySQL is *MySQL: The Complete Reference*, by Vikram Vaswani, published by McGraw-Hill/Professional, 2004. Also, as mentioned in Chapter 6, Vikram Vaswani has a great book on PHP and MySQL, published by McGraw-Hill/Professional.

Chapter 9
Putting It All Together

Key Skills & Concepts

- Design a Template
- Create a CSS
- Design a Database
- Create a Script for Authentication
- Authenticate Individual Pages
- Create a Script for Database Entry
- Create a Script for Database Update
- Create a Script for Database Deletion
- Create a Script for Database Selection
- Create a Script for Database Listing

This chapter combines many of the elements described in the first eight chapters of this book into a single application that will demonstrate how they fit together. X/HTML will of course be the foundation holding all the rest. A CSS style sheet will be used for the common styles used throughout the application. A template will be used to provide a common layout. JavaScript is used for both event handling as well as form validation. PHP will be used both for its own services and to access the MySQL databases, and MySQL will host the database tables.

In this chapter, we'll look at the design of an application, the creation of a template for the page layout, the building of a CSS file, and the initial construction of the database tables in phpMyAdmin. We'll finally go into depth on the construction of the various JavaScript, PHP, and MySQL elements of the needed scripts.

"Go into depth" is meant very literally. This chapter offers a total of 25 scripts, plus the template and the CSS. In the process, records from the several MySQL tables are written, read, selected, updated, and deleted. Multiple tables (three of them) are accessed together to utilize a relational database, and data is passed among scripts in several ways, including sending several pieces at the same time.

In summary, this chapter provides a comprehensive example of how to fully utilize X/HTML, CSS, JavaScript, PHP, and MySQL to build a significant, data-driven web site.

TIP

Remember that all the scripts in this chapter, as in the rest of the book, are available online. See the book's Introduction for details.

Application Design

In this chapter, we'll build an application for students to select and register for classes. It is based on four database tables and five components of the application as shown schematically in Figure 9-1. The components are

- Administrator Authentication

- Database Entry and Maintenance

- Class List and Selection

- Student Entry and Update

- Registration and Confirmation

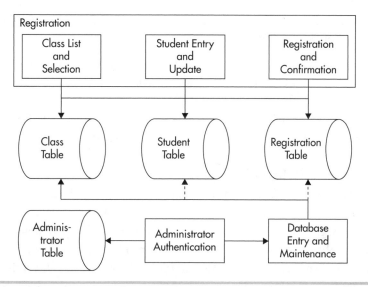

Figure 9-1   The Class Selection and Registration Application uses a relational database with five components.

These components can be grouped into Authentication, Maintenance, and Registration (where Registration contains the last three components: Class List and Selection, Student Entry and Update, and Registration and Confirmation).

Each of the components has one or more scripts and interacts with one or more tables. The Administrator Authentication component is the User Authentication application we built in Chapter 7, updated to use MySQL in place of PHP direct disk access.

TIP

While an application like this may look daunting, it was built with a lot of copying, cutting, and pasting. Many of the scripts are very similar, with only changes in the names. And you have the scripts from this book available to you online as starting points.

The functioning of the application will follow these steps:

- A student would go online, see a list of classes, and then select a class for which they want to register.

- To register for the selected class, the student would first enter his or her e-mail address. If the script finds the e-mail address in the database, the student's name and address information would be presented for the student to update. If the e-mail address is not found, the student is asked to enter his or her information.

- With the selected class information and the student's information, a registration record is built and presented to the student to confirm.

- Administrators of this system would sign on and be authenticated. With that, they can then update and maintain all of the database tables.

A major feature of this application is the passing of multiple pieces of information among the scripts by use of cookies, session variables, and as a part of the URL.

Design Template and CSS

Since you will have a number of separate web pages in this application, you want them to have a consistent look. The best way to do that is to have a template that you use to build every page. This is very easy to do with Aptana; for the period while you are building the application, simply replace the standard PHP template with the template for the application. That way each time you call for a new page, you will get the application template. You'll see how to do this in a moment.

You also want a single CSS for use throughout the application. The easiest way to do that is to build the CSS up front and attach it to the template. It will then be called in each page built with the template.

TIP

It is not easy to think through an application and decide up front how the template should look and what the styles should be in the CSS. It is easier to just start out writing the scripts and see what develops. The problem is that you will likely not get the consistent look you want, and you will probably end up going back and changing something on earlier pages. It is worth the investment to build and use these tools first and try to stay with them.

Design a Template

To create a template, the first step is to sketch out on paper what various sections of your standard web page will contain, and then how each section is sized and formatted. A common layout for a page, which will be used in this exercise and is shown in Figure 9-2, has

- A heading or banner at the top with the logo and general information

- A horizontal navigation or menu bar beneath the heading for the applicationwide options

- A vertical navigation or menu bar down the left side for local options

- One or two columns of page-specific content in the middle-right

- A footer at the bottom with copyright and contact information and possibly broad navigation options

After deciding what content will go where, the next step is to decide the size of the overall page and the individual sections. The old rule of 800×600 to fit that common size was good five to ten years ago, but today almost no screens are that small, and most screens use 1280×1024 or 1280×800. Therefore if you use 1024×768, which we will use as the overall page size, you have a safety margin. The size of the individual sections very much depends on their content. For this exercise we'll use

- **Heading**   1000 pixels wide × 100 pixels high

- **Horizontal navigation bar**   1000 pixels wide × 60 pixels high

- **Vertical navigation bar**   150 pixels wide × 500 pixels high

- **Main content**   830 pixels wide × 500 pixels high

- **Footer**   1000 pixels wide × 60 pixels high

The sections will be created using divs, floating the left and right columns in the middle to the left and right, and placing the footer at the bottom. The headings and titles

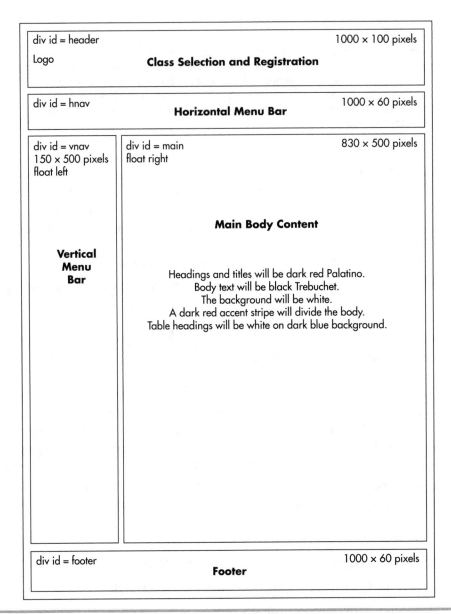

Figure 9-2 The template for the Class Selection and Registration Application

will use the Palatino font, and the body text will use Trebuchet. Both of these translate well to the Mac (Trebuchet is Helvetica on the Mac). We'll use a white background with a dark red accent stripe and dark red headings. The body text will be black, and the headings in the tables will be white on a dark blue background.

Create the Template

The template itself is just a script that is used as the starting point for all other pages. You therefore want the template to have all of the standard features you want on all pages. This starts out with the `<div>` elements that divide the page. In addition to the five `<div>` elements shown in Figure 9-2, we add one called "wrapper" that is an overall `<div>` that contains the others, but is separate from the `<body>`.

TIP

When you initially enter your `<div>` elements, enter a comment with the ID name in the ending element so that you can distinguish it from the others, like this:

```
<body>
    <div id="wrapper">
        <div id="header">

        </div> <!-- id="header" -->
        <div id="hnav">

        </div> <!-- id="hnav" -->
        <div id="vnav">

        </div> <!-- id="vnav" -->
        <div id="main">

        </div> <!-- id="main" -->
        <div id="footer">

        </div> <!-- id="footer" -->
    </div> <!-- id="wrapper" -->
```

With the `<div>` elements in place, next enter all the common elements that will appear on all pages, such as logos, titling, menus, and common footer information. This example keeps it simple, as shown in Listing 9-1 and Figure 9-3 (without formatting):

- A logo and a title in the heading
- A four-option menu in the horizontal navigation bar
- A heading and a two-option menu in the vertical navigation bar
- A heading, a paragraph, and a footnote in the main content section
- Copyright and contact notices in the footer

For the most part, everything in the template is relatively straightforward, reflecting work we have done elsewhere in this book. Two minor exceptions are the automatically updating copyright date using the PHP `date()` function and the `mailto` X/HTML construct.

The PHP `date()` function is discussed in Chapter 6, but the `date_default_timezone_set()` function was not discussed. PHP version 5.1.0 and later check to see if a valid time zone has been set and will issue a warning if it hasn't. Most Internet hosting services set this default, so if you want to use your host's time zone, you're okay.

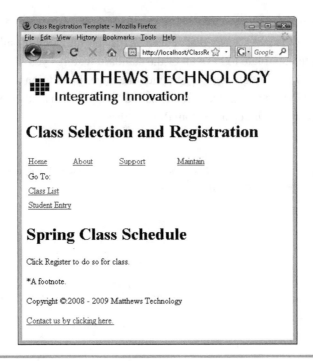

Figure 9-3 The unformatted template content

It is a good idea to set your own time zone in each script (once per script is adequate). You can find a list of supported time zone constants at http://us.php.net/manual/en/ timezones.php (not every major city is included; you must look for other cities in your time zone).

The `mailto` X/HTML construct combines with an e-mail address to open the default e-mail message client and to create a URL for sending a message to the stated e-mail address, like this:

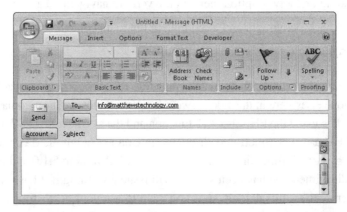

The other item whose absence you might notice is that although we said there would be accent stripes on the page, there are no <hr> elements (horizontal rules or lines) in the template. This is because Firefox does not handle the formatting (setting a height and color) of <hr> elements well, and we can accomplish the same thing with single-sided borders in the CSS.

Listing 9-1   Site template

```php
<?php
//
        ;
?>
<!DOCTYPE html PUBLIC "-//W3C//DTD XHTML 1.0 Strict//EN">
<html>
    <head>
        <title>Class Registration Template</title>
        <link rel= "stylesheet" type= "text/css"
            href= "/ClassRegistration/registration.css"/>
        <script language="JavaScript" type="text/javascript'></script>

    </head>

    <body>
        <div id="wrapper">
            <div id="header">
                <img src="/ClassRegistration/MatTechLogo.gif"
                    alt="Matthews Technology" />
                <h1 id="title">Class Selection and Registration</h1>

            </div> <!-- id="header" -->
            <div id="hnav">
                <table width="400" border="0" cellspacing="2" cellpadding="2">
                    <tr>
                        <td><a class="hmenu" href="index.php">Home</a> </td>
                        <td><a class="hmenu" href="about.php">About</a> </td>
                        <td><a class="hmenu" href="support.php">Support</a> </td>
                        <td><a class="hmenu" href="maintain.php">Maintain</a> </td>
                    </tr>
                </table>

            </div> <!-- id="hnav" -->
            <div id="vnav">
                <table width="120" border="0" cellspacing="2" cellpadding="2">
                    <tr>
                        <th class="vhead">Go To: </th>
                    </tr>
                    <tr>
                        <td><a class="vmenu" href="classlist.php">Class
                            List</a></td>
                    </tr>
```

```
        <tr>
            <td><a class="vmenu" href="nameentry.php">Student
                Entry</a></td>
        </tr>
        </table>

    </div> <!-- id="vnav" -->
    <div id="main">
        <h1 id="mainhead">Spring Class Schedule</h1>
        <p id="mainpara">Click Register to do so for class.</p>
        <p class="red">*A footnote.</p>

    </div> <!-- id="main" -->
    <div id="footer">
        <p id="copyright">
            Copyright &copy:2008 -
            <?php
                date_default_timezone_set('America/Vancouver');
                echo date('Y');
            ?>
            Matthews Technology
        </p>
        <p id="contact">
            <a href="mailto:info@matthewstechnology.com">
                Contact us by clicking here.</a>
        </p>
    </div> <!-- id="footer" -->
</div> <!-- id="wrapper" -->

<?php
    ;
?>
</body>
</html>
```

NOTE
While a template is a good idea for preparing a starting place for each page, you can't change the template and have the page it created automatically change. You can do that with the PHP `include()`, `include_once()`, `require()`, and `require_once()` functions as discussed in Chapter 7.

Create a CSS

The CSS for the Class Selection and Registration Application takes up where we left off CSS in Chapter 2's Listing 2-12, creating the final product shown in Listing 9-2. The effect that this CSS has on the template is pronounced, as you can see in Figure 9-4 (unfortunately, you can't see the color here, but it improves the visual appeal).

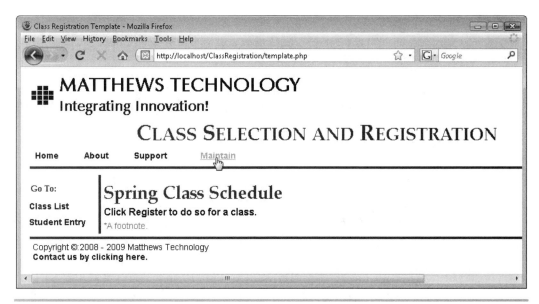

Figure 9-4   The CSS makes major changes in the appearance of the template.

The Registration CSS, for the most part, reflects the work that was done in Chapter 2 and shown in Listing 2-12. The major exceptions are the selectors for the `<a>` tag, the links used in the horizontal and vertical navigation bars. The CSS provides formatting for four states of the `<a>` tag with these selectors:

- `a:link` represents the link before it has been clicked, selected, or pointed at.
- `a:visited` represents the link after it has been clicked and the associated code has been executed.
- `a:focus` represents the link as it has been selected but not executed with the keyboard.
- `a:hover` represents the link as it is being pointed at by the mouse.

The `:link`, `:visited`, `:focus`, and `:hover` are called *pseudo-classes,* which allow you to format specific states. Actually, another `:active` is the tag as it is being clicked and the associated code executed, something that generally happens rather rapidly. The `:link` pseudo-class is the same as the tag by itself (just a), but just a also covers named anchors to bookmarks or named areas on the current page, so `:link` is preferable.

When using the link pseudo-classes, it is important to put them in the order `:link`, `:visited`, `:focus`, `:hover`, and `:active`; because of the cascading of the style sheet, the last element takes precedence, so if `:link` is last, `:hover` would not appear.

NOTE

a:focus does not work with IE 6 and IE 7, but it does work with IE 8, Firefox, and Safari, as well as Google Chrome.

Listing 9-2	Registration CSS

```css
/* registration.css */

body        {
                width : 1000px;
                margin : 0;
                padding : 0;
            }

div, h1, h2, p   {
                margin : 0;
                padding : 0;
            }

h2          {
                color : #8b0000;
                font : 600 24px "Palatino Linotype" ;
            }

P, textarea    { font : 14px "Trebuchet", "Helvetica", sans-serif ; }

.red        { color : red; }

a:link      {
                color : #00008b;
                font : 600 14px "Trebuchet", "Helvetica", sans-serif;
                text-decoration : none;
            }

a:visited   {
                color : #00ffff;
                font : 600 14px "Trebuchet", "Helvetica", sans-serif;
                text-decoration : none;
            }

a:focus     {
                color : #daa520;
                font : 600 14px "Trebuchet", "Helvetica", sans-serif;
                text-decoration : underline;
            }
```

```css
a:hover   {
        color : #daa520;
        font : 600 14px "Trebuchet", "Helvetica", sans-serif;
        text-decoration : underline;
    }

th        {
        margin : 5px;
        padding : 5px;
        text-align : right;
        color : #ffffff;
        font : 600 14px "Trebuchet", "Helvetica", sans-serif;
        background : #00008b;
    }

div#header   {
        top : 0px;
        left : 0px;
        height : 100px;
        margin : 5px;
        padding : 5px;
    }

h1#title  {
        color : #8b0000;
        font : small-caps 600 36px /1.0em "Palatino Linotype" ;
        text-align : center;
        vertical-align : top;
        padding-bottom : 10px;
    }

div#hnav  {
        margin : 5px;
        margin-left : 15px;
        padding : 5px;
        padding-top : 10px;
        border-bottom : 4px solid #8b0000;
    }

div#vnav  {
        float : left;
        width : 100px;
        margin : 5px;
        padding : 5px;
    }
```

```
#vhead    {
              color : #8b0000;
              font : 700 14px "Palatino Linotype" ;
              margin : 5px;
              padding : 5px;
          }

div#main  {
              float : right;
              width : 850px;
              margin : 5px;
              padding : 5px;
              border-left : 4px solid #8b0000;
          }

h1#maintitle  {
              color : #8b0000;
              font : 600 30px /1.5em "Palatino Linotype" ;
              text-align : left;
              vertical-align : top;
          }

div#footer  {
              clear: both ;
              margin : 5px;
              margin-left : 15px;
              padding : 5px;
              border-top : 4px solid #8b0000;
          }
```

Database Design

As mentioned earlier and shown in Figure 9-1, four tables are in the Class Registration database:

- **Class**, a list of available classes
- **Student**, a list of students
- **Registration**, a list of students registered for a particular class
- **Administrator**, a list of administrators allowed to edit the database

Three of the tables—Class, Student, and Registration—form a relational database with the Class ID and Student Email being foreign keys used in the Registration table. This allows the storing of only the keys in the Registration table and yet having available all of the information in the Class and Student tables while looking at a registration.

The tables will be built in phpMyAdmin to quickly get them online. Use these steps to do that:

1. Start XAMPP and click **Start** opposite both Apache and MySQL.

2. Start a browser and in the address bar, type <u>localhost/xampp</u>, and press ENTER.

3. Click **phpMyAdmin**. Under Create New Database, type <u>ClassRegistration</u>, click the down-arrow in the Collation drop-down list, click **latin1_general_ci**, and click **Create**.

4. Under Create New Table, type <u>class</u>, press TAB, type <u>6</u> for the number of fields, and click **Go**.

5. In the form that is presented, type in the information shown in Table 9-1. (*AI* stands for Auto Increment, which is a check box you must tab to the right to see, and is used when a key is automatically created by MySQL.)

6. Click **Save**. The Class table will be created as shown in Figure 9-5. Note that `class-id` was automatically established as the primary key.

7. Click **ClassRegistration** in the left column. Under Create New Table, type <u>student</u>, press TAB, type <u>4</u> for the number of fields, and click **Go**.

Field	Type	Length	Other
class_id	SMALLINT		AI
class_title	VARCHAR	60	
class_start	DATE		
class_descr	VARCHAR	255	
class_cost	DECIMAL	6,2	
class_instr	VARCHAR	20	

Table 9-1 Class Table

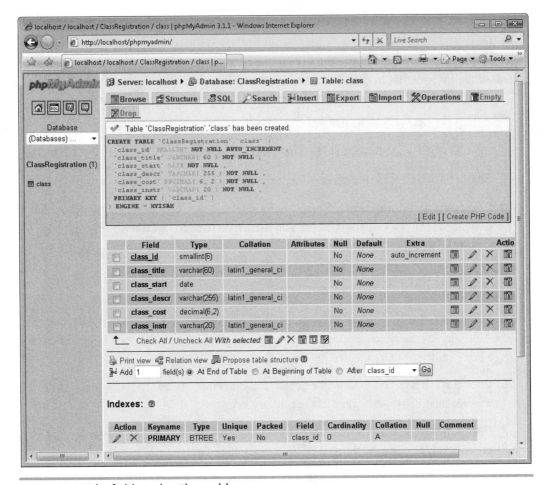

Figure 9-5 The fields in the Class table

8. In the form that is presented, type in the information shown in Table 9-2. (The Primary Key is selected in the Index drop-down list. The Current Timestamp is selected in the Default drop-down list. Null is the check box of that name. It means that the field can be left blank. **TAB** to the right to see all of these.)

Field	Type	Length	Other
student_email	VARCHAR	60	Primary Key
student_name	VARCHAR	60	
student_phone	VARCHAR	30	
student_date	TIMESTAMP		Current Timestamp

Table 9-2 Student Table

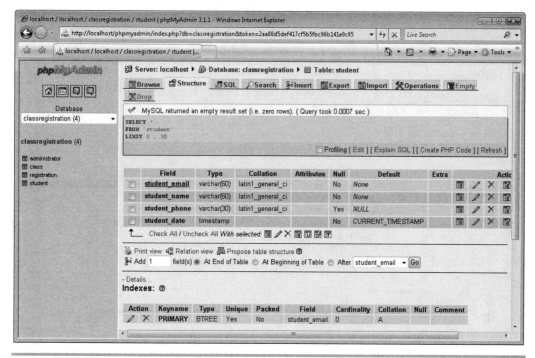

Figure 9-6   The fields in the Student table

9. Click **Save**. The Student table will be created as shown in Figure 9-6.

10. Click **ClassRegistration** in the left column. Under Create New Table, type <u>registration</u>, press TAB, type <u>4</u> for the number of fields, and click **Go**.

11. In the form that is presented, type in the information shown in Table 9-3.

12. Click **Save**. The Registration table will be created as shown in Figure 9-7.

Field	Type	Length	Other
reg_id	SMALLINT		AI
class_id	SMALLINT		
student_email	VARCHAR	60	
reg_date	TIMESTAMP		Current Timestamp

Table 9-3   Registration Table

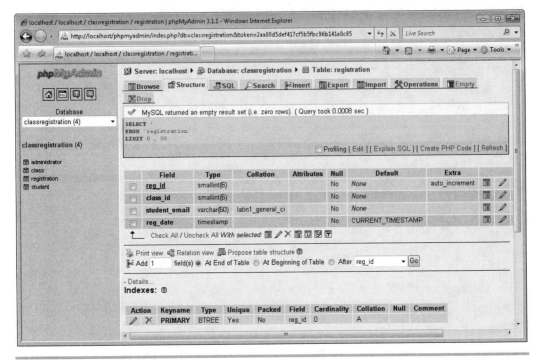

Figure 9-7 The fields in the Registration table

13. Click **ClassRegistration** in the left column. Under Create New Table, type <u>administrator</u>, press TAB, type <u>4</u> for the number of fields, and click **Go**.

14. In the form that is presented, type in the information shown in Table 9-4.

15. Click **Save**. The Administrator table will be created as shown in Figure 9-8.

Field	Type	Length	Other
admin_id	VARCHAR	20	Primary Key
admin_password	VARCHAR	100	
admin_name	VARCHAR	60	
admin_date	TIMESTAMP		Current Timestamp

Table 9-4 Administrator Table

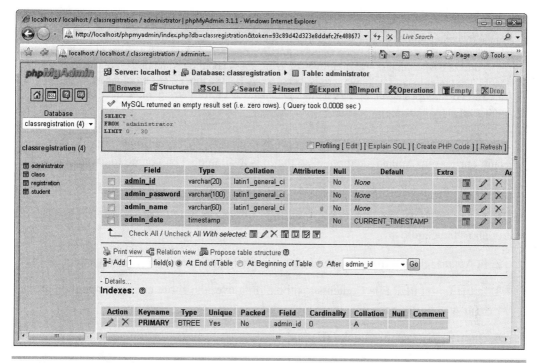

Figure 9-8   The fields in the Administrator table

Creating the Scripts

As you saw in Figure 9-1, the Class Selection and Registration Application has five components:

- Administrator Authentication
- Database Entry and Maintenance
- Class List and Selection
- Student Entry and Update
- Registration and Confirmation

Each of these components will have one or more scripts and interact with one or more of the database tables. We will address them in the order shown in the preceding list, primarily because we need a method to enter classes into the database. (The class entry could be done in phpMyAdmin, but we need an online way to do this for a complete system.)

NOTE

In the following scripts, as was true with User Authentication, often a given function is handled with a pair of scripts, one with the X/HTML and possibly a small amount of PHP, and another with just PHP and MySQL. While these could be combined on a single script, we prefer to do it with two scripts, because we believe that it's easier to debug, it keeps each script simpler, and it's a more intuitive way of transferring information to and from the PHP portion.

Before we start building the various components, copy the template.php file that you built earlier into Aptana's template, so that it is available when you go to create a new PHP script. Use these steps:

1. In Aptana, if needed, open **template.php**; press CTRL-A and CTRL-C to select and copy it all to the Clipboard.

2. In Aptana, click **Window | Preferences**. In the left column, open **Aptana** and click **PHP**.

3. In the Initial PHP File Contents text box, drag over the entire contents, and then press CTRL-V to paste in the new template.

4. Click **Apply** and then click **OK**.

Administrator Authentication

Administrator Authentication is the User Authentication application that was built in Chapter 7, except that we are now going to use MySQL and the Administrator table in place of the PHP direct disk access. As you saw in the flowchart in Figure 7-5, the User Authentication application has six scripts:

- Index.php (adminAuthen.php in Class Registration) checks if a cookie is on the user's computer.

- Registration Page (register.php) provides for the entry of a new administrator.

- Enter Name Page (enterName.php) encrypts the password and writes the record to the table.

- Sign-In Page (signin.php) provides for the entry of a user ID and password.

- Verify Page (verify.php) checks to see if the user ID and password are on the table.

- Each Page (enterSite.php) (the other pages in the application) checks if a session variable is present.

These will mostly be used as they were written in Chapter 7. Begin with these steps to create the necessary project and folder in Aptana, and then import the User Authentication scripts into it.

1. In Aptana, click **Project** in the left column. Right-click in the listing below Project and click **New | Project**.

2. Under Aptana Projects, click **PHP Project** and click **Next**. Enter <u>ClassRegistration</u> as the project name, and click **Finish**.

3. In the Project list, right-click **ClassRegistration** and click **Folder**. Type <u>Administrator Authentication</u> as the folder name, and click **Finish**.

4. Right-click **AdministratorAuthentication** and click **Import**. Accept the default File System and click **Next**.

5. Click **Browse**, locate the UserAuthentication folder from Chapter 7 (it should be in c:\xampp\hdocs), click each of the six scripts just listed, as shown in Figure 9-9, and click **Finish**.

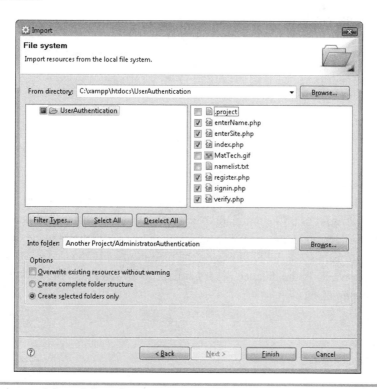

Figure 9-9 The work you did in Chapter 7 User Authentication can be imported into the Class Registration system.

6. Right-click **index.php** within the AdministratorAuthentication folder and click **Rename**. Select just the word "index," type <u>adminAuthen</u>, and press **ENTER**. We'll leave the other script names unchanged.

You can now modify each of the scripts.

Change adminAuthen.php

In adminAuthen.php, we only need to replace the cookie name `MatTech` with `Admin`. The resulting script should look like Listing 9-3.

Listing 9-3   adminAuthen.php

```php
<?php
    session_start();
    //Check if user has a cookie.
    if (isset ($_COOKIE["Admin"])) {
       //If so, set session and go to sign in.
       $_SESSION["name"] = $_COOKIE["Admin"] [name];
       $_SESSION["retry"] = 0;
       $_SESSION["time"] = time();
       header( "Location: signin.php");
       }
    else {
       //If not, go to registration.
       header( "Location: register.php");
       }
?>
```

Change register.php

In register.php, we need to embed the User Authentication `<div id= "form">` in the `<div id= "main">` of the template. Also, the vertical navigation bar needs to be turned into a placeholder, and a number of other small changes need to be made, many of which are shown in Listing 9-4. To cut down on the repetition, only the `<div id= "main">` section is shown here; the balance is very similar to the template. Figure 9-10 shows how registration.php displays.

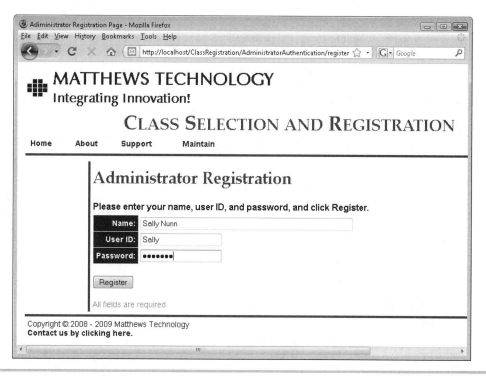

Figure 9-10 Entry of a new administrator

Listing 9-4 register.php (in part)

```
<div id="main">
   <h1 id="maintitle">Administrator Registration</h1>
   <br />
   <p id="mainpara">Please enter your name, user ID, and
      password, and click Register.</p>
   <!-- From User Authentication -->
   <div id="form">
      <!-- Go to enterName.php after clicking Register -->
      <form action="enterName.php" method="post"
         name="form1">
         <table width="300" border="0" cellspacing="1"
            cellpadding="3" >
            <tr>
               <th width="30%">Name:</th>
               <td width="50%">
                  <input type="text" name="admin_name"
                     value="" size="60" />
               </td>
            </tr>
```

```
        <tr>
           <th>User ID:</th>
           <td>
              <input type="text" name="admin_id"
                 value="" size="20" />
           </td>
        </tr>
        <tr>
           <th>Password:</th>
           <td>
              <input type="password" name="admin_password"
                 value="" size="20" />
           </td>
        </tr>
     </table>
     <br />
     <input type="submit" name="submit" value="Register" />
   </form>
  </div> <!-- id=form -->
  <!-- End User Authentication -->
  <br />
  <p class="red">All fields are required.</p>
</div> <!-- id="main" -->
```

enterName.php

While this script bears some resemblance to the User Authentication script of the same name, a lot has changed so that it could use MySQL in place of PHP direct disk access. The major parts of the script, which is shown in Listing 9-5, are

- Getting the three fields from the registration form (`admin_name`, `admin_id`, and `admin_password`), removing any white space, checking for a blank entry, removing special characters, and then assigning the results to new variables.

- Creating and setting a cookie on the user's computer with the person's name, the current date, and an expiration date 180 days in the future.

- Encrypting the password.

- Connecting to a MySQL server and selecting the ClassRegistration database.

- Checking to see if the combination of the user ID and encrypted password are already on file.

- If the user ID and password are not on the file, add a record to the administrator table so that the contents of $userid go into the `admin_id` field, $encryptpasswd goes into `admin_password`, and $name goes into `admin_name`.

- When the record has been successfully written, the adminAuthen script is reloaded. Since there is now a cookie on the user's computer, she or he is transferred to the signin.php script.

- If the user ID and password are on the file, the user has in essence "signed in," so the script writes a set of `$_SESSION` variables and leaves the authentication area.

NOTE

Remember that in Chapter 8 we recommended setting a password for the MySQL database. The scripts in this chapter support that and show "*password*" where you need to enter your own password (the word "password" is *not* a good choice for a password).

Listing 9-5   enterName.php

```php
<?php
//Remove white space, check for blanks, and remove special characters
    $name = (trim($_POST['admin_name']) == '') ?
        die ("Please enter your name.")
      : mysql_real_escape_string($_POST['admin_name']);

    $userid = (trim($_POST['admin_id']) == '') ?
        die ("Please enter a user ID.")
      : mysql_real_escape_string($_POST['admin_id']);

    $userPasswd = (trim($_POST['admin_password']) == '') ?
        die ("Please enter a password.")
      : mysql_real_escape_string($_POST['admin_password']);

//Set cookie, expires in 180 days.
    $date = time() ;
    $expire = time()+(60*60*24*180);
    setcookie("Admin[name]", $name, $expire, "/");
    setcookie("Admin[date]", $date, $expire, "/");

//Encrypt the password.
    $encryptpasswd = sha1($userPasswd);

//Connect to the ClassRegistration database
    $connection = mysql_connect("localhost", "root", "password")
       or die("Cannot connect to MySQL.");
    mysql_select_db("classregistration")
       or die("Database ClassRegistration not available.");
```

```php
//See if match in the administrator table
    $query = "SELECT admin_id, admin_password, admin_name
            FROM administrator
            WHERE admin_id= '$userid' AND admin_password= '$encryptpasswd'";
    $result = mysql_query($query)
        or die("Select from administrator failed. " . mysql_error());

//Determine if the user ID and password are on file.
    $row = mysql_fetch_object($result);
    $db_userid = $row->admin_id;
    $db_password = $row->admin_password;
    $name = $row->admin_name;

    if($db_userid != $userid || $db_password != $encryptpasswd){

        //If not on file, add record to the administrator table
        $query = "INSERT INTO administrator(admin_id, admin_password, admin_name)
            VALUES('$userid', '$encryptpasswd', '$name')";
        $result = mysql_query($query)
            or die("Insert to administrator failed. " . mysql_error());

        //Return to adminAuthen.php.
        header( "Location: adminAuthen.php");
    }
    else {
        //If on file, set the session variable, and enter site.
        $_SESSION["name"] = $name;
        $_SESSION["retry"] = "admit";
        $_SESSION["time"] = time();
        header( "Location: /ClassRegistration/Maintenance/systementry.php");
    }
?>
```

CAUTION

Due to a peculiarity of SQL, single quotes are required around all nonnumeric values, both strings *and* variables.

signin.php

As was done in register.php, for signin.php we need to embed the User Authentication `<div id= "form">` in the `<div id= "main">` of the template. Again the vertical navigation bar is simply a placeholder, and other small changes are made. Listing 9-6 shows only the `<div id= "main">` section of the script; the balance is very similar to the template. Figure 9-11 shows how signin.php displays.

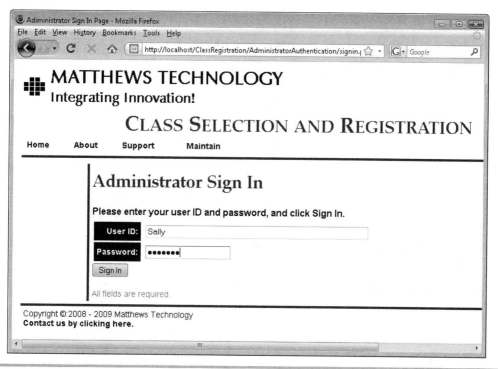

Figure 9-11   Signing in of an administrator

Listing 9-6   signin.php (in part)

```
    <div id="main">
       <h1 id="maintitle">Administrator Sign In</h1>
       <br />
<?php
    $retry = $_SESSION["retry"];
    if($retry < 1 ){
?>
       <p id="mainpara">Please enter your user ID and password, and
          click Sign In.</p>
<?php
    }
    else {
?>
       <p class="red">Please RE-enter your user ID and password, and
          click Sign In.</p>
<?php
    }
?>
       <!-- From User Authentication -->
       <div id="form">
          <!-- Display the sign-in form. After filling in, go to verify page. -->
          <form action="verify.php" method="post" id="signinForm">
```

```
<table width="200" border="0" cellspacing="3" cellpadding="5" >
   <tr>
      <th width="60">User ID:</th>
      <td width="120">
         <input type="text" name="userid" value="" size="60" />
      </td>
   </tr>
   <tr>
      <th>Password:</th>
      <td>
         <input type="password" name="passwd" value="" size="20" />
      </td>
   </tr>
</table>
<input type="submit" name="submit" value="Sign In" />
  </form>
</div>  <!-- id="form" -->
```

NOTE

The PHP code inserted at the beginning of this portion of the script calls a $_SESSION variable and therefore requires the session_start() function at the very top of the script, which is in the template.

verify.php

The verify.php script is very similar to enterName.php. userid and passwd, which are brought in from signin.php, are cleaned up, the password is encrypted, and then it and the user ID are compared with what is in the database. If they match, the session variables are updated, and the focus is transferred to the first site page. If there is not a match, the user is given three tries back in signin.php, and after which he is sent to register.php to reregister. Listing 9-7 show this script.

TIP

The result of a SELECT query is not FALSE, and the query does not fail if the sought items are not found. You must separately compare what was found to what you were looking for to determine the outcome. This is demonstrated in verify.php.

Listing 9-7   verify.php

```
//Remove white space, check for blanks, and remove special characters
$userid = (trim($_POST['userid']) == '') ?
    die ("Please enter a user ID.")
    : mysql_real_escape_string($_POST['userid']);
```

```php
$userPasswd = (trim($_POST['passwd']) == '') ?
   die ("Please enter a password.")
   : mysql_real_escape_string($_POST['passwd']);

//Encrypt the password.
$encryptpasswd = sha1($userPasswd);

//Connect to the ClassRegistration database
$connection = mysql_connect("localhost", "root", "password")
   or die("Cannot connect to MySQL.");
mysql_select_db("classregistration")
   or die("Database ClassRegistration not available.");

//See if match in the administrator table
$query = "SELECT admin_id, admin_password, admin_name
            FROM administrator
            WHERE admin_id= '$userid' AND admin_password= '$encryptpasswd'";
$result = mysql_query($query)
   or die("Select from administrator failed. " . mysql_error());

//Determine if the user ID and password are on file.
$row = mysql_fetch_object($result);
   $db_userid = $row->admin_id;
   $db_password = $row->admin_password;
   $name = $row->admin_name;

if($db_userid != $userid || $db_password != $encryptpasswd){
   //If not, add to Session Retry and test > 3
   $retry = $_SESSION["retry"];
   $retry++;
   if ($retry > 3) {
   //If greater than 3 go to register.
   header( "Location: register.php");
   }
   else {
   //If less than 3, update Session Retry and go to Sign in.
   $_SESSION["retry"] = $retry;
   header( "Location: signin.php");
   }
      }
else {
   //If on file, reset the session, and enter site.
   $_SESSION["name"] = $name;
   $_SESSION["retry"] = "admit";
   $_SESSION["time"] = time();
   header( "Location: enterSite.php");
}
?>
```

enterSite.php

enterSite.php is a snippet of code that can be either placed on each page in the site, or included on each page using the PHP require_once() function. We'll demonstrate both in the following scripts. When this is in a separate script in this application, it is called "doorway.php." This snippet checks to see if the $_SESSION variable `retry` has been set and contains `admit`. If so, it retrieves the user's name for use in the script (in real use, the `echo` statement would be removed from the snippet and placed elsewhere in the script). If not, the adminAuthen.php script is loaded.

Listing 9-8   enterSite.php (doorway.php)

```php
<?php
session_start();
//Check to see if session retry is "admit."
if (isset($_SESSION["retry"]) && $_SESSION["retry"] == "admit") {
    //If so, continue.
    echo "Hello ", $_SESSION["name"], "!<br />";
}
else {
    header( "Location: adminAuthen.php");
}
?>
```

Database Entry and Maintenance

The Database Entry and Maintenance component is used to enter, update, and delete information for the database. It is needed for all four tables, but for this exercise, we'll do it for the Class table so that we can put some classes in it. In the process, it will demonstrate the MySQL INSERT, UPDATE, and DELETE functions. Database Entry and Maintenance has three subcomponents, each with one or more scripts:

- System entry
- New class entry
- Class update and delete

System Entry

systementry.php, the starting place for Database Entry and Maintenance, allows you to choose what you want to do and then sends you on your way. It is the script to which Administrator Authorization sends you, and it's the script you return to when you are done with any of the others in this component. It has no database elements and little PHP, as you can see in Figure 9-12.

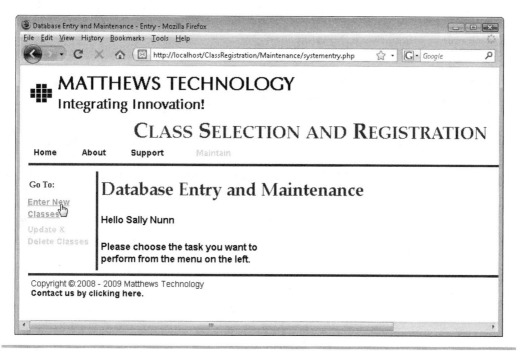

Figure 9-12 systementry.php

Begin by creating a new PHP script based on the template we've built here, cut and paste the enterSite.php snippet, modify the middle section and the vertical menu to what is shown here, and change verify.php so that it goes to this script instead of to enterSite .php. Listing 9-9 shows the PHP code at the beginning of the script that comes from the enterSite.php snippet, and the vnav and main divisions of the script. The balance of the script is straight out of the template.

Listing 9-9   systementry.php

```php
<?php
   session_start();

//Check to see if session retry is "admit."
if (isset($_SESSION["retry"])&& $_SESSION["retry"] == "admit") {
   //If so, continue.
   $name = $_SESSION["name"];
}
```

```php
else {
    header( "Location: adminAuthen.php");
}
?>
    <div id="vnav">
        <table width="120" border="0" cellspacing="2" cellpadding="2">
            <tr>
                <td id="vhead">Go To: </td>
            </tr>
            <tr>
                <td><a href="classentry.php">Enter New Classes</a> </td>
            </tr>
            <tr>
                <td><a href="classupdate.php">Update & Delete Classes</a>
                </td>
            </tr>
        </table>
    </div> <!-- id="vnav" -->
    <div id="main">
        <h1 id="maintitle">Database Entry and Maintenance</h1>
        <br />
        <p id="mainpara">Hello
<?php
        echo $name;
?>
        </p>
        <br />
        <p id="mainpara">Please choose the task you want to<br />
            perform from the menu on the left.</p>
        <!-- <p class="red">*A footnote.</p> -->
    </div> <!-- id="main" -->
```

Class Entry

Class entry starts with classentry.php, which begins with the template, adds a form
for entering new classes, JavaScript for positioning the cursor on the first field, and
finally calls addclass.php to add the class to the database. addclass.php is very similar to
enterName.php described earlier and is simpler because it doesn't need the cookie and
encryption elements. Figure 9-13 shows the screen during class entry, Listing 9-10 shows
classentry.php, and Listing 9-11 shows addclass.php.

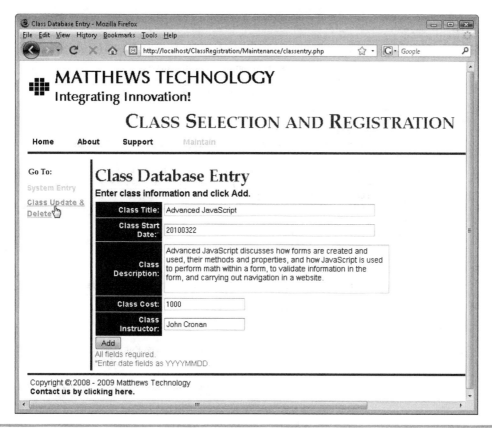

Figure 9-13 With a template, a CSS, and another page from which you can get some of the code, building a new page is relatively simple.

Most of the full classentry.php is shown in Listing 9-10 so you can see the changes in the early part of the script. The footer portion was left out because it is unchanged.

Listing 9-10 classentry.php

```php
<?php
require_once "doorway.php" ;
?>
<!DOCTYPE html PUBLIC "-//W3C//DTD XHTML 1.0 Strict//EN">
<html>
    <head>
        <title>Class Database Entry</title>
        <link rel= "stylesheet" type= "text/css" href=
            "/ClassRegistration/registration.css"/>
        <script language="JavaScript" type= "text/javascript"></script>
    </head>
```

```html
<!-- Put cursor in the first field -->
<body onload="document.form1.class_title.focus();">
   <div id="wrapper">
      <div id="header">
         <img src="/ClassRegistration/MatTechLogo.gif"
            alt="Matthews Technology" />
         <h1 id="title">Class Selection and Registration</h1>

      </div> <!-- id="header" -->
      <div id="hnav">
         <table width="400" border="0" cellspacing="2" cellpadding="2">
            <tr>
               <td><a href="../index.php">Home</a> </td>
               <td><a href="../about.php">About</a> </td>
               <td><a href="../support.php">Support</a> </td>
               <td><a href="..adminAuthen.php">Maintain</a> </td>
            </tr>
         </table>

      </div> <!-- id="hnav" -->
      <div id="vnav">
         <table width="120" border="0" cellspacing="2" cellpadding="2">
            <tr>
               <td id="vhead">Go To: </td>
            </tr>
            <tr>
               <td><a href="systementry.php">System Entry</a> </td>
            </tr>
            <tr>
               <td><a href="classlist.php">Class Update & Delete</a></td>
            </tr>
         </table>

      </div> <!-- id="vnav" -->
      <div id="main">
         <h1 id="maintitle">Class Database Entry</h1>
         <p id="mainpara">Enter class information and click Add.</p>

         <!-- Class Entry form -->
         <form action="addclass.php" method="post" name="form1">
            <table width="600px" border="0" cellspacing="1" cellpadding="3">
               <tr>
                  <th width="18%">Class Title:</th>
                  <td width="60%">
                     <input type="text" name="class_title" value=""
                        size="60" />
                  </td>
               </tr>
               <tr>
                  <th>Class Start Date:<span class="red">*</span></th>
                  <td>
                     <input type="text" name="class_start" value=""
                        size="60" />
                  </td>
               </tr>
```

```html
<tr>
   <th>Class Description:</th>
   <td>
      <textarea name="class_descr" cols="60"
         rows="4"></textarea>
   </td>
</tr>
<tr>
   <th>Class Cost:</th>
   <td>
      <input type="text" name="class_cost" value=""
         size="20" />
   </td>
</tr>
<tr>
   <th>Class Instructor:</th>
   <td>
      <input type="text" name="class_instr" value=""
         size="20" />
   </td>
</tr>
</table>
<p><input type="submit" value="Add" /></p>
</form>

<p class="red">All fields required.<br />
   *Enter date fields as YYYYMMDD.</p>
</div> <!-- id="main" -->
```

Listing 9-11   addclass.php

```php
<?php
//Remove white space, check for blanks, and remove special characters
$title = (trim($_POST['class_title']) == '') ?
   die ("Please enter the class title.")
   : mysql_real_escape_string($_POST['class_title']);

$start = (trim($_POST['class_start']) == '') ?
   die ("Please enter a start date.")
   : mysql_real_escape_string($_POST['class_start']);

$descr = (trim($_POST['class_descr']) == '') ?
   die ("Please enter a description.")
   : mysql_real_escape_string($_POST['class_descr']);

$cost = (trim($_POST['class_cost']) == '') ?
   die ("Please enter a class cost.")
   : mysql_real_escape_string($_POST['class_cost']);
```

```
$instr = (trim($_POST['class_instr']) == '') ?
    die ("Please enter an instructor.")
    : mysql_real_escape_string($_POST['class_instr']);

//Connect to the ClassRegistration database
$connection = mysql_connect("localhost", "root", "password")
    or die("Cannot connect to MySQL.");

mysql_select_db("classregistration")
    or die("Database ClassRegistration not available.");

//Add record to the class table
$query = "INSERT INTO class(class_title, class_start, class_descr,
    class_cost, class_instr)
    VALUES('$title', '$start', '$descr', '$cost', '$instr')";
$result = mysql_query($query)
    or die("Insert to class failed. " . mysql_error());

//Return to classentry.php.
    header( "Location: classentry.php");
```

Class Update and Delete

The class update and delete function has three subelements:

- Displaying the list of classes and letting the user select one to update or delete
- Displaying and updating the class selected
- Displaying and deleting the class selected

These three elements have in total five scripts, as discussed next.

Display the Class List   To update or delete a class, you must first have a list of classes from which to choose the one you want to update or delete. That is the function of classlist .php. This script begins with a PHP/MySQL section using SELECT to get all the records from the class table and ordering them by the class start date. The first record or row in the database table is then picked up and sent to an X/HTML table, which proceeds to loop through the remaining rows using a PHP do-while loop and displaying each as a row in the X/HTML table. Finally, each row of the table has two links, one for updating that particular record, and the other for deleting it. Figure 9-14 shows what the class list looks like on the screen, and Listing 9-14 shows the PHP and <div id= "main"> segments of the script to perform this function.

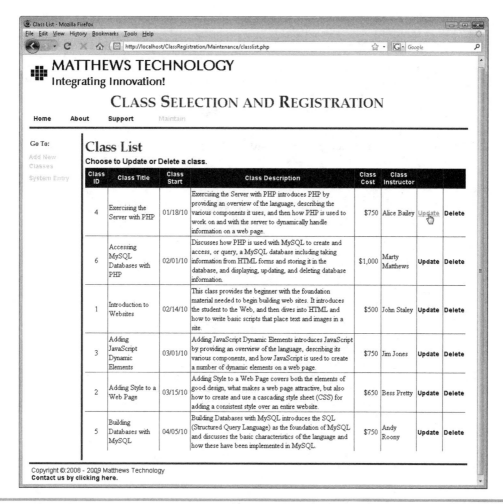

Figure 9-14   The class list lets you not only see the classes, but also choose to update or delete classes.

NOTE

The class_id used to get the correct record from the class table is passed to both classupdate.php and classdelete.php scripts in the link URL that loads them.

Listing 9-12   classlist.php

```php
<?php
require_once "doorway.php" ;

//Connect to the ClassRegistration database
    $connection = mysql_connect("localhost", "root", "password")
```

```php
        or die("Cannot connect to MySQL.");
    mysql_select_db("classregistration")
        or die("Database ClassRegistration not available.");

//Get records from the class table
    $query = "SELECT * From class ORDER BY class_start";
    $result = mysql_query($query)
        or die("Select from class failed. " . mysql_error());

//Get first class (row)from class table
    $classrow = mysql_fetch_assoc($result);

?>
```

```html
            <div id="main">
                <h1 id="maintitle">Class List</h1>
                <p id="mainpara">Choose to Update or Delete a class.</p>

                <!-- Class List -->
                <table width="850" border="1" frame="void" rules="all"
                    cellspacing="1" cellpadding="2">
                    <!-- Display the column headings -->
                    <tr>
                        <th class="list" width="40">Class ID</th>
                        <th class="list" width="110">Class Title</th>
                        <th class="list" width="60">Class Start</th>
                        <th class="list" width="400">Class Description</th>
                        <th class="list" width="50">Class Cost</th>
                        <th class="list" width="50">Class Instructor</th>
                        <th class="list" width="50"> </th>
                        <th class="list" width="40"> </th>
                    </tr>

                    <!-- Loop through and display the classes (first class
                        retrieved above). -->
                    <?php do {   ?>

                    <tr>
                        <td align="center"><?php echo $classrow ['class_id']; ?></td>
                        <td><?php echo $classrow ['class_title']; ?></td>
                        <td align="center"><?php echo date('m/d/y',
                            strtotime($classrow ['class_start'])); ?></td>
                        <td><?php echo $classrow ['class_descr']; ?>   </td>
                        <td align="right">$<?php echo number_format($classrow
                            ['class_cost'],0,'.',','); ?> </td>
                        <td><?php echo $classrow ['class_instr']; ?></td>
                        <td><a href="classupdate.php?recordID=<?php echo
                            $classrow ['class_id']; ?>">Update</a></td>
                        <td><a href="classdelete.php?recordID=<?php echo
                            $classrow ['class_id']; ?>">Delete</a></td>
                    </tr>
                    <?php } while ( $classrow = mysql_fetch_assoc($result) ); ?>
                </table>

                <p class="red"> </p>
            </div> <!-- id="main" -->
```

Updating a Class   Updating a class is a combination of entering a new one and displaying an existing one. It uses an input form like entering a new record, but provides the current value for a particular field using a PHP produced array for the class being updated. That class is found using the class_id passed from the class list and MySQL SELECT. Once the desired changes have been made on the screen, the updateclass.php script is called, and the record is replaced on the database table with MySQL UPDATE. The class_id is again passed to updateclass.php using the URL, while the other fields are brought over using the form's POST method. Figure 9-15 shows the Class Update screen, while Listings 15 and 16 show portions of classupdate.php and updateclass.php respectively.

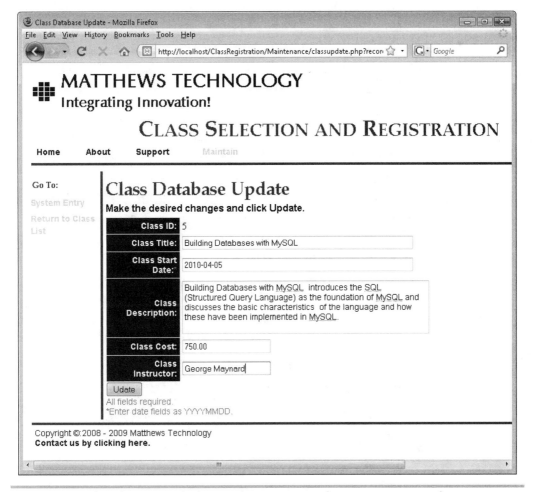

Figure 9-15   The Class List and Class Update screens and scripts are very similar.

Listing 9-13 classupdate.php

```php
<?php
    require_once "doorway.php" ;

//Get Class ID from classlist.php
    $classid = ($_GET['recordID']);

//Connect to the ClassRegistration database
    $connection = mysql_connect("localhost", "root", "password")
        or die("Cannot connect to MySQL.");
    mysql_select_db("classregistration")
        or die("Database ClassRegistration not available.");

//Get records from the class table
    $query = "SELECT * From class WHERE class_id = $classid";
    $result = mysql_query($query)
        or die("Select from class failed. " . mysql_error());

//Get class (row)from database
    $classrow = mysql_fetch_assoc($result);

?>
    <div id="main">
        <h1 id="maintitle">Class Database Update</h1>
            <p id="mainpara">Make the desired changes and click Update.</p>

        <!-- Class Entry form -->
        <form action="updateclass.php?recordID=<?php echo $classrow ['class_id'];
            ?>" method="post" name="form1">
            <table width="600px" border="0" cellspacing="1" cellpadding="3">
                <tr>
                    <th width="18%">Class ID:</th>
                    <td width="60%"><?php echo $classrow ['class_id']; ?></td>
                </tr>
                 <tr>
                    <th>Class Title:</th>
                    <td>
                        <input type="text" name="class_title" value="<?php
                            echo $classrow ['class_title']; ?>" size="60" />
                    </td>
                </tr>
                <tr>
                    <th>Class Start Date:<span class="red">*</span></th>
                    <td>
                        <input type="text" name="class_start" value="<?php
                            echo $classrow ['class_start']; ?>" size="60" />
                    </td>
                </tr>
                <tr>
                    <th>Class Description:</th>
                    <td>
                        <textarea name="class_descr" cols="60" rows="4"><?php
```

```
               echo $classrow ['class_descr']; ?></textarea>
          </td>
        </tr>
        <tr>
          <th>Class Cost:</th>
          <td>
            <input type="text" name="class_cost" value="<?php echo
               $classrow ['class_cost']; ?> " size="20" />
          </td>
        </tr>
        <tr>
          <th>Class Instructor:</th>
          <td>
            <input type="text" name="class_instr" value="<?php
               echo $classrow ['class_instr']; ?>" size="20" />
          </td>
        </tr>
      </table>
      <p><input type="submit" value="Update" /></p>
    </form>

    <p class="red">All fields required.<br />
          *Enter date fields as YYYYMMDD.</p>

  </div> <!-- id="main" -->
```

Listing 9-14   updateclass.php

```php
<?php
//Get Class ID from classupdate.php
   $classid = ($_GET['recordID']);

//Remove white space, check for blank, and remove special characters
   $title = (trim($_POST['class_title']) == '') ?
      die ("Please enter the class title.")
   : mysql_real_escape_string($_POST['class_title']);

   $start = (trim($_POST['class_start']) == '') ?
      die ("Please enter a start date.")
      : mysql_real_escape_string($_POST['class_start']);

   $descr = (trim($_POST['class_descr']) == '') ?
      die ("Please enter a description.")
      : mysql_real_escape_string($_POST['class_descr']);

   $cost = (trim($_POST['class_cost']) == '') ?
      die ("Please enter the class cost.")
      : mysql_real_escape_string($_POST['class_cost']);

   $instr = (trim($_POST['class_instr']) == '') ?
      die ("Please enter the instructor.")
      : mysql_real_escape_string($_POST['class_instr']);
```

```
//Connect to the ClassRegistration database
   $connection = mysql_connect("localhost", "root", "password")
      or die("Cannot connect to MySQL.");

   mysql_select_db("classregistration")
      or die("Database ClassRegistration not available.");

//Update the record on the class table
   $query = "UPDATE class SET class_title='$title', class_start='$start',
      class_descr='$descr', class_cost='$cost', class_instr='$instr'
      WHERE class_id='$classid' ";
   $result = mysql_query($query)
      or die("Update class failed. " . mysql_error());

//Return to classlist.php.
   header( "Location: classlist.php");
?>
```

Deleting a Class   classdelete.php has many of the elements of classupdate.php. The PHP at the beginning of the script is exactly the same and won't be repeated in the listing that follows. It simply gets the class or record that will be deleted. This record is presented in a table like classupdate.php, but here the information is just listed and can't be changed. While there are no input fields, the X/HTML table is in a form that the information can be passed on to deleteclass.php, which does the actual deletion using MySQL's DELETE. Figure 9-16 shows classdelete.php on the screen, while Listings 15 and 16 show portions of classdelete.php and deleteclass.php respectively.

Listing 9-15   classdelete.php

```
<div id="main">
   <h1 id="maintitle">Class Delete</h1>
   <p class="red"><b>If you are sure you want to delete this class,
      click Delete.</b></p>

<!-- Class Entry form -->
<form action="deleteclass.php?recordID=<?php echo $classrow
   ['class_id']; ?>" method="post" name="form1">
   <table width="600px" border="0" cellspacing="1" cellpadding="3">
      <tr>
         <th width="18%">Class ID:</th>
         <td width="60%"><?php echo $classrow ['class_id']; ?></td>
      </tr>
      <tr>
         <th>Class Title:</th>
         <td><?php echo $classrow ['class_title']; ?></td>
      </tr>
```

```html
    <tr>
       <th>Class Start Date:</th>
       <td><?php echo date('m/d/y',strtotime($classrow
          ['class_start'])); ?></td>
    </tr>
    <tr>
       <th>Class Description:</th>
       <td><?php echo $classrow ['class_descr']; ?></td>
    </tr>
    <tr>
       <th>Class Cost:</th>
       <td>$<?php echo number_format($classrow ['class_cost'],
          0,'.',','); ?> </td>
    </tr>
    <tr>
       <th>Class Instructor:</th>
       <td><?php echo $classrow ['class_instr']; ?></td>
    </tr>
  </table>
  <p class="red"><input type="submit" value="Delete" /></p>
</form>

<p class="red"> </p>

</div><!-- id="main" -->
```

Listing 9-16   deleteclass.php

```php
<?php
//Get Class ID from classupdate.php
   $classid = ($_GET['recordID']);

//Connect to the ClassRegistration database
   $connection = mysql_connect("localhost", "root", "password")
      or die("Cannot connect to MySQL.");
   mysql_select_db("classregistration")
      or die("Database ClassRegistration not available.");

//Delete a record from the class table
   $query = "DELETE FROM class WHERE class_id='$classid' ";
   $result = mysql_query($query)
      or die("Delete class failed. " . mysql_error());

//Return to classlist.php.
   header( "Location: classlist.php");
?>
```

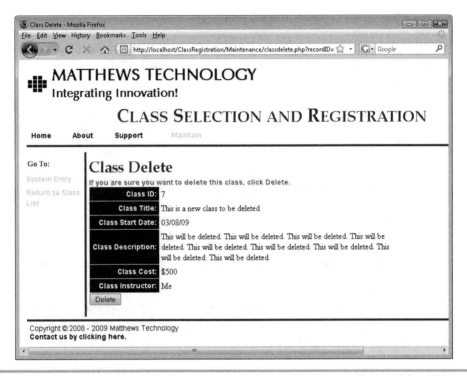

Figure 9-16 classdelete.php is getting a confirmation that the user wants to delete the record.

Class Registration

The class registration process is comparatively simple in comparison to, and after having gone through, the authentication and the maintenance processes. There are six steps to registration, as shown in Figure 9-17, each with one or two scripts.

Class List and Selection

The class list script, classes.php, is almost exactly the same as classlist.php used with updating and deleting classes. The major differences are that the Update and Delete links have been replaced by a Register link, a different script is called at the end, and some titling has changed. It is not even worth a new listing; see Listing 9-12. What you see on the screen is also very similar, as shown in Figure 9-18.

Student E-mail Entry

The student e-mail entry script brings the selected class along with it to ask students to enter their e-mail address to determine if they have previously registered for a course.

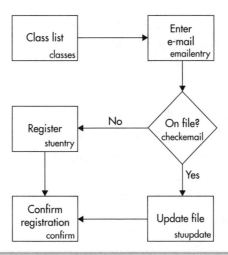

Figure 9-17   The steps needed to select and register for a class

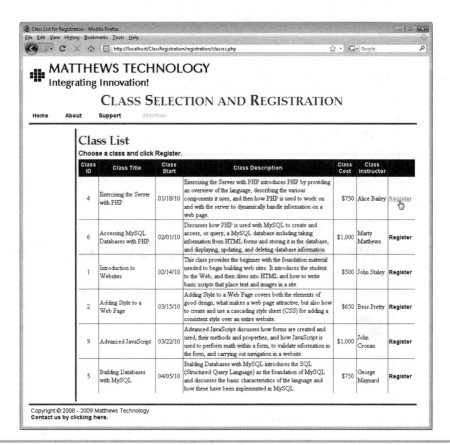

Figure 9-18   The class list for registration is very similar to the class list for updating and deleting.

If so, they are passed on to the stuupdate.php script, where they can update their student record if they wish. Otherwise they are sent to stuentry.php, where they can fill out the registration. Three scripts are used in this process:

- **emailentry.php**, an entry form for the e-mail address and its confirmation, which displays the class for which the student is registering, partially shown in Listing 9-17. Figure 9-19 shows what e-mail entry looks like on the screen.

- **emailvalid.js**, a JavaScript form validation script that checks if both an e-mail address and its confirmation have been entered, that they are both valid addresses, and that they are the same, shown in Listing 9-18. Here are three of the messages that are produced:

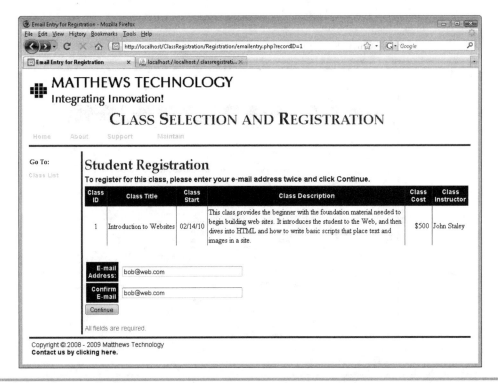

Figure 9-19   The e-mail entry carries the class information with it.

- **checkemail.php** for checking if the e-mail address is on file, shown in Listing 9-19. The student's e-mail address is compared with the e-mail addresses in the student table, and if a match is found, stuupdate.php is loaded; otherwise stuentry.php is loaded. In both cases the class ID and student e-mail address are passed on to the next script.

NOTE

The following three lines of code from emailentry.php contain two separate ways of passing the `classid` to checkemail.php. The first way uses the URL, as was done earlier in several maintenance scripts; the second uses a hidden field and `post`. Only one is needed. checkemail.php will use the second, getting the `classid` in the same way as the e-mail address. The `onsubmit` statement calls the JavaScript validation functions.

```
<form action="checkemail.php?recordID=<?php echo $classid ?>" method="post"
   onsubmit="return validate_form(this)" name="form1">
<input type="hidden" name="classid" value="<?php echo $classid; ?>"/>
```

Listing 9-17   emailentry.php

```
<div id="main">
   <h1 id="maintitle">Student Registration</h1>
   <p id="mainpara">To register for this class, please enter your
      e-mail address twice and click Continue.</p>

   <!-- From Class List -->
   <table width="850" border="1" frame="void" rules="all"
      cellspacing="1" cellpadding="2">
      <!-- Display the column headings -->
      <tr>
         <th class="list" width="40">Class ID</th>
         <th class="list" width="150">Class Title</th>
         <th class="list" width="60">Class Start</th>
         <th class="list" width="450">Class Description</th>
         <th class="list" width="50">Class Cost</th>
         <th class="list" width="50">Class Instructor</th>
      </tr>

      <!-- Display the selected class. -->
      <tr>
         <td align="center"><?php echo $classrow ['class_id']; ?></td>
         <td><?php echo $classrow ['class_title']; ?></td>
         <td align="center"><?php echo date('m/d/y',strtotime($classrow
            ['class_start'])); ?></td>
         <td><?php echo $classrow ['class_descr']; ?>   </td>
         <td align="right">$<?php echo number_format($classrow
            ['class_cost'],0,'.',','); ?> </td>
         <td><?php echo $classrow ['class_instr']; ?></td>
      </tr>
   </table>
```

```
<p> </p>
<p> </p>

<div id="form">
<!-- Display the e-mail entry form. After filling in, go
   to check e-mail page. -->
<form action="checkemail.php" method="post"
   onsubmit="return validate_form(this)" name="form1">
   <input type="hidden" name="classid" value="<?php echo
      $classid; ?>"/>
   <table width="200" border="0" cellspacing="3" cellpadding="5">
      <tr>
         <th width="100">E-mail Address:</th>
         <td width="80">
            <input type="text" name="email" value="" size="40" />
         </td>
      </tr>
      <tr>
         <th width="100">Confirm E-mail:</th>
         <td width="80">
            <input type="text" name="conemail" value="" size="40" />
         </td>
      </tr>
   </table>
      <input type="submit" name="submit" value="Continue" />
   </form>
</div>  <!-- id="form" -->

<!-- Begin from template -->
<br />
<p class="red">All fields are required.</p>
</div>  <!-- id="main" -->
```

Listing 9-18   emailvalid.js

```
// JavaScript Document
function validate_required(field,alerttxt)
{
   with (field)
   {
   if (value==null||value=="")
      {alert(alerttxt);return false}
   else {return true}
   }
}

function validate_email(field,alerttxt)
{
    with (field)
    {
    apos=value.indexOf("@")
```

```
        dotpos=value.lastIndexOf(".")
    if (apos<1||dotpos-apos<2)
        alert(alerttxt);return false}
    else {return true}
    }
}

function validate_equal(field1,field2,alerttxt)
{
    if (field1.value==field2.value)
        {return true}
    else {alert(alerttxt);return false}
}

function validate_form(thisform)
{
    with (thisform)
    {
    if (validate_required(email,"Please enter an e-mail address.")==false)
        {email.focus();return false}
    if (validate_email(email,"Please enter a valid e-mail address.")==false)
        {email.focus();return false}
    if (validate_required(conemail,"Please confirm your e-mail address.")==false)
        {conemail.focus();return false}
    if (validate_email(conemail,"Please enter a valid e-mail address.")==false)
        {conemail.focus();return false}
    if (validate_equal(email,conemail,"The two e-mail addresses are not the
        same.")==false) {conemail.focus();return false}
    if (email && conemail)
        form1.submit
    }
}
```

Listing 9-19   checkemail.php

```php
<?php
    //Remove white space, check for blank, and remove special characters
    $classid = (trim($_POST['classid']) == '') ?
        die ("Please enter a class ID.")
        : mysql_real_escape_string($_POST['classid']);

    $email = (trim($_POST['email']) == '') ?
        die ("Please enter your e-mail address.")
        : mysql_real_escape_string($_POST['email']);

    //Connect to the ClassRegistration database
    $connection = mysql_connect("localhost", "root", "password")
        or die("Cannot connect to MySQL.");
    mysql_select_db("classregistration")
        or die("Database ClassRegistration not available.");

    //See if match in the administrator table
    $query = "SELECT student_email
```

```
                FROM student
                WHERE student_email= '$email'";
    $result = mysql_query($query)
       or die("Select from student failed. " . mysql_error());

    //Determine if the student e-mail is on file.
    $row = mysql_fetch_object($result);
    $db_email = $row->student_email;

    if($db_email != $email ){

       //If not, go to new student entry with the classid and the e-mail
       header( "Location: stuentry.php?classid=$classid&email=$email");
    }
    else {

       //If on file, go to student update, with the classid and the e-mail.
       header( "Location: stuupdate.php?classid=$classid&email=$email");
    }
?>
```

New Student Entry

The student entry script (stuentry.php, shown in Listing 9-20) receives both the class ID and student e-mail address from checkemail.php. The class ID is used to display the class being registered for. The student is asked to enter his or her name and phone number (probably more fields in real life), as shown in Figure 9-20, and then, on clicking Continue, is taken to enterstu.php with the class ID and e-mail address along with the name and phone number.

Listing 9-20   stuentry.php

```
<?php
//Get Class ID from checkemail.php
   $classid = ($_GET['classid']);

//Get e-mail address from checkemail.php
   $email = ($_GET['email']);

//Connect to the ClassRegistration database
   $connection = mysql_connect("localhost", "root", "password")
      or die("Cannot connect to MySQL.");
   mysql_select_db("classregistration")
      or die("Database ClassRegistration not available.");

//Get records from the class table
   $query = "SELECT * FROM class WHERE class_id = $classid";
   $result = mysql_query($query)
      or die("Select from class failed. " . mysql_error());
```

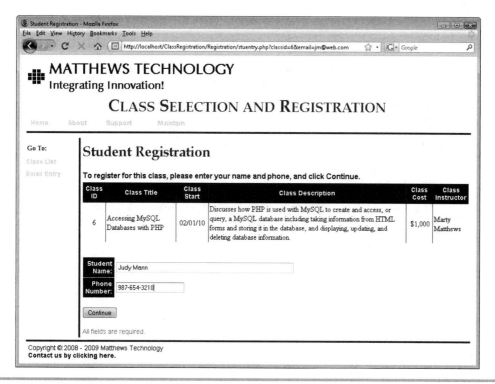

Figure 9-20 Student registration continues to display the class so the student is reminded what he or she is registering for.

```php
//Get class (row) from class table
    $classrow = mysql_fetch_assoc($result);
?>
    <div id="main">
        <h1 id="maintitle">Student Registration</h1>
        <br />
        <p id="mainpara">To register for this class, please enter
        your name and phone, and click Continue.</p>

        <!-- From Class List -->
        <table width="850" border="1" frame="void" rules="all"
            cellspacing="1" cellpadding="2">
            <!-- Display the column headings -->
            <tr>
                <th class="list" width="40">Class ID</th>
                <th class="list" width="150">Class Title</th>
                <th class="list" width="60">Class Start</th>
                <th class="list" width="450">Class Description</th>
                <th class="list" width="50">Class Cost</th>
                <th class="list" width="50">Class Instructor</th>
            </tr>

            <!-- Display the selected class. -->
            <tr>
```

```
            <td align="center"><?php echo $classrow ['class_id']; ?></td>
            <td><?php echo $classrow ['class_title']; ?></td>
            <td align="center"><?php echo date('m/d/y',strtotime($classrow
                ['class_start'])); ?></td>
            <td><?php echo $classrow ['class_descr']; ?>   </td>
            <td align="right">$<?php echo number_format($classrow
                ['class_cost'],0,'.',','); ?> </td>
            <td><?php echo $classrow ['class_instr']; ?></td>
      </tr>
      </table>
      <p> </p> <!-- Inserts two blank lines -->
      <p> </p>

   <div id="form">
      <!-- Go to enterstu.php after clicking Continue -->
      <form action="enterstu.php?classid=<?php echo $classid
        ?>&email=<?php echo $email ?>" method="post" name="form1">
        <table width="300" border="0" cellspacing="1" cellpadding="3" >
          <tr>
            <th width="30%">Student Name:</th>
            <td width="50%">
               <input type="text" name="stu_name" value=""
                  size="60" />
            </td>
          </tr>
          <tr>
            <th>Phone Number:</th>
            <td>
               <input type="text" name="phone" value=""
                  size="20" />
            </td>
          </tr>
        </table>
        <br />
        <input type="submit" name="submit" value="Continue" />
      </form>
      </div> <!-- id=form -->
```

enterstu.php (see Listing 9-21) receives the class ID and the student e-mail address, name, and phone from stuentry.php. It writes the latter three items to the student table and then loads confirm.php, passing the class ID and e-mail address to it.

Listing 9-21 enterstu.php

```php
<?php
//Get Class ID from checkemail.php
   $classid = ($_GET['classid']);

//Get e-mail address from checkemail.php
   $email = ($_GET['email']);

//Remove white space, check for blank, and remove special characters
   $name = (trim($_POST['stu_name']) == '') ?
      die ("Please enter your name.")
```

```php
        :   mysql_real_escape_string($_POST['stu_name']);

    $phone = (trim($_POST['phone']) == '') ?
        die ("Please enter your phone number.")
        :   mysql_real_escape_string($_POST['phone']);

//Connect to the ClassRegistration database
    $connection = mysql_connect("localhost", "root", "password")
        or die("Cannot connect to MySQL.");
    mysql_select_db("classregistration")
        or die("Database ClassRegistration not available.");

//Add record to the student table
    $query = "INSERT INTO student(student_email, student_name, student_phone)
            VALUES('$email', '$name', '$phone')";
    $result = mysql_query($query)
                or die("Insert to student failed. " . mysql_error());

//Go to confirm.php with class id and e-mail.
    header( "Location: confirm.php?classid=$classid&email=$email");
?>
```

Existing Student Update

Student update (stuupdate.php, see Listing 9-22) maintains the class display while displaying the student's database record and allowing the student to change the name and phone number fields, as you see in Figure 9-21. The student cannot change the e-mail address because it is the record key (this is possible, but it is a complexification—it requires the deletion of the original record and the entry of a new record), and the registration date is supplied by the system. When the student is done updating and clicks Continue, he or she is taken to updatestu.php with the information from this page.

Listing 9-22 stuupdate.php

```php
<?php
//Get Class ID from checkemail.php
    $classid = ($_GET['classid']);

//Get email address from checkemail.php
    $email = ($_GET['email']);

//Connect to the ClassRegistration database
    $connection = mysql_connect("localhost", "root", "password")
        or die("Cannot connect to MySQL.");
    mysql_select_db("classregistration")
        or die("Database ClassRegistration not available.");

//Get record from the class table
    $query = "SELECT * FROM class WHERE class_id = $classid";
    $result = mysql_query($query)
        or die("Select from class failed. " . mysql_error());
```

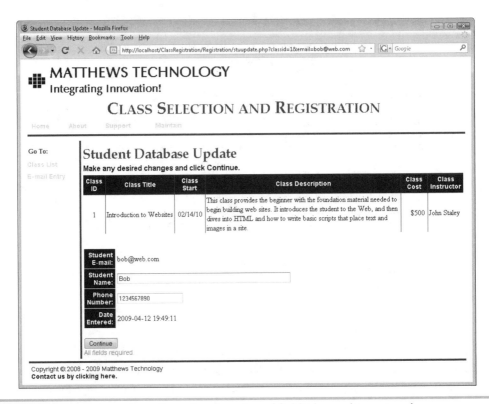

Figure 9-21 Student update allows the changing of fields the student entered.

```
//Get class (row) from class table
   $classrow = mysql_fetch_assoc($result);

//Get record from the student table
   $query1 = "SELECT * FROM student WHERE student_email = '$email'";
   $result1 = mysql_query($query1)
      or die("Select from student failed. " . mysql_error());

//Get student (row) from student table
   $sturow = mysql_fetch_assoc($result1);
?>
   <div id="main">
      <h1 id="maintitle">Student Database Update</h1>
      <p id="mainpara">Make any desired changes and click Continue.</p>

      <!-- From Class List -->
      <table width="850" border="1" frame="void" rules="all"
         cellspacing="1" cellpadding="2">
         <!-- Display the column headings -->
         <tr>
            <th class="list" width="40">Class ID</th>
            <th class="list" width="150">Class Title</th>
            <th class="list" width="60">Class Start</th>
```

```html
            <th class="list" width="450">Class Description</th>
            <th class="list" width="50">Class Cost</th>
            <th class="list" width="50">Class Instructor
        </tr>

        <!-- Display the selected class. -->
        <tr>
            <td align="center"><?php echo $classrow ['class_id']; ?></td>
            <td><?php echo $classrow ['class_title']; ?></td>
            <td align="center"><?php echo
                date('m/d/y',strtotime($classrow ['class_start'])); ?></td>
            <td><?php echo $classrow ['class_descr']; ?>   </td>
            <td align="right">$<?php echo
                number_format($classrow ['class_cost'],0,'.',','); ?> </td>
            <td><?php echo $classrow ['class_instr']; ?></td>
        </tr>
        </table>
        <p> </p> <!-- Inserts two blank lines -->
        <p> </p>
        <!-- Begin Student Update -->
    <div id="form">
        <!-- Go to updatestu.php after clicking Continue -->
        <form action="updatestu.php?classid=<?php echo $classid
            ?>&email=<?php echo $email ?>" method="post" name="form1">
            <table width="300" border="0" cellspacing="1" cellpadding="3" >
                <tr>
                    <th width="30%">Student E-mail:</th>
                    <td width="50%"><?php echo $sturow ['student_email']; ?></td>
                <tr>
                <tr>
                    <th>Student Name:</th>
                    <td>
                        <input type="text" name="stu_name" value="<?php echo
                            $sturow ['student_name']; ?>" size="60" />
                    </td>
                </tr>
                <tr>
                    <th>Phone Number:</th>
                    <td>
                        <input type="text" name="phone" value="<?php echo
                            $sturow ['student_phone']; ?>" size="20" />
                    </td>
                </tr>
                <tr>
                    <th width="30%">Date Entered:</th>
                    <td width="50%"><?php echo $sturow ['student_date']; ?></td>
                </tr>
            </table>
            <br />
            <input type="submit" name="submit" value="Continue" />
        </form>
    </div> <!-- id=form -->
    <p class="red">All fields required.</p>
</div> <!-- id="main" -->
```

updatestu.php (see Listing 9-23) receives the class ID and the student e-mail address, name, and phone from stuupdate.php. It updates the latter three items to the student table and then loads confirm.php, passing the class ID and e-mail address to it.

Listing 9-23   updatestu.php

```php
<?php
//Get Class ID from stuupdate.php
    $classid = ($_GET['classid']);

//Get email address from stuupdate.php
    $email = (($_GET['email']));

//Remove white space, check for blank, and remove special characters
    $name = (trim($_POST['stu_name']) == '') ?
        die ("Please enter your name.")
        : mysql_real_escape_string($_POST['stu_name']);

    $phone = (trim($_POST['phone']) == '') ?
        die ("Please enter your phone number.")
        : mysql_real_escape_string($_POST['phone']);

//Connect to the ClassRegistration database
    $connection = mysql_connect("localhost", "root", "password")
        or die("Cannot connect to MySQL.");
    mysql_select_db("classregistration")
        or die("Database ClassRegistration not available.");

//Update a record on the student table
    $query = "UPDATE student SET student_name='$name', student_phone='$phone'
        WHERE student_email='$email' ";
    $result = mysql_query($query)
        or die("Insert to student failed. " . mysql_error());

//Go to confirm.php with class id and e-mail.
    header( "Location: confirm.php?classid=$classid&email=$email");
?>
```

Registration and Confirmation

The final registration confirmation, confirm.php (shown in Listing 9-24), receives the class ID and e-mail address from either stuentry.php or stuupdate.php. It uses these to retrieve and display both the class and student's records from the database. The student is asked to confirm these, as shown in Figure 9-22. When they click Confirm, sendemail.php is loaded with the class ID and e-mail address passed to it.

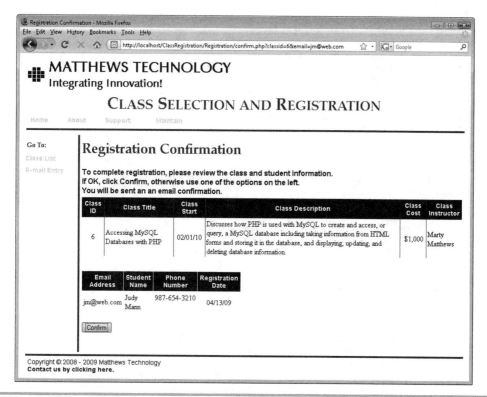

Figure 9-22   The student is given one more opportunity to make changes, and then the registration is confirmed.

Listing 9-24   confirm.php

```php
<?php
//Get Class ID from enterstu.php
   $classid = ($_GET['classid']);

//Get e-mail address from enterstu.php
   $email = ($_GET['email']);

//Connect to the ClassRegistration database
   $connection = mysql_connect("localhost", "root", "password")
      or die("Cannot connect to MySQL.");
   mysql_select_db("classregistration")
      or die("Database ClassRegistration not available.");

//Get record from the class table
   $query = "SELECT * FROM class WHERE class_id = $classid";
   $result = mysql_query($query)
      or die("Select from class failed. " . mysql_error());
```

```php
//Get class (row) from class table
   $classrow = mysql_fetch_assoc($result);

//Get record from the student table
   $query1 = "SELECT * FROM student WHERE student_email = '$email'";
   $result1 = mysql_query($query1)
      or die("Select from student failed. " . mysql_error());

//Get student (row) from student table
   $sturow = mysql_fetch_assoc($result1);

?>
   <div id="main">
      <h1 id="maintitle">Registration Confirmation</h1>
      <br />
      <p id="mainpara">To complete registration, please review
         the class and student information.<br />
         If OK, click Confirm, otherwise use one of the
         options on the left.<br />
         You will be sent an e-mail confirmation.</p>

      <!-- From Class List -->
      <table width="850" border="1" frame="void" rules="all"
         cellspacing="1" cellpadding="2">
         <!-- Display the column headings -->
         <tr>
            <th class="list" width="40">Class ID</th>
            <th class="list" width="150">Class Title</th>
            <th class="list" width="60">Class Start</th>
            <th class="list" width="450">Class Description</th>
            <th class="list" width="50">Class Cost</th>
            <th class="list" width="50">Class Instructor</th>
         </tr>

         <!-- Display the selected class. -->
         <tr>
            <td align="center"><?php echo $classrow ['class_id']; ?></td>
            <td><?php echo $classrow ['class_title']; ?></td>
            <td align="center"><?php echo
               date('m/d/y',strtotime($classrow ['class_start'])); ?></td>
            <td><?php echo $classrow ['class_descr']; ?>   </td>
            <td align="right">$<?php echo number_format($classrow
               ['class_cost'],0,'.',','); ?> </td>
            <td><?php echo $classrow ['class_instr']; ?></td>
         </tr>
      </table>
      <p> </p> <!-- Inserts two blank lines -->
      <p> </p>

      <div id="form">
         <!-- Go to enterstu.php after clicking Continue -->
         <form action="sendemail.php?classid=<?php echo
            $classid ?>&email=<?php echo $email ?>"
            method="post" name="form1">
            <table width="300" border="0" cellspacing="1" cellpadding="3" >
            <!-- Display the column headings -->
```

```
      <tr>
         <th class="list" width="40">E-mail Address</th>
         <th class="list" width="150">Student Name</th>
         <th class="list" width="60">Phone Number</th>
         <th class="list" width="450">Registration Date</th>
      </tr>

   <!-- Display the selected class. -->
      <tr>
         <td align="center"><?php echo $sturow ['student_email']; ?></td>
         <td><?php echo $sturow ['student_name']; ?></td>
         <td><?php echo $sturow ['student_phone']; ?>   </td>
         <td align="center"><?php echo
            date('m/d/y',strtotime($sturow ['student_date'])); ?></td>
      </tr>
   </table>
   <br />
   <input type="submit" name="confirm" value="Confirm" />
 </form>
</div> <!-- id=form -->
<br />
<p class="red"> </p>
</div> <!-- id="main" -->
```

sendemail.php is where we make the relational database do its thing. The class ID and e-mail address are used to build a new record that is written to the register table. Then mysql_insert_id is used to get the registration ID ($regid) that was automatically generated when the new registration record was generated. Then the class ID, the e-mail address, and the registration ID are used to retrieve records from the class, student, and registration tables respectively. This information is then used to prepare and send an e-mail confirmation of the registration. The e-mail message uses a long concatenation (the .=) of $msg_client to form the message body.

Listing 9-25   sendemail.php

```php
<?php
//Get Class ID from confirm.php
   $classid = ($_GET['classid']);

//Get e-mail address from confirm.php
   $email = ($_GET['email']);

//Connect to the ClassRegistration database
   $connection = mysql_connect("localhost", "root", "password")
      or die("Cannot connect to MySQL.");
   mysql_select_db("classregistration")
      or die("Database ClassRegistration not available.");
```

```php
//Add record to the registration table
    $query = "INSERT INTO registration(class_id, student_email)
       VALUES('$classid', '$email')";
    $result = mysql_query($query)
       or die("Insert to registration failed. " . mysql_error());

//Get the registration ID generated by insert.
    $regid = mysql_insert_id();

//Get record from the class table
    $query1 = "SELECT * FROM class WHERE class_id = '$classid'";
    $result1 = mysql_query($query1)
       or die("Select from class failed. " . mysql_error());

//Get selected class (row) from class table
    $classrow = mysql_fetch_assoc($result1);

//Get record from the student table
    $query2 = "SELECT * FROM student WHERE student_email = '$email'";
    $result2 = mysql_query($query2)
       or die("Select from student failed. " . mysql_error());

//Get student (row) from student table
    $sturow = mysql_fetch_assoc($result2);

//Get record from the registration table
    $query3 = "SELECT * FROM registration WHERE reg_id = '$regid'";
    $result3 = mysql_query($query3)
       or die("Select from registration failed. " . mysql_error());

//Get registration (row) from registration table
    $regrow = mysql_fetch_assoc($result3);

//Confirmation E-mail
$to_client = $sturow['student_name']. ' <'.$sturow['student_email'].'>';
$sub_client = 'Class Registration';
$msg_client = 'Thank you for your class registration. Here is the
                necessary information:'."\n\n";
$msg_client .= 'Registration number: '.$regrow['reg_id']."\n";
$msg_client .= 'Class ID: '. $classid . "\n";
$msg_client .= 'Class Title: '.$sturow['class_title']."\n";
$msg_client .= 'Class Start Date: '.$sturow['class_start']."\n";
$msg_client .= 'Class Cost: '. "$" . $sturow['class_cost']."\n";
$msg_client .= 'Registration date: '.$regrow['reg_date']."\n";
$msg_client .= "\n\n";
```

```
$msg_client .= 'Your E-mail Address: '.$sturow['email_address']."\n";
$msg_client .= 'Your Name: '.$sturow['student_name']. "\n";
$msg_client .= 'Your Phone: '.$sturow['student_phone']."\n\n";
$msg_client .= 'Please contact us to arrange payment at:'."\n";
$msg_client .= 'info@matthewstechnology.com'."\n";
$msg_client .= "\n\n";
$msg_client .= 'Thanks again,'."\n\n";
$msg_client .= 'Matthews Technology'."\n\n";
$addl_headers_client = 'From: Matthews Technology
    <info@matthewstechnology.com>'."\n\n";

mail($to_client,$sub_client,$msg_client,$addl_headers_client);
?>
    <div id="main">
        <h1 id="maintitle">Class Database Update</h1>
        <p id="mainpara">Thank you for completing class registration!<br />
            Please click Complete.</p>

        <div id="form">
            <!-- Go to classes.php after clicking Complete -->
            <form action="classes.php" method="post" name="form1">
                <input type="submit" name="submit" value="Complete" />
            </form>
        </div> <!-- id=form -->
        <p class="red"> </p>

    </div> <!-- id="main" -->
```

An application like Class Selection and Registration can always be expanded and improved. You make decisions as you are building it that, when you are done, you second-guess and think, in most cases for not more than 15 seconds, about going back and doing a major overhaul. Some things that might be changed in this application include

- Putting the database connection code, shown next, which is the same in every script that uses the database, in a separate script that is included in the others by using require_once. This also helps the security by putting the username and password in only one place instead of in every script. Most Internet hosting services have a way you can hide a script like this.

```
//Connect to the ClassRegistration database
$connection = mysql_connect("localhost", "root", "password")
    or die("Cannot connect to MySQL.");
mysql_select_db("classregistration")
    or die("Database ClassRegistration not available.");
```

- Expanding the database entry and maintenance component to include the maintenance of the student and registration tables. This would involve simply copying the class table scripts and changing the table names.

- Expanding the student table and the supporting scripts to include additional student fields such as address, city, state, and ZIP code.

- Adding a payment system—using PayPal makes this very easy to do. With PayPal you can accept credit and debit cards as well as bank transfers by using simple X/HTML links or a shopping cart. Check their web site at http://www.paypal.com; click **Business**, and then under Need To Accept Credit Cards? click **On Your Website**.

I'm sure you can think of many other changes to make to this application. The key is that now you have the tools to make those changes and links to many resources for additional tools. What you can do with these tools is limited only by your imagination.

Index